The Music Business for Music Creators

Industry Mechanics for Contemporary Creators

Jonny Amos

Routledge
Taylor & Francis Group

LONDON AND NEW YORK

Designed cover image: junce via Getty Images

First published 2024
by Routledge
4 Park Square, Milton Park, Abingdon, Oxon OX14 4RN

and by Routledge
605 Third Avenue, New York, NY 10158

Routledge is an imprint of the Taylor & Francis Group, an informa business

British Library Cataloguing-in-Publication Data
A catalogue record for this book is available from the British Library

Library of Congress Cataloging-in-Publication Data
Names: Amos, Jonny, author.
Title: The music business for music creators : industry mechanics for contemporary
    creators / Jonny Amos.
Description: Abingdon, Oxon ; New York : Routledge, 2024. | Includes index.
Identifiers: LCCN 2023055931 (print) | LCCN 2023055932 (ebook) |
    ISBN 9781032589121 (paperback) | ISBN 9781032589138 (hardback) |
    ISBN 9781003452119 (ebook)
Subjects: LCSH: Music trade—Vocational guidance. | Musicians—Vocational guidance.
Classification: LCC ML3795 .A8256 2024 (print) | LCC ML3795 (ebook) |
    DDC 780.23—dc23/eng/20231213
LC record available at https://lccn.loc.gov/2023055931
LC ebook record available at https://lccn.loc.gov/2023055932

ISBN: 978-1-032-58913-8 (hbk)
ISBN: 978-1-032-58912-1 (pbk)
ISBN: 978-1-003-45211-9 (ebk)

DOI: 10.4324/9781003452119

Typeset in Goudy
by Apex CoVantage, LLC

Supporting materials can be accessed at: www.jonnyamos.com/music-industry-resources/. Assets and resources include a song copyright split sheet, a sound recording copyright split sheet, a producer release agreement, a performance release agreement, a music publishing short-form contract example document, a record company short-form contract example document, a metadata template and a press release template.

Contents

Contributors

Denise Beighton, Artist Manager, Upside UK Music Management, UK.

Alex Bestall, Chief Executive Officer, Rightsify and Global Copyright Exchange, USA.

Rudolfs Budze, A&R, Universal Music, Latvia.

Kevin Charge, Songwriter and Producer, TG Management/Publishing, Soundgraphics, UK.

Chris Clark, Bassist, Daytime TV and Session Musician, UK.

Jonas Ekdahl, Songwriter, Producer and Drummer, Evergrey, Sweden.

Adam Ficek, Clinical Psychotherapist and Counsellor, UK.

Lorenzo Filippin, Label Manager, Milleville Music, Italy.

Meldra Guza, Director, The SongLab, UK.

Ricky Hanley, Songwriter, Producer and Vocal Arranger, Hanley Music, UK.

Karen Harding, Recording Artist and Songwriter, UK.

John Hart, Manager, John Hart Music Management, UK.

Kate Hendry, Head of Label Operations, Absolute Label Services, UK.

Bryan Hinkley, Owner, Gratitude Sound, USA.

Laurence Hobbs, Founder, SAFO Music, UK.

Emily Jackson, Assistant Head of Distribution and Quality Control, Horus Music, UK.

Martin 'Magic' Johnson, Freelance Drummer, UK.

Natalie Major, Singer-Songwriter, USA.

Misstiq, Music Producer and Content Creator, Australia.

Gavin Monaghan, Music Producer, UK.

Erik Nielsen, Director/Consultant, Wingnut Music, UK.

Steve Osborne, Music Producer, UK.

Andy Rea, Co-founder, 2000trees Festival; Founder, Redtarn PR & Events; University Lecturer, UK.

Paul Rogers, Production Music Creator, Flexitracks/Universal Music, UK.

Sipho, Record Artist, Dirty Hit, UK.

David Stark, Editor/Publisher, SongLink International, UK.

Kieran Thompson, Artist Manager, UK.

Greig Watts, DWB Music (Music Publisher), UK.

Tilly Wellard, A&R Consultant and Co-owner, Bonded, UK.

Tersha Willis, Co-founder, terrible*, UK.

Preface

This book was written for people who create original music and wish to build a career out of their passion. It also aims to serve those who support music creators on their path to growth in the music industry.

Gaining an understanding of the mechanics of the music business can unlock abundant opportunities for music creators. This is an industry that has an undeniable air of mystique about it and that can sometimes seem closed off to the uninitiated. Except it is not. Because the doors are not locked. The doors are in fact open to anyone who is brave enough to try. This book enables music creators to know what to say and what to expect when they open those doors. The music business needs music to survive as a business and music creators need to know how the business of music functions.

In recent years, I have witnessed a growing need for a comprehensive guide that demystifies the music industry and its operations. This book is the result. The decision to write this book was informed by my professional and academic experiences. I work with a wide array of young music creators, many of whom exude enthusiasm and talent, but lack a cohesive understanding of the business that underpins the landscape around them. I have attended many international songwriting camps and worked with writers and producers who don't fully understand their intellectual property rights and how their rights are collected and exploited. I have worked with a great deal of emerging artists who don't understand the contracts put in front of them. I see bands who are confused by the roles played by their managers, their booking agents and their promoters. I see DJs who don't know how to take their product to market and gain growth online. I see many of my students overwhelmed by the abundance of information around them who trip themselves up and struggle to find their feet.

In the 2020s, a major generational gap has emerged between those who were born in the information age of digital technologies, social media and advanced internet capabilities and those who were not. As someone in their 40s, I am familiar with both generations and I see mismatched expectations and behaviours between them. This is especially prevalent in many industries and music is no different. There is often an expectation that the younger generation are fortunate because they have all the information that they need instantly available to them. There is thus an assumption that they should be multifaceted and self-educated. But the reality is that the information age can be quite overwhelming for many music creators and knowing where to look to find the information they need to build a career can be extremely complex, for a whole multitude of reasons. This book seeks to address that.

I get asked a great deal of questions by artists, composers, producers, band members, DJs, songwriters and performers, and I can't think of a single question I have ever been asked that is not answered in this book.

Author: Jonny Amos. Photo by SS Creative Photography.

Acknowledgements

This book was created with invaluable input from several people. Special thanks go to Erik Nielsen, Alex Bestall, Kevin Charge, Dr Adam Ficek, Dr Paul Rogers, David Stark, Ricky Hanley, Misstiq, Martin 'Magic' Johnson, Denise Beighton, Steve Osborne, Emily Jackson, Natalie Major, John Aagaard, Kieran Thompson, Sipho, Tersha Willis, Julie Knibb, Gavin Monaghan, Andy Rea, Laurence Hobbs, Lorenzo Filippin, Rudolfs Budze, Jonas Ekdahl, Karen Harding, Bryan Hinkley, Greig Watts, Chris Clark and Kate Hendry. Extra-special thanks go to John Hart, who not only contributed with his interview but also ran a fact-checking edit on the entirety of the book.

Gratitude and acknowledgements are also due to the sources which were very useful in the research for the book. These include the International Federation of the Phonographic Industry, Music Tomorrow and Music Business Worldwide.

A big thank-you to Hannah Barnes-Rowe at Routledge for instantly understanding the need for this book and its context in the marketplace. Thanks also to Emily Tagg, Evie Evans and the rest of the team at Routledge.

Thanks to James Black, Paul Mead, Darren Loczy and Steve Dunne for riding the rebellious rollercoaster with me. It has shaped us all.

I would also like to thank my parents, Pauline and Keith, who have always shown unconditional love and support for every path that music has taken me down; and to my big brother Geoff, who has always got my back.

And most of all, thanks to my dear wife, Meldra Guza, for supporting me through the process and for contributing Chapter 34 on portfolio careers – a subject on which she is one of the leading experts. Meldra, you are an inspirational leader and the epitome of perfection. You only think you know how much I love you.

Introduction

The ability to create music is a gift that only some possess. It is a natural aptitude that is perhaps attributable to an individual's unique make-up. Once that giftbox is opened, this skill begins to develop through experimentation, passion, tenacity and curiosity. For someone with heightened creative abilities, there is an itch that can only be scratched by creating more. This may lead to a desire to pursue music as a career; but for this to be a fruitful path, it is crucial to understand what that might look like. By learning the key aspects of the business, you can ensure that this path is an enjoyable and sustainable one. I wish I had known that when I was 17.

I am a music creator, which has allowed me to write this book through the lens of a music creator for the benefit of other music creators. It is worth mentioning too that I do not feature in this book. I refer to myself only in the introduction and the conclusion. That is because the book is not about me. It is about you. Allow me, however, to offer a little insight into my past.

It was October 1997. I was 18 years old. I was living in a suburb of Birmingham – the second-biggest city in England. I was a singer-songwriter who could not find a band committed enough to create, rehearse and perform music with the same level of enthusiasm that I possessed myself. Therefore, I was on my own and singing my own songs. I had written and recorded some songs that I thought I believed in, and I had a box of 100 demo cassette tapes that featured four of my songs. I had used some of those demo tapes to gain work and build my reputation locally. I was playing regular gigs in pubs, cafes, bars and restaurants. I wanted to get a manager to work with me on taking my career further, but before the arrival of the internet, it was difficult to know where to start trying to find one. The only places I could think of were the ads in the back of *The NME* (a weekly music publication in the UK) and the back of *The Stage* (a weekly publication catering largely for the theatre world, but which sometimes featured ads posted by managers and record companies that were looking to work with recording artists). The way to pitch yourself back then was by sending a demo tape and covering letter in the post. If a telephone number was included in an ad, it would be a landline, because mobile phones had not yet become mainstream at the time. I sent demos to many managers and heard nothing back, so I plucked up the courage to start making calls instead. I was met with a great deal of answering machines; but one day, one of my phone calls was answered.

'Yes?' the man replied in a gruff but cut-glass English accent.

'Hello!' I said with enthusiasm. 'My name is Jonny Amos and I am a singer-songwriter who is looking for a manager. I wonder if perhaps that might be you? Would you like me to send you a demo tape for your consideration?'

I heard him exhale in annoyance down the phone. 'Are you a professional?' he asked in a sharp and frustrated manner.

'Not yet,' I answered.

'Then why are you bothering me? I only deal with professionals,' he snapped as he put the phone down.

It is moments like this that can shape our understanding of how things work when we know no different. I knew that not all managers would be rude. I was brought up to be polite; but I also knew that my enthusiasm and manners would not always be matched by others. In a situation such as this, taking the path of least resistance could perhaps have been the easiest thing to do to. I could have let it go and moved on. However, I wanted to stand up for myself, so I called him back.

'Hello – it's me again, Jonny Amos, the singer-songwriter from Birmingham. I think the line went dead as we were talking,' I said, knowing full well that he had cut me off previously.

'Yes, what do you want?' the manager asked bluntly.

'I want to find a manager and I'd like to see if you would be interested in listening to my music, because you might like it,' I stated with confidence laced with a purposeful sense of innocence.

'But I only work with professionals, so why are you bothering me?' he asked aggressively.

I could tell that the phone call was close to being ended once more. 'Because I'm going to be a professional. I'm not yet, but I will be; and I'm going to need a manager. And I think you should be more polite in your tone when you talk to me,' I said.

I heard him gasp. The nature of the call changed.

'Okay,' he said in a softer tone. 'What's your name again?'

I replied, 'I'm Jonny Amos and I represent a new generation.' To this day, I don't know where that line came from. I seemed to just pull it out of the sky somehow in a moment of panic and my voice was wobbling with nerves as I said it.

'Okay, Jonny – let's see what you've got,' he said calmly. 'Send me your tape and write your name on the top-left corner of the jiffy envelope, so I know it's you who is sending it. I'll look out for it.'

I posted the tape package that same day.

A week later, I got home one day and my mum said there was a message on the answering machine for me from a manager from a music company. 'He sounds very posh,' she said. As I tried to access the message, I thought to myself that the greeting on the machine was my mum's bright and friendly voice. 'Welcome to the Amos family answering machine. Please leave a message after the tone,' was the automatic message that anyone heard when the phone rang out in my family's home in the late 1990s. I cringed a little inside – this did not fit well with the professional image I was trying to portray!

'Hello Jonny, it's Derek. Well, I'm glad you stuck up for yourself, young man, because I've listened to your music and it's superb. Just superb. Let's arrange to meet.' He signed off leaving the same telephone number that I had called him on only a week before.

My dad and I duly went to meet Derek for coffee in the Waldorf Hotel in London's West End. He was small in height, with a long, black coat that almost skimmed his ankles. He was well dressed yet looked unloved and malnourished. He did not look like how I thought he would. He was probably in his 60s. He would talk a great deal about himself, pause for some coffee and a long drag on his cigarette, and then talk about himself some more. Then he moved on to how hard it was in the music industry these days. 'These days' can be any days in the eyes of the negative, I've since discovered.

Derek chain-smoked throughout our meeting and the long cylinders of tobacco ash would balance on the end of his cigarette as he consistently dictated the conversation in a commanding fashion. He then looked my dad in the eyes and said, 'Keith, from one father to another, I'll take care of your boy.' He then asked my dad for what he referred to as 'publicity fees', which my dad kindly paid on my behalf. 'I just need to cover the costs for when I take people out for dinner to discuss Jonny's career,' he said in a calm and confident manner. We figured this was normal because we had no basic understanding of how things worked. From that day on, I never saw Derek again and he never returned my calls. I had been hustled.

Perhaps that's why Derek had ads in publications. Perhaps this was how he made his living. Perhaps the staff at the hotel had no idea. Perhaps his originally putting the phone down on me was his way of filtering out those he thought would be unwilling to pay his 'publicity fees'.

This was an undeniable setback. I figured I was back to square one; but really, I wasn't. You're never back to square one if you learn something. I would not let what happened define my outlook on myself and my music. Neither would I allow it to stain my understanding of the music industry or any other manager I would go on to work with.

In June 2022, 25 years after first meeting him, I bumped into Derek again by chance. He was looking in the window of a bookshop on Charing Cross Road – a mere stone's throw from where I had last seen him over two decades previously. He was old, very old. I approached him. He didn't recognise me. I had always wondered what I would say if I ever saw him again. I surprised myself. I took immense pity on him. He looked lonely. I made small talk with him about the bookshop. We then talked about how much London has changed in recent years and how different everything looked around us. It felt symbolic. I was a successful songwriter by this point. I had become a music professional who had learned to make smart choices. We ended our brief chat and I wished him a good day.

It's often said that the two most important days in your career are the first and the last, because that's when you learn the most. I don't know what my last day in the music business will look like, but my first was when I met Derek and I learned a great deal. Mark Twain once said, 'The two most important days of your life are the day you were born and the day you find out why.' This also resonates with me and so many others who pursue the creation of original music as their lifelong goal.

My first day in the job taught me a lot. I figured that if I learned about how the business behind the music works, I would be able to protect myself. I was right.

That was then and this is now. The music industry I signed up to barely exists anymore. It has been replaced by something far greater, in my opinion. There are fewer 'jobs' than there used to be; but there is more work than there has ever been before. We are in the information age: an artist-centred, data-driven, multifaceted global gig economy that is teeming with opportunities, some of which have only just begun to emerge. This is, however, still an industry that rewards tenacity, consistency, courage and evolution in the same way it has always done.

This book explores in depth the mechanics of the music business, with a focus on the perspective of the music creator. It begins by exploring the key aspects that underpin the traditional elements of the music business, which are centred around intellectual property. It then moves on to focus on life through the lens of a recording artist, followed by a collection of chapters that put the spotlight on releasing music into the digital sphere. The book goes on to explore how music creators can create income streams to build their careers, before concluding with a series of chapters on the future of the music business.

You don't need to worry about the Dereks of this world – you have me in your corner now, and you have this book to turn to anytime you like.

Part 1

Song and Recording Copyrights

1
Understanding Copyright

What Is Copyright?

'Copyright' is the right to copy.

There are two forms of copyright attached to a song's audio content. First, there is the copyright of the sound recording, which is most commonly referred to as the 'master rights'. Second, there is the copyright of the musical work. To be more precise, the latter is the identity of the song and the copyright that is retained within the composition. The basic legal outline of copyright ownership works in much the same way throughout most of the world, in that copyright is granted automatically when an original work is created. There is no official register of copyright works in many countries. For example, there is no such system in the UK and therefore there are no fees that need to be paid to any official organisation to validate or protect a copyright. From here on in, the book refers to a musical work as a 'song'.

A song's copyright is defined by three key factors:

- the lyrics;
- the melodies; and
- the chords that are used to create harmony.

It is the combination of these three ingredients that defines an original song's identity and subsequently its copyright.

Automatic copyright protection in most countries is granted to original literacy, musical and artistic works, and this also extends to illustrations and photography. In the context of original music, chord patterns alone cannot be copyrighted. However, lyrics and melodies when combined, or lyrics alone, can be. Most commonly, it is the combination of lyrics, chords and melodies that determines a song's copyright.

DOI: 10.4324/9781003452119-2

The three key requirements for copyright protection are as follows:

- It must be a work of authorship;
- It must be original; and
- It must be fixed in a tangible means of expression.

A breach of copyright is most commonly referred to as an 'infringement'. This is defined by somebody using either the whole song or a substantial part of the song without the copyright holder's permission.

How to Protect Your Copyright

Copyright protection is automatic from the moment of creation. However, someone's word is not enough to prove copyright ownership should a situation arise where the copyright's owner is being questioned about the originality or ownership of the idea. It is important to prove ownership. The most effective solution here is a digital time stamp of the song's digital identity.

A digital time stamp can be documented in several ways. The most common form is for the songwriter/s to record a version of the song on a smartphone or tablet by using an app that can record and document the time and date of the process. Another form of time stamp creation is to record the song on a digital audio workstation (DAW) software application on a computer. This offers the copyright owner further options for multitracking additional parts or layers to the original idea. This is especially useful for songs that have arrangement ideas (eg, rhythmic and melodic sequences) which form part of the uniqueness of the song's identity. DAW software applications also tend to have back-up files and extended details on times and dates of when specific parts were recorded or edited.

To ensure further peace of mind, it is recommended to export the song in MP3 format from either of the above methods, email a copy of the MP3 to yourself and save it to a folder on a web-based email account. This action will add a new time and date as to when the file was sent, and this process can be used in a court of law to provide evidence of ownership.

How Long Does Copyright Last?

A song's copyright lasts for the creator's lifetime plus between 50–70 years after the death of the creator, depending on the country where the creator is based. If the song was co-written, the duration will be 50–70 years after the death of the last cowriter to pass away. After this period has elapsed, the song's copyright expires and in many countries this means that the song then enters the public domain.

There are many songs that are now in the public domain which date back several hundred years. We are yet to witness the dawn of pop hits entering the public domain, but under current legislation this will happen one day.

A song's copyright is a form of intellectual property that can be assigned or licensed to a music publisher for the purposes of administration, exploitation and royalty collection.

2
What Are Master Rights?

Master rights relate to the copyright of a master recording of a song.

Often referred to as the 'sound recording copyright', they constitute the intellectual property of a recorded song – not the song itself, but the recording of the song.

For the purposes of clarification, master rights and master recordings have nothing to do with the term 'mastering'. 'Mastering' relates to the process of rendering the audio content of a song for commercial release.

A master recording is deemed to be the sonic identity of a studio version of a song. The master rights relate to whoever owns those rights to the recording. Master rights are typically owned by whoever facilitated the recording. In a professional context, this will usually be a record company. On a grassroots level, ownership of the master rights is often more complicated. The owner could perhaps be the artist, a manager, a financier, a producer or another entity.

New master rights are created every time there is a master recording of a song. Therefore, one song could have more than one master related to its identity.

Who Owns Your Masters?

This can be a difficult subject to unpack due to the wide number of variables in place, so let's explore some different scenarios.

Scenario 1: Band's Demo Masters

A band has self-produced a catalogue of songs that they plan to use for their debut album. They recorded the songs themselves in their own portable set-ups

DOI: 10.4324/9781003452119-3

using their own instruments, recording equipment and software. The band own their own masters. Several months later, the band sign a record contract. The record company finances the recording of the same songs in a professional studio with a producer and a recording engineer. The masters are now owned by the record company, but this is a brand-new recording. Even though the band played the same arrangements as their demo recordings, this is a brand-new set of master rights because it is a brand-new recording that is owned by the record company.

Scenario 2: The Uncle and The Shed

A four-piece band record their EP. They are on a tight budget, so the singer's uncle offers to record the band for free in his shed. The uncle records the band's songs and then the guitarist from the band mixes the songs on his laptop. Who own the masters here? The uncle states that he does not want a fee, but that does not mean he's not entitled to a good portion of the masters – especially if the recordings find success in the future. The guitarist may stake her claim to co-ownership due to the time that she has put into the mixing of the songs. The best solution here is to have a mature conversation with all parties present about master rights; but in this case, that conversation doesn't take place. This prevents the band from being able to license the songs into sync opportunities, so the master rights need cleaning up.

This could be a solution to the above scenario:

The uncle recorded the band over two days on his property with his equipment. These were 7.5-hour sessions each day with a one hour break. This totals 13 hours.

The guitarist spent two evenings working on the mixes in her own home on her own laptop using software that she had paid for previously. She worked for 3.5 hours per evening. This totals 7 hours.

13 hours (uncle) = 65%
7 hours (guitarist) = 35%

It could perhaps be said that the above split is a fair option for master rights ownership; but what about the rest of the band? In the end, the solution was to give 50% to the band, with the uncle and the guitarist splitting the rest according to the equation above.

Master rights ownership:

Band = 50%
Uncle = 32.5%
Guitarist = 17.5%

Scenario 3: The College Campus Session

A producer works with a three-piece punk band on their next single. The producer and the band are all students at the same college. The recording session takes place at the studio of the college. No fees are paid by any parties. They agree to work on a speculative basis and to split the masters evenly between themselves.

Band Member 1 (drummer) = 25%
Band Member 2 (bassist and vocalist) = 25%
Band Member 3 (guitarist) = 25%
Producer = 25%

What they did not know was that the college has a clause in its service-level agreement which states that it owns 10% of the masters of any recordings which take place in its facilities. This is surprisingly common for many educational settings. However, what these institutions do to administrate and regulate this policy may be questioned.

Scenario 4: Self-produced Artist Who Outsources the Mixing

An indie folk artist has recorded their debut single. The artist produces the track themselves and outsources the mixing. The artist exports the stems and sends them to a mixing engineer who has been recommended to them. It is at this point that the artist and the mix engineer must negotiate on this transaction. The mix engineer can either:

- offer their mixing services for a fixed price;
- offer to work for 'free' in exchange for 10% ownership of the master rights; or
- offer a deal where they take 5% of the masters and charge half their normal rate.

It is at this point that the folk artist can decide whether they wish to invest the money and keep 100% of their master rights or to save the money and offer a part of their masters in exchange for the time and services of the time engineer. There is no right or wrong: everything is negotiable.

The Benefits of Owning Master Rights

Master rights are one of the most important forms of intellectual property in the music industry. Today, many artists choose to own their own masters rather than sign to a traditional record company. Artists that own their own masters are entitled to trade freely with whichever entities they wish to do business with. This is especially lucrative when it comes to licensing the use of their recordings with brands, ad agencies, videogame creators, film production companies, TV companies and a whole host of other audio-visual synchronisation opportunities. This is because all of the upfront fees go directly to the artist. This route relies on the artist being self-motivated and connected to the right industry personnel to make this a viable option.

Another option artists have is to choose to partner with a label services company which they effectively hire to manage their release campaign, rather than relying on the services and personnel of a record company. Streaming royalties are also much more favourable for those that own their masters.

What Are 'Points'?

'Points' are percentage points on record sales. This is something that some producers expect when they produce a record. This should be part of the negotiation process when working with a producer. Perhaps the producer is being paid a flat fee for each song, a day rate or even an hourly rate. On top of this, the producer could ask for points from sales. If this is the case, it is important to determine whether this relates to the dealer price or the retail price. Point scales tend to vary from 1% to 5% but may increase if sales reach a specific threshold. This should all be a part of the negotiation process. Producers' point requests are not always met; in fact, some could even argue that it is a practice from a bygone era. Many labels no longer negotiate on points and only offer flat fees to producers. Nevertheless, it is another consideration in the context of master rights.

Master rights are a valuable source of income in the global music industry. It may be that an artist is comfortable with relinquishing these rights in exchange for the services that a record company can offer. Perhaps the record company is offering an advance to the artist or is offering an equal-split profit-share deal.

Perhaps the artist wishes to remain flexible and empowered by the freedom that master rights ownership offers them, so that they can do business their own way and retain ownership.

In all cases, an agreement in writing is of paramount importance as to who owns the rights to the masters.

3
Song Splits

Song splits relate to how a song's copyright is split between its co-creators. A song split represents royalty share and percentage of ownership.

Most commonly, song splits concern the copyright of the song. However, there may also be the subject of the copyright of the sound recording, also known as the 'master rights'. For the avoidance of doubt, when referring to splits with co-creators, it is always recommended to ensure clarity and transparency on two key issues:

- what rights you are splitting; and
- what the shared percentages are of the rights you are splitting.

It is not only how you are splitting your rights but also what rights you are referring to. So much information can be lost in translation, jargon and assumption.

Songwriting in Bands

Bands have a sense of cohesion and togetherness, and often share a unity of collective thinking. Band members may well be investing equally when it comes to covering the costs of marketing, merchandise, travel, accommodation and other such collective outgoings. This can often lead to the understanding that all profits should be split evenly as a result. This is perhaps both fair and accurate to a certain extent. It does not necessarily mean, however, that song copyrights should be split evenly. A song's copyright is defined by lyrics, melody and harmony. Band members may often argue that they 'wrote their own part'. It could be argued that this is a musical contribution to a recording and is acknowledged and remunerated as a neighbouring right or a digital performance royalty (depending on which country you are based in). It may perhaps be suggested that this does not necessarily contribute to the songwriting process and

DOI: 10.4324/9781003452119-4

therefore is not part of the copyright equation. This can be difficult for many band member musicians to understand, as they are often present during a song's original inception and therefore feel connected to its authorship. This is where clear lines of communication are necessary in the interests of all parties.

Let's imagine the following scenario: the singer of a band turns up to a rehearsal with some new lyrics and some ideas for a new song. The guitarist starts to play some chords that put the singer in the creative zone, so that they can add their lyrics and attach melodies to those lyrics. There are two songwriters here. Unless a further creator contributes towards the underlying lyrics, melodies or harmonies, there is no case to add another songwriter to the copyright ownership of the song, even if they were present and added their instrumental backing.

In this scenario, the singer and guitarist are quite happy to split the songwriting evenly in the band because they feel pressurised into doing so. There are now five equal portions of 20% across all five band members.

A year later, the bass player leaves.

The following year, the song gets a placement on a trending TV show on Netflix, in a videogame and on two editorial playlists on Spotify; and it eventually makes a chart entry.

The original bass player who didn't contribute to the songwriting process still gets the same royalties. Forever. How would you feel about that as the singer?

In this scenario, the band looked at their intellectual property in the same way as they looked at their other band-related outgoings and income streams. The singer and the guitarist were being loyal, noble, kind and considerate to their band member; but it could also be said that they were doing themselves an injustice.

There are plenty of bands that split their songwriting evenly and there's nothing morally flawed about this, even if it is only one or two members of the band that create the lyrics, melodies and harmonies. If there is a written understanding between all parties, it is less likely to create misunderstandings and friction further down the line. There are also other bands that split their copyrights only between the members who contributed to the songwriting. In either case, it is about finding a workable solution that offers transparency and understanding for all parties. It is too easy to blur the lines between composition, performance and recording, and therefore bands are always encouraged to have open and honest conversations about their song splits. In some cases, bands have written agreements (often referred to as 'inter-band agreements') in place which agree on various aspects of the business between members in the context of their band. This works to safeguard the interests of all band members and offers clarity on various business-related matters. It could be argued, however, that this is less effective for agreeing on song splits because the splits may vary from song to song. The more viable solution is perhaps to have a song split sheet in place between all writers for each song.

Songwriting with Producers

The lines between songwriting and production have long been blurry in contemporary music. It could be argued that the lines are even blurrier in today's era of the rapid development of affordable music-making software. Songwriters, artists and producers should always have an open discussion about song splits before the creative session takes place. It might be assumed that all parties will take an even split on the songwriting; but try never to allow assumptions to get the better of you and your situation. In truth, nothing can be assumed. The two key issues to be clear on when working with producers is what the splits look like on both the songwriting and the master rights.

Scenario 1

A songwriter is paying a producer for their time. The producer verbally agrees to relinquish all songwriting credit despite having a case for a percentage because they contributed towards structural changes, arrangement, chords and lyrical and melodic changes. The master rights are acquired in full by the songwriter because they paid the producer for their time. The producer gets a name credit on any subsequent release. A scenario such as this seems quite clear and straightforward, but it is not. Unless these agreements are made in writing, the producer could claim percentages on both the songwriting splits and the master rights further down the line. If this song goes on to gain commercial success, sync licence fees and royalties could be received, and the producer may have a change of heart about how they feel about waiving their rights. This problem could have easily been overcome by signing a split sheet for the songwriting splits and the master rights split at the time of or on completion of the recording session.

In theory, a songwriter should acquire the full master rights of the recording from a producer if they pay the producer for their time. However, in practice, it is not always as simple as this. Only when it is put in writing is there a watertight, legally binding agreement. Some producers will want to have splits on master rights even when they have been paid a fee for their time. There is no right or wrong here. Most sync licensing agents will want to see a producer release which states in writing that the producer/engineer/studio stakes no claim to the master rights of a recording. This is so that the sync agent puts themselves in a position where they can license the recording into TV or film placements without any risk of copyright claims further down the line from a party that they were unaware of. The solution to this scenario is for the songwriter and the producer to establish a clear agreement in writing in the early stages of their working relationship.

Scenario 2

A songwriting artist collaborates on a song with a producer. There are no fees exchanged and they are working on a speculative basis with the view that both parties stand to benefit should the song be successful in some form in the future. The producer creates the chords and the structure of the song and provides all the instrumentation and programming of the musical parts to the production. The songwriting artist creates the lyrics and the melodies that attach to those lyrics; this is most commonly referred to as a song's 'topline'. In this scenario, the producer and the artist agree to a clean 50/50 split. A 'clean split' in this scenario relates to both the songwriting copyright and the master rights. They fill out a split sheet which states their splits and they both sign it.

Songwriting splits

Producer = 50%
Songwriting artist = 50%

Master rights splits

Producer = 50%
Songwriting artist 50%

Twelve months later, the producer reaches out to the artist to ask if they plan to release the song. The artist has decided that the mood and feel of the song no longer fit their style and direction. The producer then asks if the artist has any issue with the producer pitching the song to other artists through their music publisher. The artist is open to this suggestion. Five months later, the song is placed with a different artist who is signed to a record company. The process of music creators placing a song with an artist is most commonly referred to as 'a cut'. In this scenario, the producer relinquishes control of any ownership of the master rights to the record company in exchange for a fixed fee and listed credit. This is because the record company feels not only that the song is suitable for their artist, but also that the production values meet its expected standard. The record company could choose to record a new version of the song, which would mean that it owns the master rights of the new version. Instead, it pays the original producer because it wishes to use their production. The producer delivers the stems (wav files of all individual instrument files) to the record company and the new artist from the record company records their own version of the lead vocal for the song. The lyrics and melodies are not adapted or changed from the original version. The songwriting splits are clear in this arrangement. They are put down in writing: 50/50 between the producer and the song's original artist. However, the producer keeps 100% of the master rights fee that is received from the record company. The song's original artist queries this with the producer and reminds them of their original agreement, which states in writing that they each own 50% of the master rights. The producer defends themselves by saying that none of the vocal files that the original artist recorded were used on the final version of the recording because the vocals were replaced by the new artist, which therefore removes the original artist's contribution to the recording. The producer has a valid point here. However, this is not what they agreed in writing. The splits agreement did not state that the original songwriting artist should only retain 50% of the master rights should their vocals be used. The split sheets merely state a 50% clean split on both copyrights. Both the producer and the songwriter amicably agree on this and take 50% of the fee from the record company. Both parties are credited as songwriters on the release and the producer is credited for producing the track.

There are several lessons to learn from this scenario, but let's simplify them into two key areas. First, the producer could have placed a clause in the song split agreement that protects their full ownership of the master rights should any musical performances from the song that was pitched be removed from the final master recording. This clause would have entitled the producer to the full fee from the record company. Second, perhaps one of the key discoveries for both parties here is how keen record companies are to buy out masters from original track producers. This is most certainly more common today than it used to be. We are in an era where we are seeing less demo recordings followed by brand-new master recordings. This could largely be due to advancements in portable recording technologies and the affordability of professional solutions for music production. There have been many hit songs that were recorded as demos that became master recordings. 'Someone Like You' by Adele (XL Recording, BMG Publishing) is a good example of this. It was a demo recording that was licensed by the record company for release. Adele and her co-creator Dan Wilson are the songwriters, with Wilson having the production credit. The song is merely piano and a lead vocal, with no added layers of other instrumentation. There was clearly something very special that the record company liked about this original recording: a sense of heartache, vulnerability and perhaps a moment of magic in the performance that was captured on the day it was recorded. In any case, it is always worth considering the role that the original recording could play in the future and what the splits are for the ownership.

Differences in Cultures and Genres

There are cultures that are attached to genres in the same way as there are cultures that are attached to countries or groups of countries. It is important to absorb and respect different approaches to cultures when navigating the subject of song splits. For instance, the typical Nashville culture is to have even splits across all writers before the songwriting process begins. This leads to a mature and open process where all parties know where they stand.

In electronic dance music (EDM) culture, the track and the song are often viewed as separate entities. This often suggests a 50/50 split between the producer and the topline songwriter. It is not uncommon to see that the original vocals are kept in the final production and the topline vocalist then becomes the featured artist and can receive a payment for the performance on the recording in addition to backend royalties for the songwriting. This is often due to the culture of EDM whereby many dance music labels like to sign and release on a song-by-song basis rather than investing in an artist's wider body of work. This culture is not hugely dissimilar to hip hop and its associated sub-genres, where there is a distinctly different split of rights between the track and the vocal.

In the world of commercial pop music, it is often standard practice to split the songwriting evenly across all parties that contributed. However, it is also quite common for the original splits to be decreased when bringing in other writers, musicians, producers, DJs and mix engineers to contribute additional hooks and ideas to an edit of the song which enhances the chances of its future success. Cardi B's single 'I Like It' featuring Bad Bunny and J Balvin (Atlantic Records, 2018) has a total of 17 credited songwriters. This does not discredit the artist or any of her co-creators, but offers a glimpse into the ever-evolving industry of commercial chart music when it comes to the subject of song splits. Such a high number of creators can often to be accredited to the number of revisions that take place before the song is complete. Tasks such as melodic revision, hook enhancement, lyrical edits, beat making, programming, significant instrument additions and even audio engineering can often attribute towards being listed as a credited composer. This type of high numbered collaboration is generally restricted to the East Coast and West Coast of the US in the context of hotly touted and highly funded major label acts with big Billboard Hot 100 potential.

In Europe, it is not unusual for songwriters and producers to offer something in the region of 5% to 10% of a song's copyright to a music creator who can add a new dimension to a song's presentation prior to be it being pitched to record companies for potential placement with a recording artist. To try to secure the 'cut', songwriters and producers may make this offer to a creator who can help to embellish the song's pitch potential. This could perhaps be a vocalist who can represent the song, a guitarist who can bring a new sense of identity to a song's perception or maybe even a DJ who can add flair to the song's rhythmical sections. In this scenario, the creator is not necessarily contributing to the song's key compositional aspects of lyrics, melody and harmony, but is instead assisting with the performance and arrangement of the song. If all original songwriters agree with this action, the scenario sees non-songwriters become credited songwriters. While this type of decision is perhaps open to criticism on a moral level, it is common in the world of commercial songwriting in the modern era.

Views on this overall subject matter can and do vary significantly, but can usually be attributed to a shift in genre and culture. For instance, producers in the genres of rock and metal rarely assume that songwriting credits will be given to them, even if they make reactive suggestions on lyric, melody and harmony changes. There is perhaps an unspoken code of conduct for music producers not to ask for or expect a split of a songwriting credit because they are often not present at the time when the song was composed. The producer's role here is therefore in working with a complete song and finding the best possible ways to arrange, record, produce and perhaps even mix the result. A modern change in this area relates to technology and ease of access. Songwriting often happens at the computer in many cases. When working with bands, it could be argued that a producer's role is very different from that in the previous examples in the world of pop music. Even if the producer has more influence on changes to key compositional elements when working with a band, it is not assumed that their name will be on the songwriting credits. This contrasts quite significantly to a beat maker or a recording engineer in the commercial pop world, who may be given songwriting credit even if they do not alter the lyrics, melody or harmony.

UK-based music producer Steve Osborne (KT Tunstall, Happy Mondays, U2) considers his role of positively influencing the end product more important than negotiating on rights, even if he contributes to compositional changes:

> In my productions, I've changed chords; added riffs; changed arrangements, key signatures, tempos . . . There is not much I haven't done apart from getting involved with the lyrics. I only once got publishing which was kindly offered by Deacon Blue on one of their songs that I'd changed quite a lot.

The reality is I was paid well and got producer points. My prime concern is always to get the best possible record made. I've always felt that if the question of publishing were to arise, then it could give the impression that I was making changes to make money. It's hard enough trying to make changes without this being in the back of people's minds and I would rather get the best result possible for the record.

While Steve's insight is transparent, traditional and noble, he concedes that there has been a cultural shift in this subject matter irrespective of the genre. 'In today's climate, if I was making the same contribution, I would want an agreement about publishing before starting a project,' he adds. This shift, it could be argued, is perhaps because there is less money to be made from recorded music today when compared to bygone eras: the producer points no longer yield the kinds of returns that they used to and therefore the remuneration comes with a higher expected return in the form of additional credit. Perhaps we are witnessing change across the board in all genres, where producers expect to gain a greater stake of a copyright than they used to. If pop and hip hop do it, why can't rock and metal?

An alternative and widely acknowledged perspective on song splits is to make a clear three-way distinction between the three compositional elements.

'I see it as lyrics 33%, melody 33% and harmony 33%, irrespective of the number of writers involved in the process,' says Laurence Hobbs, chief executive officer of Safo Music Group, London (Pixie Lott, Sam Smith, Shayne Ward).

But this theory – however fair it may seem – can cause misunderstandings among some creators. For instance, a lyricist who offers their lyrics to a songwriting collaborator may see their instant song split as 50% because they provided a full lyric sheet with an indication of built-in or suggested form. It could perhaps be argued that standalone lyrics that possess clear lyric metering considerations and rhyme structures in their phrasing but don't contain melodic attachment to the words could only relate to one-third of a copyright. It's certainly a plausible figure to justify, on paper at least.

By way of contrast, some performing rights organisations (PROs) in Europe split copyright ownership into 12 units, with six units being assigned to music and the remaining six being assigned to lyrics. This leaves open an area of subjectivity, which is whether the attachment of melody to the lyrics is classified under music or lyrics. This somewhat grey area is further complicated when the lyricist and the melody writer are different people – perhaps from different countries with different music publishers and different viewpoints on the division of lyrics and melody.

Translation

Another aspect to consider in how copyright ownership is split is in the translation of a song into a different language. A good example of this is when songs that are composed in English are translated into either Japanese for the J-pop market or Korean for the K-pop market. It is standard practice that both markets expect between 30% and 50% of the copyright ownership in exchange for translation. This is a high percentage for songwriters to have to relinquish. It is always made abundantly clear at the start of any communication from a music publisher in Japan or South Korea that this is the case. There are three main reasons for this.

First, both languages are syllable heavy and therefore hold a different depth of rhythm in their natural metering. Translating 'Hello' to 'Konnichiwa' involves switching two syllables to four. With this basic example in mind, songs do not and cannot simply translate in a way that one might expect. Either the melody or the lyric must be compromised. The Far East upholds a highly etiquette-driven and honourable culture, and this attaches itself to music composition in the same way it does to many other aspects of life. Therefore, the song's melodies are kept perfectly intact in the way that they were composed in the song's original language. The melodies are treated with honour and meticulously imitated with the highest respect. This means that the lyrics must be compromised in order to adhere to this approach. A song's lyrics can change so drastically that the entire narrative may need to be rewritten. This task cannot be achieved by a standard translator. It is a task that can only be undertaken by a professional songwriter.

A second reason is that the business behind the placement of translated songs is complex and intricate. The process requires two music publishers: one that represents the song in English, which is pitching the song; and one based in Asia that knows the local market. When two music publishers work together like this, it is known as a music publisher working with a sub-publisher. Songwriters in this scenario assign their copyright to a music publisher's control. This means giving up a split of the copyright ownership in exchange for the services of the music publisher. Once the song's copyright has been split with all parties (songwriters and music publishers), the songwriters' split is reduced.

(Based on two songwriters plus translator):

Writer 1 = 50%
Writer 2–50%

This then becomes:

Writer 1 = 33.3%
Writer 2 = 33.3%
Translator songwriter = 33.3%

Now let's add the percentage due to the music publishers and let's assume this is a 50/50 split between writers and music publishers, because this is often the case.

Writer 1 = 16.65%
Writer 2 = 16.65%
Translator songwriter = 16.65%

Music publisher 1 = 33.3% (Writers 1 and 2's 50% splits)
Music publisher 2 (sub-publisher) = 16.65% (50% split of translator songwriter)

The third issue to understand here is the lucrative markets that we are talking about when it comes to Japan and South Korea. Japan is the second-largest music market in the world (behind the US) and South Korea usually ranks either sixth or seventh, depending on which report you read and when it was published. Both are big markets with very high sales of CDs and DVDs. This means that songwriters, music publishers, recording artists and record labels generally stand to earn more money from physical sales than they would in most Western markets. A smaller copyright percentage not only is a necessity in getting a song translated and placed in one of these markets, but also can be a profitable one despite the seemingly small figure. If you are perhaps wondering why countries such as Japan and Korea (among others) don't just source all songs domestically, it is generally because they hold a high level of respect for international songwriters and music creators who influence and help shape of their musical culture.

Producer points are generally not granted to music producers in these markets, but producers can be expected to be fairly paid for the master rights buyout of their production by the record companies should their tracks be used.

Put It in Writing

Everything that you've just read in this chapter means nothing if it's not agreed in writing. Nothing.

One of the more common ways to agree on song splits is for all songwriters to fill out a split sheet. Split sheets usually include the following information:

- the names of the songwriters as they appear in their PRO. This is the name that is on their passport rather than a stage name;

- a postal address for each writer;
- the role of each writer (lyricist, producer, melodies);
- the percentage split of each writer;
- the Interested Party Information (IPI) number of each writer (see the glossary);
- each writer's publisher's name and IPI number;
- the date of birth and signature of each writer;
- the title of the song; and
- the length of the song.

Filling out song split sheets makes the process of song administration easier for songwriters and music publishers. If the splits are agreed in writing in some form, this becomes a legally binding agreement, which is an important factor as it safeguards the interests of all parties involved in the ownership of the copyright. Split sheets are an ideal solution, as they are a tangible document that exhibits a range of information about the song and the songwriters. However, even a handwritten note or an email exchange between all involved parties will often suffice.

Professional song camps that are arranged for songwriters and producers to collaborate on song projects for specific artists and labels (often assembled by music publishers working in partnership with record companies) are typically active in using split sheets; but when it's just a regular song collaboration between two or three writers, there is a tendency to merely clarify that it is even splits in the copyright in an email between one another before or immediately after a collaborative session has taken place.

There is no right or wrong in any of these cases. It is always down to the creators of the song to decide how the splits should look on both the songwriting and the master rights. It need never be an awkward conversation or an embarrassing moment because this is rarely a crystal-clear subject, except perhaps for writing partners who work together regularly. A songwriter's intellectual property is their bargaining power and it is important to always be transparent and open with all parties when it comes to the subject of song splits.

Part 2

Music Industry Structures and Roles

4
What Is Music Publishing?

Music publishing is a crucial sector of the global music business. It relates to the administration, exploitation and royalty collections of song copyrights. Let's try to remove the jargon here so we can understand what music publishers do for songwriters.

What Do Music Publishers Do?

Music publishers sign songs and songwriters. They then seek opportunities for those songs and songwriters to make money. This perhaps could be in the form of pitching songs to record companies that are looking for songs for their artists; but it could also involve seeking to license the use of songs in TV programmes, movies, videogames, ads, media campaigns and just about any other tangible form of multimedia use where songs and music aid visuals. Publishers then look to monitor usage and collect and distribute royalties to the songwriters. Music publishers make their money by taking a split of the songwriting royalties. No money is ever paid upfront by a songwriter to a music publisher for their time and services.

Think of a music publisher as a songwriter's friend. In all actuality, many independent music publishers are songwriters themselves who have found their path into music publishing by understanding the business of songwriting.

Music publishers specialise in the administration of song copyrights by registering songs with the relevant performing rights organisations and ensuring that collection methods are taking place in accordance with song usage by music users.

DOI: 10.4324/9781003452119-6

In addition to their primary roles, music publishers often undertake other duties. Songwriting camps are an investment often made by music publishers as a way to get songwriters together for several days to create new songs which can then be pitched and exploited for mutually convenient commercial gain. Music publishers are often great networkers who have good relationships with many different people in the music industry, but especially with record companies, licensing agents, music supervisors, artists, artists managers, producers and – most importantly – songwriters. Music publishers can often be great mentors to songwriters.

Music publishing companies can vary significantly in terms of roster size, company structure, territories covered and genre specialism. It is common practice for small independent music publishers to partner with other music publishers in foreign territories. This is referred to as 'sub-publishing'. This enhances opportunities as the songs are plugged into further networks for both exploitation opportunities and collection management. Sub-publishers in foreign territories also connect songwriters with each other and sometimes handle translation of languages in songs.

Case Study: DWB Music

DWB Music works with a wide range of multi-genre songwriters in Europe who write songs for the J-pop (Japanese) market. DWB Music pitches the songs to its sub-publishing partner, Soundgraphics, in Japan. Soundgraphics has a strong reputation in Japan for providing high-quality songs to artists and labels, in addition to being able to navigate language translation and specialised collection methods. This type of strategic partnership work allows for international writers to gain entry to the lucrative J-pop market.

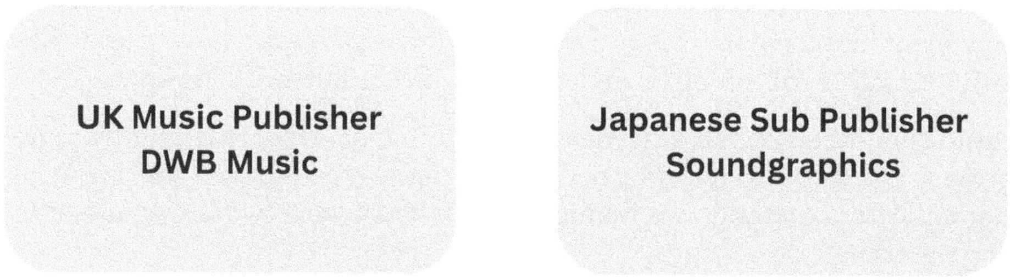

UK Music Publisher
DWB Music

Japanese Sub Publisher
Soundgraphics

Figure 4.1 The Role of a Music Publisher and a Sub-publisher Partner

Interview: Greig Watts, Director, DWB Music, UK

DWB was formed in 2004 as a songwriting and production team consisting of Paul Drew, Greig Watts and Pete Barringer. By 2006, DWB Music had developed into an independent music publishing company, which started to expand into signing and developing other songwriters. Since then, the company has grown to represent songwriters and producers from all over the world, selling over 100 million units in the process. The company is particularly well known for its work in the Japanese and South Korean markets and Eurovision, although the ethos of the brand is to go to places where other people do not. Today, DWB Music continues to thrive and grow: Pete Barringer continues to write and produce at a prolific rate, while Paul Drew focuses largely on the video production side. Greig Watts leads the music publishing department and develops and mentors music creators, while also running international song camps in various countries.

DWB is hugely active in identifying territories of growth that need songs. What have you learned over the years that has surprised you?

DWB's brand and identity come from the core value of wanting our writers' music to be heard – whether that be at Number 1 in the Billboard charts or when we get into a car and hear our song on the radio. We always seek to find homes for our songs and we learned very early on that there are many music markets throughout the world that need songs – it's just a matter of us finding them! In Japan, we were lucky enough to be in early on the first wave of Western writers in the market; it helped us to recognise the importance of being early in a marketplace before it becomes saturated. I think it is surprising that more writers and publishers don't do the same. So often, many focus solely on the UK and US markets, where everyone is trying the same route. We of course work those markets too; but we don't make them our focus, as the competition is tough, so sometimes it's good to go where the competition is less intense.

How important are your sub-publishing partners to your overall business?

Our sub-publishing partners have been very important to our business model, for a couple of reasons. First, when we have been successful in a territory, it's usually because we found a hungry song plugger who believed in our catalogue, and they helped place our songs and taught us the culture of where we were pitching. It's been so important to have the help of someone with local knowledge to guide us through placements, negotiations, contracts and much more.

The business is about relationships – so where our relationships are good, so are our results. Having several different song pluggers/sub-publishers in different territories means it's not just us that pitch the songs, but a team of people working on placing them in different places.

Second, we have found it much better to collect our income through sub-publishers, who again know the ways and cultures of the local collection societies. Throughout our career, we have often had co-writers ask us whether we have received our money and usually we have, while they are still waiting for a collection society to pay out. I learned in my early days not to rely on this. We are a small business and the writers are all small businesses, so we need the money to flow through so that we can carry on writing the next hit. Sub-publishers have really helped with this.

The collection of royalties is, of course, an important part of your practice. Do your collection methods ever expand outside of performing rights organisations (PROs) and sub-publishers?

Most of our writers' royalties are collected through sub-publishers and PROs. Of course, sometimes we have to do deals in territories where neither of these is efficient enough; in those cases, we have learned to ask for fees upfront, as often royalties in certain places will never come through – so you also learn not to work in those territories too much!

You receive a great deal of information and data from record companies regarding which songs they would like to receive for their artists. Do you tend to spot patterns that you then try to make sense of when creating opportunities for your writers?

There are certainly patterns and trends in the leads and briefs that we receive. But actually, we tend to try to encourage our writers not to work to specific briefs too much, but rather to continually write with knowledge of the current trends. We also encourage our writers to be leaders and innovators rather than followers. I have learned, as an artist and repertoire (A&R) person, how many songs are received and the quality is usually quite high. However, in the end, I (or the A&R person in charge) had to make a choice, and often it was the song that stood out or that was slightly different from the formulaic lead that won the race. In creativity, business and many aspects of the world, if we follow others, we will always be behind; so we really try to take our own path and keep writing great songs. I don't believe songs like *Bohemian Rhapsody* were written to a lead, and not many of our biggest hits were. Or sometimes they were written to a lead and we missed the target but hit another, because we were striving to deliver the best we could.

You are a well-loved mentor to many songwriters from all over the world. What advice can you offer to emerging songwriters who wish to write songs for recording artists?

My best advice is always to find yourself a team. Songwriting alone can be isolating. The business is full of rejection and can be hard to handle sometimes. If you have a team around you, they can act as a support network and this can really help you to get over the rejection and keep going. I believe that the most successful songwriters are those who overcome rejection and keep going. They see rejection or failure as a step in the road to success – something to learn from and build upon. This is very hard to do without people around you to support you. So, if you are a songwriter, melody writer, lyricist or producer, try to find people who complement you and can do the other jobs that you aren't so good at. Work to your strengths and theirs, and don't try to be a jack of all trades. I was someone who could write and produce, and also sing; but to become successful, I had to find my strengths, which were more on the melody side and lyrics, and also leading and directing sessions. I only really discovered my strengths when I found Paul and Pete, who were both great producers and musicians. As we wrote together, we complemented each other's skillsets, and I focused on my strengths and so did they. So, find a team; find your strengths; keep focused; find ways to be inspired (song camps being one of the best, as you meet likeminded people); and most importantly, believe in your talent and never give up.

So, Music Publishing Isn't Actually About Publishing Music?

No, it's not. In fact, it's a rather confusing name for such a prominent sector of the global music industry. Let's simplify this. To 'publish' something is to prepare, issue and distribute it for public consumption. Like a book, for example. However, music publishing is not about publishing music – so where did the name come from?

The origins of music publishing can apparently be traced back to the 19th century. At a time that was dominated by religious hymns and music from the classical realm, a bohemian neighbourhood of lyricists and music creators known as Tin Pan Alley emerged in New York City. This cohesive community collectively created and released original music. Music at that time was not documented by means of audio recording but through sheet music, which was published and made available through print.

That's where the name came from and it's never changed since. It could perhaps be said that this is a dated and confusing term, given the misleading inaccuracy of the name of the sector – especially in the age of digital distribution, when artists can 'publish' their own music. It's confusing for many; but try not to think of music publishing and digital distribution as the same thing. They're not. They sit in completely different places in the landscape of the music business.

Types of Music Publishing Contracts

Single Song Assignments

A single song assignment (SSA) is an agreement between a songwriter and a music publisher for one song only. Typically, royalty rates are split 50/50 between both parties. This may vary depending on negotiation, but not hugely. There is a set term which does not usually surpass 20 years in the modern era in most countries, although this can vary in different cultures. SSAs or 'one song deals' are a great entry point for songwriters starting out their careers and are also a favourable route for songwriters who are looking to split their risk by not putting all their eggs in one basket by signing an exclusive catalogue deal with one music publisher. SSAs are a great way for songwriters to understand the practice of music publishers while widening their network and their understanding of the business behind songs.

Exclusive Songwriting Agreements

Exclusive songwriter deals signify a stronger partnership between a songwriter and a music publisher, as they involve the exclusive assignment of a songwriter's catalogue to a music publisher. Agreements can and do vary significantly. For instance, a back catalogue deal usually covers everything that a writer has ever composed. This would earn the writer the right to ask for an advance, which would be recoupable but not returnable. This means that the publisher would recoup the advance that it has paid to the songwriter by keeping the songwriter's royalties until the advance is paid back to it. If, however, the advance is never recouped due to a lack of song success, the songwriter need not return the advance. The music publisher bears the risk. It could be that the songwriter only signs their future catalogue. It could be both. Regardless of the hugely negotiable variables, this contract would be binding for at least five years in most cases, although rolling one-year contracts are a more flexible and favourable modern alternative for many. Royalty rates typically vary from 70/30 (in the songwriter's favour) to 50/50. In the US, this contract is commonly referred to as a 'staff writer deal'.

Administration Deals

Administration deals tend to be quite popular for (but not limited to) songwriters with a previous back catalogue of successful copyrights. The songwriter does not need to assign their copyrights to a music publisher but instead licenses the publisher to carry out specific tasks such as collection or sync. A much more favourable royalty rate is agreed and typically sits between 75/25 and 90/10.

Purchase Agreements

Purchase agreements cover the purchase of an entire catalogue of song copyrights. For instance, Michael Jackson purchased the right to a large proportion of the Lennon/McCartney catalogue in 1985 for $47 million. Purchase agreements are acquisitional transactions which often blur the lines between sales from one entity to another with company mergers. Deals of this nature happen regularly.

Key Terms of a Music Publishing Contract

Contracts come in two forms: short form and long form. A short-form contract (sometimes known as a 'heads of agreement') acts as a summarised version of the contract, with the key headlines of the offer outlined briefly. A long-form contract is the same contract but in full legal language with fully expanded terms, conditions and clauses included. Contracts are formal and legally binding, and should be drawn up by lawyers. Contracts should conform to legal jurisdiction, which is why they can be jargon heavy and confusing for many. Let's simplify the key terms of a music publishing contract.

Rights

Rights are either assigned or licensed in the context of how songwriters work with music publishers. When rights are assigned, a music publisher has control over how copyrights are used. When rights are licensed, the writer retains control. The licensing of rights is more typically associated with administration deals. In most instances, the assignment of rights is the more common practice between songwriters and music publishers. When assigning rights to a music publisher, it might be that a songwriter prefers to specify what their music supports and what it does not support. For instance, a songwriter may not want their songs to be used in a TV show that compromises animal rights. This kind of stipulation is referred to as a 'moral right' and can be requested by the songwriter and negotiated with the music publisher.

Term

This relates to the length of time for which the songwriter assigns or licenses the rights of their works (songs) to the music publisher.

Retention

This relates to the length of time after the term for which the music publisher can still exploit and collect on the copyrights.

Collection Period

This is a specific amount of 'mop-up' time in which the music publisher collects the royalties that were accrued during the retention period. Royalties can sometimes take a substantial amount of time to be received, so a collection period can be useful for a publisher. Collection periods are usually between one and two years. For instance, if a retention period elapses in 2034, collection could run until 2036.

Date

As simple as it may sound, all contracts must have a date. In this context, it is a fixed point in time at which the contract is executed. This is highly significant in the years that follow.

Jurisdiction

This relates to the laws of the territory to which the contract is bound. Copyright law is generally quite similar in most Western countries. Every contract should always state the jurisdiction so that any legal action can conform to a recognised set of domestic principles and laws.

Audit

Songwriters have the right to an audit if they wish to gain clarification on the accounting methods of a music publisher. This is typically at the cost of the songwriter who requests the audit, as they will need to hire an accountant. In more recent years, songwriters' requests for audits have decreased in number – perhaps due to advancements in digital technology and the transparency and accuracy that software applications can offer. It is, however, a right that needs acknowledging in a contract.

Royalties

This relates to how income streams will be split between the songwriter and the music publisher. This section of a contract should clarify how income is split in percentages between the songwriter and the music publisher in relation to performance, mechanical, print and synchronisation. Many contracts will refer to 'any other income' or 'catch-up income', which typically refers to income streams which are yet to be defined or created in technology but relate to the use of a copyright. A songwriter can only assign or license their portion of any song that is co-written and not the entirety of the song.

Territory

This term specifies which countries, groups of countries or continents are covered in the agreement. Most publishers will want the whole world covered but this is negotiable. One of the more modern words used in relation to territories is 'universe', which covers territories outside of planet Earth.

Advances

This outlines any upfront contractual payments which are agreed from the publisher to the writer. Typically, these payments are spread over the course of the contract's term. They will be outlined in a contract along with a specified timeline.

Minimum Commitment

Sometimes referred to as 'minimum delivery', this relates to how many works (songs) a music publisher expects to receive from a songwriter in a calendar year.

Accounting Period

This term relates to when royalties are typically distributed. Traditionally, this was twice a year, in June and December, but most publishers and PROs now distribute royalties on a quarterly basis. Some music publishers are now moving to a monthly distribution model, but this is more to do with their own reporting rather than the speed of collection.

Considerations for Songwriters

IPI Number

Music publishers will want to know your IPI number. This is a unique and internationally recognised identification number which usually consists of nine or more digits. Each songwriter and music publisher is given their own IPI number by their PRO when they sign up for membership. In the UK, the PRO is PRS For Music, and it often refers to an IPI as a 'Composer, Author, Editor' number. It is the same thing.

Perpetuity

When reading through a music publishing contract, be careful of the word 'perpetuity' in the context of a term. The word 'perpetuity' means 'forever' or 'with no fixed maturity'. This is often otherwise referred to as 'life of a copyright'. It relates to a songwriter assigning control of their rights to a music publisher for the lifetime of the songwriter. It is still standard practice for some countries to expect songwriters to agree to perpetuity. This can create a clash of cultures when it comes to negotiating on contracts because it is a rather dated protocol in most countries today.

Negotiate

Know that you can negotiate. It's human nature sometimes to think that when something is written down in front of us in black and white, it is definitive; but it's not. It is completely acceptable to negotiate on any of the terms of a contract, provided that all parties act and behave responsibly and politely. Perhaps there is one specific term that doesn't sit right with you. Query this term with the publisher, because they may well offer a rational explanation for it; but you won't know if you don't ask, so please know that you can. It is not a sign of naivety or weakness – quite the opposite, in fact.

Transatlantic Terminology

Copyrights and music publishing function and operate in much the same way in the UK as they do in North America. However, the terminology is different and this can confuse some songwriters. In the US and Canada, each song is given a writer's share and a publisher's share. Each adds up to 100%. In the UK, we only refer to the entire copyright combined.

Don't be confused by this. It's the same thing. In the US and Canada, songwriters and publishers will often refer to these shares separately. Writers could perhaps negotiate to have 100% of the writer's shares and 20% of the publisher's share. This is called 'co-publishing'. In the UK, we do not use this terminology. We would just refer to this as a 60/40 split of the song copyright.

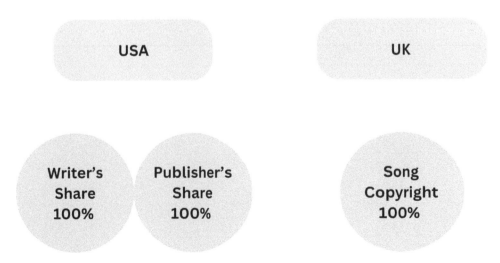

Figure 4.2 US and UK Examples of Song Shares

Summary

For a songwriter assigning their rights to a music publisher in the form of a music publishing contract, this can feel like a huge achievement. However, it is not a guaranteed gateway to success. Depending on the goals of the songwriter and the intended use of their songs, it could be argued that signing to a music publisher is no longer as necessary as it once was. Songwriters now have more options available to them when it comes to self-publishing because of the emergence of the internet and the digital age. It could be said that some songwriters who are efficient with their paperwork, administrative procedures, song split sheets, collection methods and networking building may be more suited to retaining their own copyrights. There are, of course, advantages of plugging a song or catalogue of songs into the network of a music publisher's exploitation and collection protocols – especially if the music publisher takes a proactive approach to finding placements for a songwriter's works. It is always recommended to research any music publisher before signing a contract.

5

The Role of a Record Company

The core purpose of a record company is to release and promote recordings of music.

In one bold sentence, that is their primary aim – in addition to being profitable in the process. However, there is much more to understand about the different roles played within a record company and the variations between different types of record companies.

A record company manufactures, distributes and promotes music recordings and music videos of the artists that it signs to its roster. There are broadly two main types of record companies: majors and independents (indies). At the time of writing, there are currently three major record company groups in the world: Universal Music Group, Sony Music Entertainment and Warner Music Group.

Record companies which are not major labels or part of the 'big three' are known as 'indie labels'. Indie labels can range from small or large organisations and are not affiliated with the corporate governance of a major record company group. While more traditional corporate structures exist in many larger independent labels, smaller independent labels can and do exist, with one or two people running the organisation. Widely regarded to be less mainstream and more genre specific in their core values, many indie labels are often considered to be more artist friendly, as they allow their artists to retain more creative control, in addition to offering more favourable royalty rates. Indie labels are often known to offer 50% profit share deals with their artists, whereas a royalty rate for a new artist on a major label can be as low as 13%–18%.

What Do Record Companies Do?

- Scout, sign and develop recording artists.
- Work with the artist to select and agree repertoire (songs) for the recordings.

DOI: 10.4324/9781003452119-7

- Organise songwriting collaborations and recording sessions to take place between artists and producers.
- Pay for the costs associated with recording the music that is planned for release. This includes the fees for producers, recording engineers, studio hire, additional performing musicians who are not the signed artist(s), mixing, mastering and the overall completion of the final rendered audio or audio-visual project.
- Pay for the creation of artwork and any associated digital assets.
- Arrange the pressing and transportation of the chosen format for release (physical releases are more common than many people think).
- Liaise with distribution partners on digital store delivery.
- Design the release campaign and associated actions.
- Create and fund the press campaign.
- Fund the radio campaign by hiring a radio plugger.
- Create a digital campaign for playlist curation.
- Fund promotional events.
- Find synchronisation placements for their recorded catalogue of music in TV programmes, films, videogames and other multimedia. This will also be done by music publishers, as they have an invested interest in the song's copyrights – as opposed to the record companies, which have an invested interest in the recordings of the songs rather than the copyright of the songs themselves.

Artist Option 1: The Major Label Route

In addition to fronting the costs of product creation, larger record companies will usually offer upfront money to the artist in the form of an advance on future royalties. The amount of this advance is negotiable, along with the proposed royalty rate for the artist. The purpose of the advance is usually to ensure the financial sustainability of the artist while they commit to recording, promoting and touring the product, before they start earning money and seeing a financial return for themselves. The circumstances of the artist's lifestyle and the projected amount of time it will take to generate an income can be difficult to calculate in advance, so this is an issue that needs strategic forecasting and planning.

There is an undeniable risk to the record company in this situation, which is much more in line with the practices of a major label. To offset the risk, the record company will seek to take a substantially higher royalty split than the artist. If the artist fails to recoup the advance that the record company pays them, it is very unlikely that the artist will be expected to return the money; although this will be negotiated prior to signing of the record contract. An artist will pay back the advance to the record company in revenue once the negotiated sales threshold has been met. If the expected sales are not met, it is the record company that loses out more often than not. Major record companies will also often pay for the legal costs associated with drawing up the artist's contract once the terms have been agreed.

Signing to a major label may be the most suitable option for an artist, especially if the artist, in the eyes of the label, holds global mainstream appeal. A major label may have a larger marketing spend and often a wider global reach and a greater capacity to push an artist internationally, due to the worldwide company structures it has in place. A major label artist is often deemed to be a commercially viable act and the costs involved with taking a popular music act to market are generally much higher than those associated with a niche genre.

Artist Option 2: The Indie Label Route

Indie label artists generally receive a lower advance and a higher royalty rate. Recording artists should be aware that indie record labels tend to have more financial restrictions than major record companies. This can sometimes mean that artist recognition and overall profile building are more gradual processes, with a larger body of releases required to gain traction among the public.

Independent labels are often associated with specific genres. With this often comes specialism and recognisable routes to market through trusted and existing networks such as genre-specific tastemakers in the form of journalists, radio DJs, playlist curators, YouTubers, promoters and festival bookers. An indie label brand can often have a strong sense of identity and character; but this can also be said of many other labels that fall under the umbrella of a major record company.

Types of Record Deals

Licensing Deal

In this type of record deal, the artist licenses the label to use the master recordings that were created by the artist, as opposed to the record company arranging and financing the recordings. The licence permits the label to manufacture, distribute and sell copies of the recordings, among other negotiable variables, such as licensing for multimedia use. This type of contract is well suited to a well-developed or self-produced artist who can create high-quality master recordings that the record company approves of. In this deal, the label need not put in as much time, which is usually reflected in a better royalty rate for the artist.

Exclusive Recording Contract

This is a traditional record deal, whereby the record company invests financially in the recording process in addition to the other areas of expenditure such as manufacturing, distribution, marketing and promotion. This type of contract often gives the label the right to renew the contract for a further period. The contract could be for one single, one album, three albums or more. A substantial investment of time and resources is made in the artist under contract, especially for artists who are under longer contracts than just one product release.

360 Deal

In this type of contract, the record company benefits from all income streams that relate to the artist's career. These could include shared revenues from such things as live ticket sales, music publishing rights, merchandise and sponsorship deals. The deal may even extend to broader ventures such as acting, writing, fashion lines and more.

270 Deal

This is the same as a 360 deal but without signing music publishing rights. If a songwriting artist signs a 270 deal, this affords them the flexibility to gain an additional advance from a music publisher, for which they will have a separate agreement covering the assignment or licensing of their song copyrights.

Development Deal

This type of contract involves a lower risk on the part of the record company, especially when compared to a traditional and exclusive deal. It sees an artist commit to recording a small collection of demo songs which are funded by the record company. Under these agreements, artists more commonly commit to a specific length of time than to a specified number of songs. Traditionally, no advance is paid to the artist under this type of arrangement. A development deal is often viewed as a record company putting an artist on hold and trialling them before either committing to further investment or terminating the agreement once it has run its course. This gives the artist the chance to impress the label. In many cases, there is a clause stating that the option to extend is in the power of the record company, which safeguards its investment.

Production Deal

Under this agreement, a recording artist does not contract directly with a label for its full services, but only for the business of recording. This is typically an offshoot business of a record label. This type of contract is more commonly associated with a production company or a partnership between music industry professionals. The person or company that is offering the deal will almost certainly be looking for exclusivity from the artist, with the aim of then either shopping the artist and the recordings to a record label or working in strategic partnership with an artist management company and a distributor to further the career of the artist for the mutual benefit of all parties involved.

One Song Profit-Share Deal

This is a 50/50 profit-share deal on one single between a recording artist and a record company. This type of contract is more typical for small independent labels which are looking to release multiple singles by multiple artists, often with a view to including them on compilation albums. These types of agreements are more commonly associated with electronic genres such as house, drum and bass and techno. Often the label will look to sign one single with the artist, with the option of a further single. Artists in these genres often seek to build their careers by releasing multiple singles across a range of independent labels in order to raise their profile and create leverage that they can use to forge new partnerships with professionals such as sponsors, brands, booking agents, music publishers, artist managers and larger independent or even major labels.

Company Structures

There have never been as many record company structures as there are today. A small but reputable label can often be an offshoot of a live promoter, a producer, an artist or some other music business-related venture. This – among a whole multitude of other significant changes in the landscape – is why we now see such a wide range of forms and structures for new and emerging record companies around the world. The key indicator that dictates the structure of a label is the number of tasks it takes on in-house versus the number of tasks that are outsourced. Let's understand this a little more by exploring some sample structures.

Sample Structure: Major Label Company Structure
(All positions are salaried employees)

Chief Executive Officer (CEO)
President
Vice President

Director of Marketing
Director of Sales & Distribution
Director of A&R
Director of Publicity
Director of Legal & Business Affairs

Digital Marketing Team
Retail Marketing Team
Accountancy Team
A&R Team
Product Management Team
Publicity Team

A&R Scouts
Assistants
Coordinators
Interns

Figure 5.1 Sample Company Structure for a Major Label

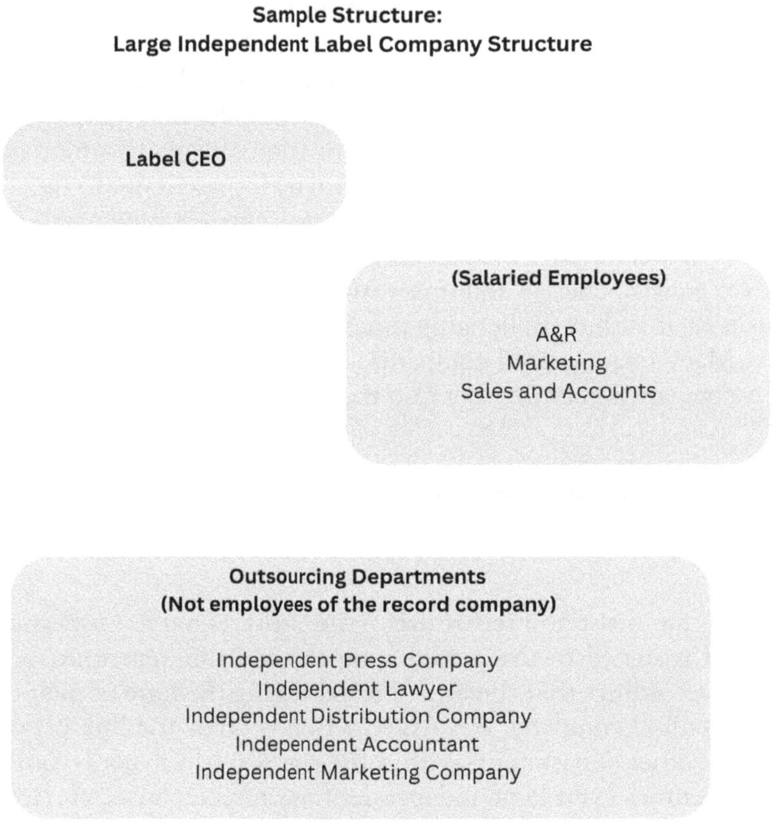

Sample Structure:
Large Independent Label Company Structure

Label CEO

(Salaried Employees)

A&R
Marketing
Sales and Accounts

Outsourcing Departments
(Not employees of the record company)

Independent Press Company
Independent Lawyer
Independent Distribution Company
Independent Accountant
Independent Marketing Company

Figure 5.2 Sample Company Structure for a Large Independent Label

Sample Structure:
Small Independent Label Company Structure

Director

Everything else outsourced

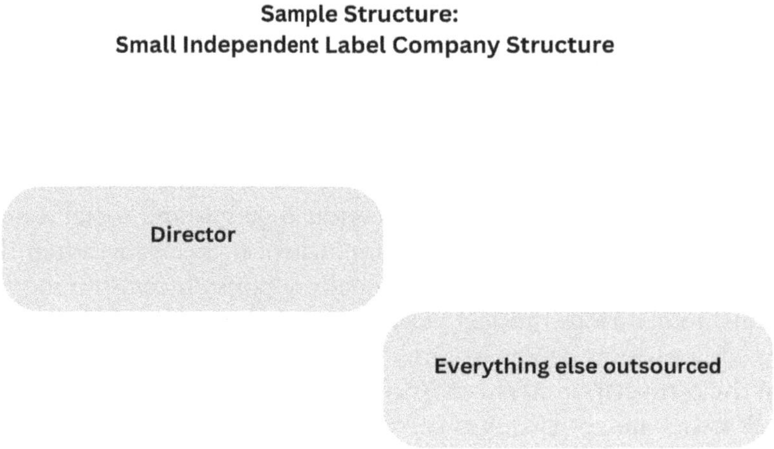

Figure 5.3 Sample Company Structure for a Small Independent Label

Strategic Changes in a Period of Constant Evolution

The 2020s are an exciting period of change for the recorded music industry and the players that are thriving are those that are not afraid to morph their business model into something new. Today, many corporate giants are struggling to see a future because they are unable to control their present due to the structure and philosophy of their business. At the same time, exciting, genre-bending music scenes are emerging, with small labels headed by digital natives with a keen eye on growth, change and innovation. If history has taught us anything about business, it is that challenging times force change through foresight and initiative. Many major record companies are thus now seeking to change not only their company structures, but also their strategic approach.

Roles Within a Record Company

A&R

'A&R' stands for 'artist and repertoire' – the 'artist' being the performing musical act that is signed to the record company and the 'repertoire' being the catalogue of recordings that the artist creates during the term of their contract with the recording company. An A&R person is often the link between the artist and the other departments within the company. In major record companies and sometimes even large independent record companies, an A&R position can be categorised according to the holder's level of experience and track record in the field.

A&R Scout

A scout is often, but not exclusively, an emerging young music professional looking to build their reputation in the industry by showcasing their ability to source talent, which they then recommend to senior personnel in the department. Scouts typically attend lots of live music events in order to identify new talent and research emerging underground genres and social trends that could potentially appeal to a mainstream audience. Scouts are often the first gatekeepers to emerging talent and are usually responsible for listening to demo submissions from various musical acts. They tend to move around companies regularly early in their career in order to build their networks and climb the ladder in the competitive world of A&R. Typically young, passionate and hungry, A&R scouts are go-getting types who communicate well with others and are not afraid of working antisocial hours in order to get ahead in the music business.

A&R Manager

Typically the next in line in a corporate structure, A&R managers are often reported to by scouts. It is the A&R manager's job to filter through the talent that the scouts pitch to them while using various other methods to track emerging talent. Artificial intelligence (AI) now plays a key role in locating talent from around the world as musicians find their own ways to reach their audience through algorithmic growth on audio-streaming services such as Spotify and Apple Music, audiovisual streaming sites such as YouTube, social media platforms such as Tik Tok and Instagram, live streaming platforms such as Twitch and more genre-specific platforms such as Soundcloud. All of these platforms generate data on emerging talent which can be tracked by various AI tools (some of which are even owned by the major record companies). A&R managers are often the go-to contacts for numerous acts on the label and liaise between various parties in relation to the recordings of artists. These could include, among others, recording studios, recording engineers, songwriters, music producers and additional contributors to recordings, such as orchestras and outsourced arrangers. A&R managers also typically receive song submissions from music publishers and songwriters that are pitching songs to a specific artist on the label's roster. This is especially true for pop acts that need songs, tracks or co-writers. It is often the A&R manager's responsibility to oversee all these processes and liaise with the recording artist at the same time. An A&R manager can often play a significant role in song selection for the recording artist and suggest which songs would be most suitable as single releases. A&R managers often play a role in the sonic identity of an artist because of the developmental process through which the artist progresses during their term with the label, especially early in their career.

A&R Director

The A&R director is usually the most senior A&R person within the corporate structure of a record company. Often considered to be the key decision makers, A&R directors do much to shape the role of music in popular culture due to their influence on the record company's identity and success rate. The director dictates the entire output of the A&R department while also reporting to the chief executive officer or president of a corporate entity.

A&R Consultant

An A&R consultant's job is to offer specialism across the entire spectrum of A&R. Typically a freelancer or self-employed professional, or perhaps the director of their own company that offers services to other companies, an A&R consultant is often someone who has previously enjoyed significant success within the structure of record company A&R departments or a music professional who has built a good reputation for themselves and can charge fees for their time and services.

Marketing and PR

There is a distinctive difference between PR and marketing. 'PR' stands for 'public relations' and in short aims to secure a good reputation in the media; while marketing aims to successfully communicate a product in the marketplace. In the context of record label operations, the two blend well together, even if one is done in-house and the other is outsourced. This is for the simple reason that the two disciplines are symbiotic in their relationship and goal: to push product onto consumers and to pull in listeners in the process. A marketing team or marketeer is tasked with designing a release campaign that involves a solid cycle of activity, pushing a music product into the awareness of as many listeners as possible. Marketing techniques can and do vary depending on budget but are more commonly associated with traditional advertising and social media campaigns. A press campaign would also fit inside a key release cycle and focus on the narrative of the artist (PR) and the details of their release (marketing). This could variously take the form of press interviews with artists, reviews for releases, blog features or editorial articles focusing on the profile of the artist and a particular journalistic narrative with a softer focus on the release.

Promotional Roles

This area deserves its own category even though it involves a combination of duties that are often shared or spread across different departments, depending on the size of the record company and its budget. These roles rely on a high-quality network and are often outsourced due to their specialism, particularly by independent record labels.

Radio Plugging

The role of a radio plugger is to promote a single, EP or album to key tastemakers in radio. This will predominantly take place during the pre-release period of a product's commercial release. The role of radio in the promotion of music is under continual threat due to the changing ways in which consumers discover and listen to music. That said, it is still a reputable, desirable and recognised medium to reach a listener base. Radio pluggers have extensive databases of decision makers, gatekeepers and relationships with many key professionals in the world of audio broadcasting. There are different types of radio pluggers: some who hold specialisms in specific genres and others who have significant influence on mainstream stations. Then are those who specialise in pitching to college radio in the USA; bringing new or trending artists to local and regional radio or internet stations; or gaining rotation on national shows which are then also available through on-demand application-based services. A high-quality radio plugger will be a respected professional with a good ear and an understanding of the current landscape of wherever their specialism lies.

Playlist Pitching and Curation

An undeniably important role when it comes to the promotion of music involves how and where a song is being placed in playlists on audio streaming platforms. One of the hallmarks of a record label's identity is its reach and one of the quickest ways to analyse this is through its ability to plug a single into its existing playlist network. If a label can instantly place one of its new releases into its self-curated playlists, this generates an early and stable level of traction and growth (provided that the playlists have a good level of engaged listeners). For labels to achieve this, they must be consistent in how they curate their playlists and how listeners engage with them. A typical playlist collection run in-house by a label is depicted in Figure 5.4.

Figure 5.4 Record Label Playlist Network

It could be that approximately 75% of the tracks on these playlists are not signed to the label. This neatly demonstrates how many labels are curating their own platforms to stabilise their in-built reach. It also allows labels to partner with other labels of similar styles on playlist support to add crossover and listener engagement, while simultaneously providing symbiotic assistance to one another.

It is also the job of a label to pitch its releases for playlists curated by third-party organisations and individuals, in addition to the editorial departments within the digital service platforms themselves. Many of the spots on Spotify's key editorial playlists, for instance, are taken up by acts on major labels. Pitching songs for playlists takes research, time and knowledge. Many labels have their own database of curators who specialise in specific moods, seasons and genres, and finding placements on as many playlists as possible is a sure-fire way of gaining visibility and organic growth.

Licensing

One of the key income streams attached to the operations of a record company comes from how its catalogue of recorded music is used. There is often an individual or an entire department committed to finding placements for the company's catalogue. This entails licensing recordings for various uses such as film soundtracks, compilations or synchronisation opportunities in TV programmes, games and ads.

Creative and Product Management

A key link between A&R and sales is the creativity behind the products. It is perhaps fair to say that music is more visual today than it has ever been, so there is a vital need for aesthetically pleasing assets that align with and support a release. Recording products (EPs, singles, albums or compilations) must have visual assets that support a digital or physical release package, including the following:

- artwork;
- photography;
- branding;
- logos;
- thematical design;
- graphics;
- squares, banners and visualisers for all platforms (sizes and shapes vary considerably between social media platforms and digital service platforms);

- videos;
- canvas for audio streaming platforms (three to eight seconds of a visual loop that forms a backdrop for a release);
- font design;
- instore displays; and
- ads.

It is important that any aspect of intellectual property inside the design of a release is cleared with the creators, as the copyright of the artwork is something that a record company will be looking to acquire. This is an issue that some independent creators can easily overlook.

Sales and Distribution

Sales departments are responsible for making music releases available to music listeners. This could be in the form of physical products, digital packages or both. It is crucial that the sales department has a strong understanding of how to make music releases available to as many consumers as possible throughout the world. Working relationships with record stores, online music stores, download sites and streaming platforms are key to success – especially in an age when the digital retail landscape is rapidly evolving.

Distribution has long been a crucial role of a record company. For the major labels, their distribution protocols and partnerships are a valuable commodity in their own right. This is because major labels offer their distribution arms to many independent labels due to the extended reach they can offer. Distribution is often outsourced by many independent labels to independent distribution companies which offer delivery to the digital stores together with detailed analytics providing insights into how, when and where music releases are being consumed on different digital service platforms in different territories. This is comparable to how independent artists use digital aggregators to deliver their music to digital platforms.

Royalties and Accounts

Keeping track of the flow of revenue from various income streams relating to the consumption and use of recorded music is a task that must be administered with transparency and clarity due to the high volumes of data being shared. There are multiple types of physical and digital retailers that make music available to listeners, and transactions and usage are tracked and calculated by royalties and accounts departments. Metadata is a key component for tracking, understanding and categorising digital usage. Income streams from recorded music can include both how music is consumed by listeners and how music is used in TV programmes, films and other media. The recording royalty shares of the artists are processed in accordance what has been agreed in their recording contract with the record company.

Legal Services

These can be provided by an in-house lawyer, a legal department or an out-sourced legal firm. It is the responsibility of the legal party to draw up the contracts between the record label and the recording artists that the label works with. Negotiations with artists, artists' managers and artists' legal teams are handled by the record company's legal representative. Legal action of any kind will always be handled by the label's legal team. A legal department will also be responsible for contractually clearing any issues around intellectual property such as the use of samples in a recording. In addition, a legal department will oversee any contracts involving brands and the licensing of a record company's recorded music in conjunction with the media.

Interview: Lorenzo Filippin, Label Manager, Milleville Music, Italy

Established in 1989, Milleville Music is an independent record label, music publisher and production company based in Italy. With more than three decades of experience and activity, Milleville continues to evolve by developing big hits and great artists across a range of musical genres.

What qualities do you hope to hear in a song that is submitted to you?

When I listen to a new song, I focus on several qualities. First and foremost, it should sound excellent in terms of both production and recording quality. The overall quality needs to be professional, meaning that the song should sound good on all sound systems, with a balanced mix and a powerful master. The second aspect I look for is a well-crafted arrangement. Each section of the song should have its own space and the sequence of sections should be arranged in a manner that's pleasing to the ear. The third element involves creativity. I pay attention to the melodies, the choice of sounds and the overall vibe of the song. Everything should harmonise well with the rest of the track. Additionally, I personally value the overall innovation in a song. There are many well-produced songs that sound good, but often that's not enough to make a hit. Therefore, I warmly welcome artists who experiment with new ideas in areas such as arrangements and sound design.

How important is it that the artists you sign understand some of the key aspects of the music business?

I believe it's in the best interests of artists to familiarise themselves with the basics of the music business. By doing so, they can safeguard the rights associated with their creative work and gain a better understanding of contractual agreements. This knowledge also helps to prevent potential issues such as unintentionally granting the same rights to multiple parties simultaneously.

How much of your label operations takes place in-house and how much do you outsource?

Our responsibilities encompass a wide range of areas, including promotion, talent scouting, managing social media, creating content, addressing legal aspects and registering songs with collecting societies. However, we outsource certain tasks such as the distribution of music to digital stores and specific IT-related work such as website content creation and design.

What is your strategy for gaining playlist spots for your releases?

We utilise a diverse range of strategies. To begin with, we manage our own playlists, providing our releases with immediate visibility. Additionally, we collaborate with a multitude of other labels and curators, engaging in 'trades' every Friday. This process involves an exchange of songs between playlists, expanding the audience reach for each track. Furthermore, for every single release, we pitch to the editorial playlist of each digital provider, which can significantly boost the song's growth if selected. We also advise our artists to make their own personal pitches to platforms such as Spotify, effectively doubling their chances of being featured. Lastly, we encourage our artists to curate their own playlists. This allows them to build a ready-made fanbase that will be eager to listen to their new releases.

What changes do you foresee for the future of the recorded music industry?

Currently, the music industry is undergoing rapid and significant transformations. With each passing month, we are introduced to new innovations that redefine our listening habits and new ways in which we experience music that were previously unimaginable. The lion's share of the business has transitioned to the digital realm and the world of computing. The music industry is progressively aligning itself with the tech sector. The rise of streaming services has revolutionised how consumers access music, leading to a decline in physical sales and downloads. AI is being used to create new songs, suggesting that the future might see more AI-composed music. This opens up a whole new realm of possibilities for music production and composition. Virtual reality concerts and performances are gaining popularity, providing fans with immersive musical experiences and the possibility of participating from wherever they are. This trend is likely to continue as technologies advance and become more mainstream. Social media platforms are also playing a significant role in music discovery. Platforms such as YouTube, Facebook, Instagram and TikTok are becoming increasingly important for music discovery. In particular, TikTok has become a major platform for music discovery and promotion.

In conclusion, the future of the recorded music business lies in its ability to adapt to technological advancements and changing consumer preferences. It will continue to evolve with the rise of new technologies and platforms, offering exciting opportunities for artists and listeners alike.

Record Label Offshoots

Vanity Labels

A 'vanity label' is a label brand that is often designed to look like it is owned by an artist but in fact is owned by a record company. It differs from an imprint because it focuses largely, if not solely, on one artist – perhaps sometimes stretching to acts that are affiliated with the primary artist through genre alignment, tour supports, collaborations or remixes. A vanity label can also aid a scene or a movement in a particular style. This fictitious model can also be used as a PR plan to make an artist appear empowered and independent to consumers, when in all actuality the situation involves nothing more than a traditional label-to-artist record deal. This is a model that yields effective outcomes for many artists and it is used in various genres.

This is not to be confused with artists who start their own label which is then later purchased by a larger corporation. This approach often leads to artists being able to retain more creative control and secure more favourable terms in contracts.

Imprints

An 'imprint' is a division of a record company that represents its own label identity and brand but falls under the legal structure of its parent company. Typically associated with a genre specialism or a particular value or message, an imprint is not a standalone company but a unit of a larger company. Imprints often have their own trademarks, branding and artists but are governed by their parent company in terms of legal and business affairs. Imprints are often influential entities and are often associated with breaking artists; they may even brand their own label merchandise range. Imprints are a popular model for record companies that may be looking to extend their reach into a new or established marketplace by having a specific brand that is associated within a genre or sub-genre.

Case Study: Beggars Group

UK-based Beggars Group is one of the largest independent record company groups in the world.

Each of its imprints adopts a unique approach to its values and roster, and some boast their own in-house departments but use the Beggars Group infrastructure for legal, finance, production, licensing and administration.

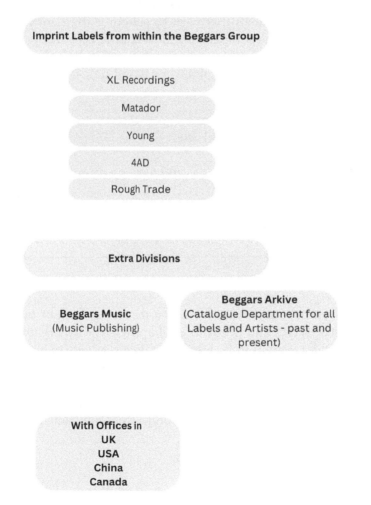

Imprint Labels from within the Beggars Group

XL Recordings

Matador

Young

4AD

Rough Trade

Extra Divisions

Beggars Music
(Music Publishing)

Beggars Arkive
(Catalogue Department for all Labels and Artists - past and present)

With Offices in
UK
USA
China
Canada

Figure 5.5 The Structure of the Beggars Group

6
Artist and Label Services Model

A fully managed artist and label services model is a highly suitable choice for independent artists and labels that wish to outsource their entire release process to a third party. Some companies will work only with independent labels, while others are open for business to both labels and independent artists alike. This service model effectively enables labels and acts to hire a company to undertake tasks such as:

- digital and physical distribution;
- manufacturing, production and sales;
- international reach;
- synchronisation of music into TV and film opportunities;
- marketing;
- PR campaigns;
- radio campaigns;
- playlist pitching;
- rights collection; and
- analytics.

One of the advantages of this model is that the services can be tailored to suit different budgets, scales and needs. It could perhaps be said that this model is seen as less risky for a small indie label, as it does not have to hire its own staff or compromise its vision for an artist and their release. A services model is a favourable choice for independent artists who have the budget to hire professionals to work on their release campaigns, as the ownership of their master rights is not relinquished when working under this arrangement.

Case Study: Absolute Label Services

With a core staff of approximately 30 people, this UK-based label services company has been running successfully since 1998 and boasts an array of highly

DOI: 10.4324/9781003452119-8

knowledgeable and cutting-edge professionals. Having established an impressive track record in this ever-changing landscape over the past two decades, Absolute Label Services has all the know-how and efficiency needed to take product to the global marketplace. One of the most interesting aspects of the company is its versatility, as it specialises in pretty much every contemporary genre.

'We become your record label; while you retain all your rights' is its motto, and the flexibility in its business model is reflected by the range of acts it has served, from chart-topping bands to emerging rappers.

Interview: Kate Hendry, Head of Label Operations, Absolute Label Services, UK

Are there any specific standards or expectations that you have from an independent record company that wishes to work with you?

We work with companies of all shapes and sizes, from small labels to big ones; from artists who have turned themselves into a self-managed cottage industry business to big management companies with many artists and their own label arms, brands who want to get into the musical landscape and everything in between. I'd say the thing they all have in common is a focused vision of what they want their projects to say; and – more simply and practically – they are as responsive to us as we are to them, which breeds a partnership vibe.

Which of your services tend to be the most popular with independent labels?

Distribution, project management, promo team building, project budget building and maintenance, with a major focus on digital service provider (DSP) playlist pitching and support.

What is your approach to pitching songs for DSP playlists? For instance, do you tend to find that you yield greater results by trying to target specific playlists that align in genre and mood with releases; and do you pitch to third-party playlists in addition to the DSPs?

We focus on editorial playlist support only and as a distributor partner, we aren't allowed to pitch for specific playlists. We use our editorial relationships, direct comms and pitching tools to best direct our releases to the right editor, who will then push them to appropriate curators as they see fit according to the various pitching criteria such as genre, mood, theme, lyrical content, campaign points and overall sound.

Many artists who were formerly on the rosters of major labels are now seeking to move to a position where they have more control of their rights. Do you think that artists in this position would be best off working with you as an artist or setting up a label brand that has an identity before working with you?

We have many of these types of artists on our roster and they are really their own label brand, as they are self-releasing and their label is all about them and their creative output, so they can work with us as an artist and have their own label brand too.

Are there any changes in the global landscape that you are witnessing that may have a bearing on the future?

The emphasis on content is hugely important for an artist to get their message out there – short-form content is, of course, the content type of the day, and being as creative as possible with it is central to any campaign we run or craft.

It is worth thinking about something important, which relates to purpose and strategy. If a label goes to a label services company, it is because they have created a story, a campaign and a product that is ready to go to market. The services company helps to exploit that overall package through channels that can give it visibility, strength and growth. If an independent recording artist goes to an artist and label services company, they will also be expected to know what that package looks like. This is something which is not impossible to achieve on your own. However, without creative guidance, input and the collaboration of other professionals who are less emotionally invested and more objective, it is very difficult.

Enter the artist manager . . .

7
What Do Artist Managers Do?

Artist managers work on behalf of the music creators they represent by promoting their music, running their business affairs and guiding them through their careers with strategy, purpose and mentoring. Managers are usually experienced professionals who have played previous roles in the music industry, which means that they know what is needed to manage an artist. Managers must have a very well-rounded skillset and knowledge base, as they must combine an understanding of the business aspects of recorded music, music publishing, marketing, publicity, the live music sector and digital growth with the interpersonal skills of conflict resolution, communication, negotiation and positivity. Combine this with the ability to listen to songs and identify their faults, their strengths and their route to market and you suddenly have a much smaller pool of music professionals who can excel in this high-pressured hybrid role. The duties of managers can perhaps be sub-divided into business duties, personal duties and creative duties, but this may vary depending on the type of manager and the needs of the creator.

The duties of managers include:

- guiding the careers of music creators;
- negotiating the best deals and fees;
- advising on career decisions and strategies;
- understanding and generating press attention;
- managing media relations;
- working closely with A&Rs to coordinate an artist's strategy;
- collaborating with booking agents and promoters to schedule live appearances, tours and festivals;
- booking and arranging creative and recording sessions with studios, engineers, producers, songwriters and performers; and
- helping artists to grow and be profitable.

DOI: 10.4324/9781003452119-9

Types of Managers

There are some artist managers who represent recording artists, but there are also managers who exclusively manage producers, songwriters, recording engineers or mix engineers. Some managers may be genre specific, while others have a much wider remit across various music genres, styles and cultures.

The backgrounds of managers can vary: some may come from an artist or performer background, while others may come from a music business background. This often determines the type of manager that they become. For instance, managers who come from an artistic background often have a much more personal and empathetic management style, involving themselves with the creators they manage on a day-to-day basis. This could include offering creative and styling advice, managing a creator's diary and serving as a constant point of contact. Other managers are much less supportive on a personal level and instead play more of a business role as an objective strategist who builds business plans that are measurable and scalable within the term of the contract agreement. These more business-focused types of managers will typically negotiate on behalf of the artist with record companies, music publishers, booking agents, sponsorship partners, accountants and lawyers, and manage budgets across various aspects of the artist's career.

There are, of course, hybrids between these two types of managers. There are also management companies in which different members of staff play different roles when managing a creator's career.

When Does a Music Creator Need a Manager?

Music creators often ask this question and the answer is not always simple, because it varies based on numerous factors. Loosely, however, it boils down to how close the creator is to becoming a fully fledged music professional. The usual answer is: 'When an artist can't manage themselves anymore.' However, it could be argued that this is somewhat flawed, as it depends on the type of person the artist is and how organised they are. Many music creators would love, I'm sure, to have the support of an artist manager as early as possible in their career. However, attracting the attention of a manager with a proven track record is less realistic if the artist does not have a track record of their own. Many artists often assume that it is their talent and potential that make them appealing to more established managers, when actually it is usually their ability to test themselves in the marketplace and generate growth. This is especially true today, when it is arguably much easier for artists to self-launch their careers and gain traction in the form of artist data, which can then be used as leverage to further their careers and attract the interest of proven managers. 'Artist data' is defined by metrics such as social media following and engagement, number of streams and live activity; but indications of growth can also include self-created press attention in the form of blog reviews and interviews, obvious knowledge of their genre and artistry, combined with a commitment to growing their own network – or in other words, reputation.

It is important that creators think about what their offer is to managers in addition to what a manager's offer is to them. Managers are music professionals who need to make a living from their time, efforts and services, and a good intention to work for free is as noble as it is unsustainable. In assessing when the right time is to work with a manager, a music creator must also ask when the right time is for a manager to work with them.

If you can explain to yourself why you need a manager, exactly what you expect of them and what you can do for them in return, you are already several steps closer.

Interview: Denise Beighton, Artist Manager, Upside UK Music Management, UK

With a wealth of experience, knowledge, passion and insight into various aspects of the music industry, Denise Beighton comes from a major label background, having achieved an array of accolades throughout her career. After establishing Upside UK alongside her colleague Simon Jones, today Denise plays a crucial role in managing artists who have gained big success on major labels.

When considering working with an artist, what skills do you look for the most?

Talent, without question; but also, they must show real drive, ambition and passion for the music they're making. I avoid artists who just have a desire to be rich and famous at any cost. I like people who are true to themselves and who are motivated by making great music first and foremost; and if that leads to the trappings that go with success, then great. To manage effectively requires a lot of mutual trust, respect and loyalty; and if that's not there, it's not going to work.

What level of experience do you expect to see from an artist before you work with them as their manager?

This is a tricky one. In the past, I'd have said that experience wasn't that relevant. For me, it's always been about feeling a vibe about the people involved and sharing a vision of how we might develop their talent. But nowadays, artists need to get themselves to a certain level before they even approach management. This should be across the board, including songwriting, recording, live and social media.

I won't take anyone on unless they already have a great sense of their identity and musical direction. It's becoming increasingly hard to get artists signed to labels, as they mostly look at statistics and numbers before the music. And without a label, they'll need investment.

I wish that wasn't the case. When we first signed Karen Harding, she was a young singer from Newcastle who had never even set foot in a recording studio. It has been extremely rewarding to be part of her journey and watch her grow into a hugely successful singer/songwriter with a fantastic catalogue of songs, including a million-selling single and almost 1 billion streams under her belt.

Sometimes, if I'm approached and I think the artist has something special going on, but is a little early for management, I might mentor them a little and make suggestions on how they can grow and keep them on my radar. I have a couple of people I'm looking at currently who show a lot of promise. But even then, once I've decided to take someone on, I don't actually sign them for another six months, which is a long enough time to see whether we can have a great working relationship or not.

There are some artists who think that once they have a management deal, they can sit back and let you do it all. This is so wrong; the artist should always be in the driving seat. I always tell them, 'This is my job, but it's your career and – more importantly – your dream, and you should never put that in someone else's hands.'

On an operational level, what duties tend to take up most of your time when working with artists?

It differs depending on the level of success an artist is at. At the beginning, it's tapping into the contacts and labels to see who will work with your artist. That also involves a lot of chasing, as the music industry isn't renowned for responding too quickly when an artist is just starting out. This does change, however, once they hit a certain level!

When there are deals in place, it can be chasing the various teams, record labels, live agents, publishers etc to make sure they're across all of their contact bases to push your act. Reaching out to other songwriters/producers etc that your artist might aspire to work with is also important.

It all changes again when we have a track due: everything is focused on that. We have our own mailing lists and contacts; it also involves social media planning and chasing the label for assets. We need to ensure everyone has all the relevant info and that the tracks are getting registered correctly etc. There will also be a lot of diary planning if there are a lot of people on radio and in the press who want to talk to the artist.

The release times are my favourite kind of busy! Generally, though, no two days are the same.

At what point in an artist's career would you suggest they seek artist management?

Once they have developed themselves as far as they can and can show that they have initiative, an identity and a vision. Also, try to remember that it's a business. If they are doing regular paid gigs (no matter how small) and have tracks on the various platforms, that will show a manager that if they can reach a certain level without professional help, there's potentially a market for them.

Is there any advice you would offer to early career stage music creators?

Get as much music out there as you possibly can. You can make the best record in the world, but if it's sitting on your computer with no one hearing it, then it's pretty pointless. Reach out to other musicians who are in a similar lane to you, to collaborate or work with them. This could be in the studio or on the live circuit. One of the acts I'm talking to at the moment is booking venues and promoting his own gigs and works with acts on a similar level. Currently, none of the acts could sell out the venues he's booking, but collectively they can. Working with other artists can help you to think out loud with people who can relate to the highs and lows of starting out. It can also mean growing your fanbase, as people may discover you through an artist they are following and vice versa.

Believe in yourself and what you're doing – make music that you love! Most creators I know are by default sensitive souls, so try to develop a thick skin. The music industry is full of rejection and it's an opinionated business, but if someone doesn't like your music, it doesn't make them right and you wrong. Some of the world's biggest artists were turned down and criticised at every step on the way up the ladder. Every artist I've ever met will take the negative comments to heart. They can post a clip of music on a platform and if they have 99 great comments and one bad one, I can guarantee it's the negative comment they'll talk about and remember. It's hard, but accept it: not everyone will like what you're doing.

Finding a Manager

On the one hand, we are firmly in the information age, when we can find so much of the information that we need through internet search engines. On the other hand, there's so much information available that it can be overwhelming, so knowing where to start can be difficult to navigate.

Research Creators Similar to You

Identify creators who are like you in style, genre and market. These should be specific recording artists if you're an artist; DJs in your sub-genre if you're a DJ; commercial songwriters who cover your intended territories if you're aiming to write for and with artists; producers doing the work you want to do if you're a producer; or bands similar to yours if you're in a band. Once you have identified the creators who are similar to you in style, research who manages them. Then do a separate search on the management company or manager and understand the role they play, how to submit to them and what their specialisms and musical interests are. Beware of premature introductions in a world where it's so easy to direct message on social media. Instead, be patient, be professional, put together your offer and email them.

Research Music Universities and Colleges

In the same way that regional radio is bursting with emerging talent in the form of broadcasters, tastemakers, journalists and presenters, educational settings such as colleges, universities and contemporary institutes are also brimming with emerging artist managers who are desperate to find new acts to champion. It is good to explore this on a local level by identifying the right educational settings. This can be achieved by using internet search engines to identify music business courses in your area and skipping past the initial ads that pop up for their courses. Once you've found the right educational settings with the right courses, reach out to the music business department with a polite email introducing yourself and state that you're looking to partner with an emerging artist manager. This could very well lead to you being asked to come in to audition and talk with undergraduate-level learners who are soon to become music professionals, allowing access to a range of emerging and motivated people who have been studying the routes to market that you are trying to identify yourself. If you don't hear anything back, turn up at reception and ask for the course leader who runs the music business courses and introduce yourself to them. At the very worst, you'll get a polite 'no'; but you'll be remembered and respected.

Research the Music Managers Forum

It is also advisable to read up on the Music Managers Forum (MMF) (https://themmf.net) and how it functions. This is the largest representative body of music managers in the world. Its purpose is to educate, innovate and advocate for music managers, and to serve as a collective society for music professionals and companies from different styles of management and from different parts of the world. Understanding more about the MMF will educate music creators on what to expect from a manager. In 2022, the MMF published *The Essentials of Music Management*. Together with its *Music Manager's Bible* and its listings of hundreds of managers, this is a valuable resource through which music creators can learn more about the MMF.

Research Listings of Managers

There are numerous publications available for researching artist managers. One option for the UK market is *The Unsigned Guide* (www.theunsignedguide.com), which lists many music managers alongside their genre specialism, together with a host of other crucial music business contacts. The *Music Week Directory* (www.musicweek.com/music-week-directory) also includes a database of music managers alongside various other sectors of the music industry.

Ask Those You Trust

This will depend on who is in your network, but it can be very effective. When talking to other music creators who have their own managers, it can be useful to gain an understanding of what those managers do and what you can learn from this. The key is in subtle soft-skill networking ability:

- Question 1: 'I really want a manager; can you help me?'
- Question 2: 'Who's your manager and how do you find working with them?'

In essence, these are the same questions, but they will be perceived differently. The first creator is starting a conversation with the second creator about artist management with the aim of understanding what their manager does for them, while softly considering whether they would want that manager themselves. It could be said that Question 1 comes off quite desperate. The word 'help' is a dangerous word – it feels like a plea. Question 2 is the first creator being interested, which is more interesting to the person being asked the question. In Question 2, an opinion is being sought, which is different from asking for help. Question 1 is a closed but wide question. The answer from Question 1 is arguably being answered much better as a result of the questioning technique of Question 2. The first creator will gain a more informed understanding of what a manager does and will also strengthen their relationship with the second creator. Question 1 could have perhaps scared off the second creator from future conversations.

It is also a good idea to ask around your own network as to what makes a good manager and who the right person for you might be. Asking local promoters, producers, recording engineers, music educators, festival bookers and just about anyone else on a local grassroots scene can be useful. Once a creator's career has progressed outside of their local area and onto the national scene, it is good to continue asking this same question of a wider pool of music professionals.

Making a Manager

One of the changes in the music management landscape since the turn of the millennium is the increase in music managers under the age of 30. This is perhaps due to heightened awareness of artist management as a viable career route for emerging music professionals. It could also be due to the amount of information available to us in the modern era, combined with the development of contemporary music institutions that are educating new learners on the mechanics of the music industry at the undergraduate and postgraduate levels. The latter is something which was not widely available before the turn of the century. Nonetheless, the majority of music managers are over the age of 30 and, as previously mentioned, come from a background in the music industry, albeit not artist management. Therefore, there is a turning point at which music professionals take the leap to become music managers, which starts by managing a musical act. That could be you. Perhaps there is somebody you are aware of that you think would be a great music manager for your career. They might be a producer, a promoter, an A&R scout, a journalist, a lawyer or someone else from a different field within the music industry who is looking to branch out in a new direction. You could be the first act they manage, if you are brave enough to approach them – and it could be a pivotal moment in your career and theirs.

What Kind of Commission Does a Manager Take?

Typically, between 10%–25% of a creator's collective income. It has become more common in recent decades to see sliding scales of percentages against total revenue – for instance, 20% on the first £15,000 and 15% on the remaining income after that. This will usually sit inside the term (eg, three years) of a contractual agreement rather than a typical tax year. It is often worth a creator considering whether any pre-existing income streams that were self-generated prior to the appointment of a manager should be commissionable. This subject is often overlooked in contracts and can lead to unnecessary fallouts, so it is always imperative that exactly what is commissionable is laid out clearly in the agreement.

Interview: John Hart, Manager, John Hart Music Management, UK

John Hart is a UK-based music industry professional who manages five self-releasing artists, including Blair Dunlop, Kitty Macfarlane and Rory Butler. John's approach to artist management is different from Denise Beighton's, in that he looks to set up self-sustainable business strategies for artists who don't require the funding or backing of a major label.

John is the director of Etude Music Ltd, which is developing a new app for self-managing artists. In addition, John is a published songwriter with BMG and a world-travelled musician in his own right, and also operates as a music industry consultant with clients that include UD Music and the Association of Independent Music. John is also a visiting senior lecturer in music business at numerous UK educational institutes.

What kinds of artists do you look to work with?

The artists I work with tend to be acoustic singer-songwriters rooted in the world of folk and related genres. I work with artists who might have traditionally been called 'unsigned' in the old industry. However, the landscape nowadays means that there are an increasing number of artists who have no desire to have a label on board. We work hard to manage all potential revenue streams around the artist and essentially set them up as label and publisher themselves. They become their own label. The theory here is that if we manage things with tight reins, the pennies all add up as there are no big chunks disappearing to rights owners. All revenue is coming to the artist. This is becoming increasingly difficult with the continued decline away from physical sales; but it does mean the artist keeps more control of their intellectual property and related areas.

What qualities do you look for in an artist?

I want to see the artist understands the independent approach we take and subscribes to the methodology somewhat. However, the main thing for me is always the songs. The songs are important, as is the ability to perform them . . . Same as it always was! I want them to be engaging to audiences in the room and online, and be able to think of interesting and innovative ways to engage with fans. It's very hard to create an authentic voice on socials, so engagement here is important.

What is your approach in creating sync opportunities for your roster?

One of the reasons we work to become rights owners is that it gives us a greater potential chunk of sync revenue. However, access to sync opportunities is challenging as independents, so we work with a range of partners in this area. Often, we will try to do a publishing deal if it feels right and sync will be an important part of that conversation. On the recording rights side, our distributor (Absolute Label Services) has roots in sync opportunities and as part of a campaign I will work closely with my label manager there to maximise opportunity. I also keep a close eye out myself and often pitch things independently.

What kinds of partnerships do you establish for your artists when developing live and touring plans?

Agents are essential here. It's impossible for us to take this on as well and a good-quality booking agent is worth so much. We will try to get the right agent in place early on and work closely with them to build touring plans in various territories. We often have different agents by territory (North America, Australia, the UK and Europe), and try to build realistic touring plans around releases and activities working with them. At the level our artists are at, it's unusual – but not unheard of – to have national tour promoters on board (we are generally in 100/200-capacity venues), so we also work hard with local promoters to ensure that touring is promoted.

What advice would you give to emerging recording artists who are less interested in the major label route to market?

Be prepared to work hard to generate your fanbase. You will gain them in ones and twos, but they are critical to your growth. Treat them well and offer them opportunities to engage with you as much as possible (without hassling them!). Understand the importance of owning your own rights and recognise that you now have the duty of a label/publisher to exploit them in the best way possible. If you don't recognise this, there is no point in working to retain them! Treat the business like work and go to work every day . . . If you don't have a show, it doesn't mean you don't have work to do. Think strategically and as long term as you can.

Do Managers Invest Financially in Artists?

A key part of a management agreement concerns how the manager will recoup expenses on the artist's behalf. Expenses incurred by the manager on the artist's behalf are unavoidable and should be built into the agreement. Spending caps are rarely agreed in contracts, so it is important that there is transparency and openness between an artist and their manager when it comes to this subject. What tends to be more common in a management agreement is a clause for larger expenditures (eg, £5,000) to be agreed upon in advance in writing with the artist's approval.

It is not uncommon to see a manager invest larger amounts of money in a music creator's career. This could perhaps be to cover the costs of recording, promotion, small-scale touring or photo and video shoots. This is often regarded as an advance against future earnings rather than a loan which is repayable. Again, this will need to be agreed in advance and then put in writing to protect all parties.

Experience or Passion?

Both are important, but they don't always come hand in hand. An experienced manager is often the sought-after choice because they have a track record and an existing network. However, a less experienced but really passionate manager may be what's required to take a creator's career to the next level. A good example of this is USA-based Myles Shears, who catapulted Norwegian producer Kygo to become the first billion-streaming artist on Spotify within a relatively short space of time. Shears was in his early 20s at the time and had previously only managed one act. Norwegian producer Kygo had composed a song which had generated some early career buzz on a Hype Machine-listed music blog. Having listened to his music on Soundcloud because of the blog feature, Shears was quick to spot Kygo's pioneering sonic capabilities. This early career intervention, together with Shears' extrovert character and fearless approach, made for a yin and yang-style partnership with the more placid Norwegian. On the other hand, Ed Sheeran's long-time manager, Stuart Caves, had a solid track record of managing successful UK pop acts – including James Blunt and Lily Allen – before he signed Sheeran to management in 2010.

By contrast, there are managers who have drawn on both experience and passion to evolve and develop into greater versions of themselves and move adeptly with the times. A good example of this is UK-based artist manager Stephen Taverner, who successfully managed UK rock band Ash for almost two decades. Taverner had previously reshaped the careers of indie pop duo The Ting Tings, taking them from their less successful incarnation as Dear Eskimo and turning them into a Billboard chart sensation with critical acclaim on both sides of the Atlantic before they switched to US management giants Roc Nation. A less passionate manager could quite easily have become justifiably disenchanted; but a defiant Taverner instead went on to enjoy even greater success with Alt-J and Wolf Alice.

Network

There's an old saying: 'Your network is your net worth.' The music industry has long been a largely people-based business that thrives on connections between key individuals working together with strategic purpose. A manager is often expected to have a wealth of connections across the music industry so that they can build the right team around the artist and their goals.

A network can be grown quickly when a hungry manager is motivated, so the ability to grow a network is a crucial skill. A network must also be sustained, and it takes effort to continually feed it in this rapidly evolving industry. Therefore, a manager needs interpersonal skills, patience and the ability to meet people and make things happen. In an industry where things change quickly and people move on, managers who rely on their contacts from a bygone era tend to fare poorly.

Trial Period

A trial period between a creator and a manager is often a good idea. This will usually be a fixed period of between three and 12 months which allows all parties to decide whether they wish to carry on and progress their partnership or move on from one another. Earlier in this chapter, Denise Beighton said: 'Once I've decided to take someone on, I don't actually sign them for another six months, which is a long enough time to see whether we can have a great working relationship or not.'

A trial can be a non-contracted period, which perhaps puts some risk on the manager – especially if they make significant improvements to the career of an artist who then moves on to a different manager. The manager could safeguard their position by putting in place a contractual agreement from the very beginning which outlines their option to cancel or continue with the arrangement at their discretion following on from the trial period.

Double Interview: Artist and Manager

Recording artist: Sipho
Label: Dirty Hit
Genre: R&B, gospel and alternative indie hybrid

Artist manager: Kieran Thompson

UK-based singer-songwriter Sipho's genre-bending sound beautifully represents his uniqueness as an artist. His stunning vocal ability blends seamlessly with his brutally honest and heartfelt lyrics to create a compelling act that has won significant critical acclaim early in his career. Sipho captured the attention of iconic London label Dirty Hit when he auditioned at a label showcase set up at BIMM Institute while he was studying on his songwriting degree. Having already formed a trusted bond with his manager, Kieran Thompson, prior to the label introduction, Sipho and Kieran began to build their team.

Interview 1: Sipho, Recording Artist, Dirty Hit, UK

Did creating your sonic identity come naturally to you or was it the result of artistic experimentation?

For me, it was time and experimentation and finding reference. It was seeing all the parts of other sonic identities you love and appreciate, learning the purpose of those features and how they make you feel. That, combined with happy accidents and habits you make for yourself, tends to draw you closer and closer to a sound. My advice is not to force it, just like your own personality. It's naturally unique to you.

How involved do you like to be in your aesthetic styling and branding?

I like to be as involved possible. That video, that cover – whatever it is – is what represents your creations. It tells people how to feel about what they're hearing. It informs so much. You don't have to be an expert – I'm not – but studying your favourite visual references definitely helps. Even if you're absolutely stumped, which I am at times, at least put it in the hands of people you trust and make sure every aspect is done with purpose or you'll end up with a poorly curated mess.

What have you learned about the music industry since you became a signed artist that you did not know before?

From the very start, it was meeting all the people involved in what I do. It made me realise that, as much as we're taught to look at this all as a massive machine, there are real people behind these operations. Especially my team. They text you, call you, laugh and cry and drink and eat with you, and make great things happen for so many people. I'm grateful to have them.

Are there any aspects of the music business that you would encourage emerging artists to understand better before starting their professional careers?

LEARN HOW TO READ YOUR CONTRACTS!!! You don't have to be an expert – that's what your lawyer is for – but gaining a general understanding of what they're asking for is important, especially in relation to what they're giving and taking. Understand what you're owed and where you can and should get paid from. You're not just an artist; you're a business. Right now, as much as we sensationalise the new generation of artists every year with lists and articles, and get excited about their creative pursuits, we're still looking at emerging start-up businesses. They can either go up or down. And you need to know your rights. I'm still learning so much. You're not going to come in fully clued up, but always keep yourself open to information and the growth and changes of your industry.

How has creative collaboration developed your sound as an artist?

It's been very important. As much as I like to be stubborn and sit by myself and craft everything to my own taste, it can put you in an echo chamber and send you insane if you lock yourself away. The only thing that makes us human is other humans. If you isolated a person their whole life, they would not come out resembling anything close to what we know as human. It's the same with the creative process. You could come out with something great by yourself, but sometimes that sounding board to tell you what's good or bad can really speed up and add a new quality to your work.

Interview 2: Kieran Thompson, Artist Manager, UK

What qualities do you look for in an artist?

I look for something unique. I love it when, even though you may be able to see an artist's inspirations or what you may think you know about what their inspirations are, they are still uniquely themselves in their creative output across the board, from sound to style and branding. I believe that great artists have a level of depth that goes beyond the surface level of what you may see as a manager or a consumer. There is a sense of fascination about tapping into who the artist is and it is nice to learn more about them in and outside of the music. I think this is what determines the longevity of an artist's career. If your whole story can be told in just one project, there's no sense of growth that can allow others to help your world grow and allow consumers to grow with you. If that's not there, you won't be around for a long time.

What other skills would you hope to see in an artist before they start working with a manager?

I love when an artist is so much more than just what they can do in the studio. Music is changing. It's no longer just about the music; obviously, that's the most important thing, but people buy into people. Whether it be your personality or your live show, what else do you have to offer?

I wouldn't necessarily say it's a skill, but there needs to be a level of hunger. How badly do you want this? Are you willing to improve? How well do you take criticism? Are you professional? How do you treat people around you? It's about assessing a person on a human level.

In regard to your role as Sipho's manager, what kinds of duties take up most of your time?

I handle everything that would take away from my artist being creative and making music. Artist management is a selfless position. It's about understanding where you're best served and what skills you have that will ultimately help what the artist is doing in the studio to translate outside of the studio. You must build a relationship with your artist on a personal level before you can even begin to understand what they are trying to achieve on a creative level. I'm essentially a PA, a confidant, a creative director, an executive producer – but most importantly, a fan.

How did your professional relationship with Sipho develop from being interested in his music on Soundcloud to becoming his manager?

My professional relationship with Sipho developed quite easily. I DM'd him on Instagram and said I'd love to meet to discuss his music. We sat down and discussed him, his music and what his goals were, and I showed him where I thought I could fit in and add value. Like any relationship, you're going to have to build a level of trust and understanding before an artist feels comfortable enough around you to allow you to get to work.

Are there any tips or advice you can offer to emerging artists who are interested in finding the right manager for their career?

Take the time to understand yourself as an artist and how you want your art to be positioned, consumed and understood. Ultimately, it's about being honest with yourself as an artist. A manager can only work with what you give them. Timing is the most important thing. If you get a manager too early, before you understand who you are and what you want, you could be easily led and end up doing what your manager's vision for you is instead of what you envision for yourself. There's no rush – the music industry isn't going anywhere!

8
What Do Lawyers Do?

Music lawyers are the cornerstones of a successful recording artist's career. They are also important for songwriters, composers and producers. They understand every component of the music industry, especially around the intricacies of intellectual property.

Key duties include:

- providing legal guidance;
- advising on contracts;
- negotiating on a creator's behalf;
- offering strategic career guidance;
- helping creators to understand their value in the business;
- using their initiative to foresee potential difficulties further into a creator's career;
- helping creators to make informed decisions; and
- using their network to advance a creator's career.

When Should a Music Creator Hire a Lawyer?

The simplest answer is: when the creator is offered a contract that they don't fully understand. Knowing when is the right time can be difficult, as it might be that the creator understands many of the key concepts of a contract but struggles with some of the more extended long-form details. It is often the case that the creator is excited by the prospect of a contract and likes the person they are dealing with, and therefore overlooks some of the fine print or misunderstands some of the core details of the contractual relationship. Many lawyers are brought in further down the line to unpick problems that could easily have been resolved earlier on. Another common thought that many creators have is, 'This is the only contract I am being offered right now, so I may as well just

DOI: 10.4324/9781003452119-10

go for it.' Receiving a contract can be used as leverage to build interest among similar parties and music lawyers can be crucial in generating interest among other professionals while also brokering a deal with more favourable terms for their client. For some creators, a lawyer is the first member of their professional team, and together the creator and lawyer build the rest of the team. However, in some cases, creators work too early with music lawyers – especially if the creator is yet to build an investable proposition for labels, managers, booking agents or publishers to invest their time in. Lawyers excel at advancing a creator's career when they are artistically developed and have realistic and professional goals.

What Deal Should a Creator Expect from a Lawyer?

The typical starting point for a working relationship with a lawyer is a letter of engagement. This usually follows on from an initial conversation in which a lawyer or a member of their legal team conducts a basic needs analysis assessment regarding the client's specific requirements. The letter of engagement is the official document that starts the formal engagement of a lawyer's services. It will outline the fees for different tasks or provide a breakdown of how the lawyer records their time; in either case, you will gain a full understanding of how to use their services and what the costs will be. A lawyer or legal firm is generally quite fixed in their pricing structure and less open to negotiation. The letter of engagement will also provide details on:

- the lawyer-client legal relationship;
- the lawyer's contact information;
- the lawyer's insurance;
- their lawyer's complaints procedure; and
- the ways in which the lawyer's services can be used.

9
What Do Accountants Do?

A music business accountant is typically a professional who is added to a creator's team once initial income streams are being generated. The needs of music creators are often quite different from those of professionals in other industries, so music accountants offer a more tailored service which caters to this specific profession.

Typical accountancy duties include the following:

- tax calculations;
- preparation of tax returns;
- financial reporting to the state/government;
- handling the closing of tax years;
- payroll;
- business forecasting of accounts;
- assessment of business status;
- up-to-date knowledge of legislative changes to the economic landscape; and
- advice.

Qualities that are more specific to music business accountants include the following:

- the flexibility to offer bookkeeping services for a creator's week-to-week income and expenses;
- specialist knowledge of royalty collection and data interpretation, with a focus on discrepancies and inaccuracies in reporting;
- industry-specific knowledge of typical areas of spending, especially in relation to touring and music-related events;
- the ability to educate and inform a creator of changes in the economic landscape of the music business;

DOI: 10.4324/9781003452119-11

- the ability to communicate expertly with other professionals on the creator's team; and
- the flexibility to offer more time to a creator who has specific questions about music industry accounting.

An accountant can be an asset when it comes to budgeting, forecasting and planning strategic growth. Some creators misunderstand the role of an accountant by assuming that they will add to the creator's overall costs, when the truth can often be the opposite. Accountants are experts in their field who understand the legalities and loopholes of financial interest. This can and often does save creators a great deal of unnecessary expense. It could be argued that perhaps a creator could handle some of these tasks themselves, which would help to bring down their annual accountancy costs. These could include tasks such as doing their own bookkeeping, for which many great software applications are available.

10
Understanding the Live Sector

Today, there are bands that have millions of streams on Spotify and yet would struggle to pack out a 200-capacity venue in their hometown. Those bands walk the same streets as other bands that could sell out a 200-capacity venue quite easily and yet don't have the streams to use as leverage to attract a successful booking agent or manager.

Growing a fanbase on the live circuit is a key driver of growth for any artist that isn't a straight-up pop act or a studio-only concept. Live music has stood the test of time throughout all the changes that the music industry has witnessed in recent decades. The economics have switched, though: acts used to tour to sell a record, but today acts use streaming as a marketing tool to attract a live following. However, the art that is shared on stage remains the same.

Live music is undeniably special. It is difficult to articulate just how special it is, but there is something tribal about standing in a large crowd of people all enjoying an atmosphere and sharing the energy that is created by a gig. If you were to ask any emerging artist what they want out of their careers, scaling up their live music presence would probably be mentioned in some capacity in the first half of their answer. For some creators, it is *the* thing that defines their musical identity. Let's unpack some of the key roles in the live sector.

Promoters

Promoters at all levels are a cornerstone of the live sector, with several purposes, roles and duties. Promoters can be either individuals or companies, and their core aim is to promote live music and artists. Promoters range from those who book artists to play at small grassroots venues to those who book huge festivals. Often the venue itself may be the promoter. Promoters secure bookings for venues that can range from bars to clubs, halls, arenas and festivals. They enter into contracts with the venues or event organisers which outline the

DOI: 10.4324/9781003452119-12

terms of the agreement reached between the two parties. The promoter then books artists to play; promotes the event through posters, banners, social media and ad campaigns; and engages with the press to secure further coverage. Duties will vary depending on the size of the artist and the venue. Promoters are responsible for the audience experience, which includes security, ticket sales and logistics. Promoters also negotiate on the fees for artists in advance. They have a wide network of music professionals – especially booking agents, artist managers, venues, event organisers and artists themselves. Promoters at a grassroots level, who tend to work in regional areas, are often quite useful to talent scouts and A&R personnel who are keen to find emerging talent in the area. Promoters on a national or international scale tend to be more proactive in the promotion of live music events where the emphasis is on gaining visibility for the artist's tour dates.

Booking Agents

Sometimes referred to as 'talent agents' or simply 'agents', booking agents are music industry professionals or companies that secure live bookings for artists by working in partnership with promoters, venues, event organisers and festivals to secure gigs. Often working closely with artist managers and artists, booking agents are responsible for booking tours and one-off live performances. Booking agents excel at contract and fee negotiations and take a commission on the artist's fee in exchange for their services. Booking agents excel at the logistics of things such as travel arrangements, itineraries, backline and technical arrangements, and accommodation. Booking agents often support the marketing of live performance events alongside the promoter and the artist team, although this can vary depending on scale and territory. Many booking agents also help an artist and their team to make informed decisions about strategy and market trends in relation to the upscaling of their live music plans.

Festivals

In addition to providing support slots for headlining acts, music festivals play a crucial role in bringing new artists to a wider audience. As the experiential economy has boomed since the turn of the century, music festivals have enjoyed continued growth and now appeal to a much wider demographic: today, many major festivals around the world cater for families and a broad age mix in addition to the younger generation of listeners. Festivals can range from small-town fusion festivals combining food, culture and local music to mega festivals such as Glastonbury in the UK, Coachella in the USA, Primavera Sound in

Spain, Montreux Jazz in Switzerland and Canada, and Rock am Ring and Rock im Park in Germany.

As for many other aspects of the music industry, it is important that recording artists research the festivals to identify those which they would be best suited to, as well as the application process and deadlines. Many booking agents and managers expect bands and artists to scale themselves up and build their stage show through appearances at local and regional festivals; but there are also many emerging artists who get a break at major festivals through networking. Sponsors can be influential in suggesting acts for festival slots; as can contemporary music universities and regional radio. It is a festival promoter's job to be aware of emerging artists who are building their reputations, as many large festivals want to be associated with breaking talent in addition to booking legacy acts.

Interview: Andy Rea, Co-founder, 2000trees Festival; Founder, Redtarn PR & Events; University Lecturer, UK

2000trees is a magnificent festival experience. You have truly created something unique that embraces stages, tents and forests, and that extends far beyond merely an event. Was this always the intention or have the ideals evolved over time?

Honestly, as six friends with a punk-rock dream of starting a festival from scratch with very little experience, we had no idea if we could even organise the first event; so to succeed and then keep it going as an independent over the next 15 years has been one of the most rewarding achievements of our lives! I like to think it shows that through strong audience connections, a great atmosphere and everyone having a fantastic time in a field together.

There is a loyal 'Trees' community, without which we are nothing. The original idea emerged around a campfire when we attended a major UK rock festival with which we found many, many faults, so we were inspired to create the antithesis: a fan-friendly event which was not the corporate 'pursuit of profits at all costs' model we endured that weekend in 2006. Today, we remain fiercely independent and customer focused, and all six friends continue to work together to create the kind of festival that we would love to attend ourselves.

From that starting point, we developed company values incorporated into our first marketing tagline in 2007: 'A Green, Ethical, Music Festival.' Those ideals still hold today as we try to focus on sustainability, value and quality entertainment.

However, while we have always held true to our core ethics and ethos which were there from the start – of being a festival 'for music fans, by music fans' – there has also been an evolution, in terms of ideals, content and an overarching drive to learn from failure by continuously seeking improvement. We have developed our knowledge, skills and experience across the business; and we have evolved our practices such as our marketing tagline – which has changed a few times over the years – and our programme offering, which has become increasingly diversified. We are focused on continuously improving the amazing atmosphere and the positive, inclusive, 'be yourselves and be happy in that space' vibes experienced by customers when attending.

In relation to how you populate your line-up of artists, do you set your ideals for who you want to play and then reach out to booking agents for those acts or do you have booking agents reach out to you to pitch their acts?

The short answer is both. We have a list of bands we want to approach, but we also take submissions from booking agents – particularly the ones we know have a history of breaking bands.

In regard to the booking process for independent music creators, do you have an open-door policy for independent artists and if so, what do you hope to hear or see in the pitch?

Yes, absolutely, as we appreciate it can be a thankless task as an unknown artist in a competitive industry. While it can be overwhelming with the sheer volume of submissions, we are always open to finding new talent with the drive to work hard at their craft. One example is George Ezra, who played our festival about a decade ago. He performed to 50 people on a bale and look at him now!

We're interested, first and foremost, in the art created, so making it easy for us to see and hear the music is vital. It helps for those who are already on their artist journey if they can show some positive elements, such as venues played previously (with capacities), other artists supported and so on. Finally, it is no coincidence that most, if not all artists who succeed work incredibly hard, so evidence of growing an online presence is helpful too.

At 2000trees, you have a fantastic philosophy towards accessibility and inclusivity. We are now in an age when virtual festivals are beginning to evolve with the development of immersive audio and 4K resolution screens which allows for an even higher level of inclusivity and access. How do you see the future of this aspect of the sector?

I'm a big fan of technology and seeing how we can utilise it; but even if I wasn't, it's important to try to keep an eye on the direction of travel in the live music and events industry, as well as the wider 'leisure pound' experiential economy.

There are pros and cons here, but one constant is that it must work seamlessly to meet customers' expectations. To take an extreme example, if everyone decided that an augmented reality festival experience were preferable to actually attending the event, we would be out of business. To elaborate, a widely held view is that the 'live experience' is irreplaceable, but that doesn't mean we shouldn't explore opportunities to include those who cannot attend – subject to reasonable budgets. And the more the technology is harnessed, the more cost effective and widely used these solutions can become.

You are also very active in PR with Redtarn PR and Events. Is there any advice you can give to emerging music creators on how to build a buzz around their act?

One important factor is to enjoy this fickle business of the live music and events industry. Intrinsic motivation is so important for success, so finding something you truly love doing will get you over the line, alongside all the hard work, creativity and administration. It's all about the journey, rather than the destination; and if you believe this, you may find yourself happier at the end of it all.

Another is to check who you're working with on PR and avail of their network of contacts. For example, if a label offers you a radio plugger as part of the deal, explore what that really means: who they are and what connections they have; which radio stations they have contacts at. Immerse yourself in the detail before committing to anything.

Have something to say to fans, to the media and to the industry, which comes from building resilience and self-esteem. I remember Justin Hawkins (The Darkness) saying he knew how to play the media game, so when many journalists were after a feud with other bands, he played along. He had something relevant, pithy and humorous to say, and he didn't take himself too seriously.

Seek advice. Some people believe you should 'stay in your lane' and there is a lot to be said for focusing on your music, your act and your core role. Others believe that they can do a multiverse of things to help their act to succeed with wider-ranging skills beyond being an artist. At either end of this spectrum, good advice is good advice, so seek out those mentors, experienced tastemakers and influencers who can help you along the way.

Live Streaming

The live streaming of music performances experienced a major boom in 2020 due to the outbreak of Covid-19. As the pandemic was brought under control, demand for in-person live performances began to rebound; and by the time the World Health Organization declared the pandemic over in May 2023, the live sector was once again booming as the major festivals in the northern hemisphere exploded in their usual summer glory. However, some of the patterns established in lockdown became habitual: think of video meetings, enhanced pre-booking and remote working, among others. The pandemic fuelled significant technological advancements in the live streaming field, especially in relation to the user experience. Interest is growing in the capabilities offered by immersive audio, 4K and other technologies as replacements for the in-person experience. The beauty of these technologies is that they cater to those who are unable to experience in-person live music due health conditions or impairments. Innovative new methods of live music streaming emerged at the height of the pandemic; time will tell whether these technologies embed themselves further in the immersive and revolutionary world of live streaming to the point where they achieve mainstream acceptance.

Tour Managers

A tour manager plays a crucial on-the-ground role in the success of a tour. A tour manager is often defined by their ability to juggle logistics, time and people management, emergencies and crisis response, while simultaneously supporting the audience experience and handling travel arrangements for artists and crew, budgeting, health and safety and artist support, among a host of other unexpected tasks. The tour manager's role is an around-the-clock responsibility, which in many cases starts months in advance of a tour through efficient planning and culminates with the show dates, when their usual responsibilities are augmented by a wide variety of preparation duties. The success of a tour is often dictated by the strength and attitude of the tour manager.

Grassroots Growth

Many music creators are keen to win fans in the world's major cities, but it is healthy to question whether this is always the right approach.

When it comes to building a following on the live circuit, smaller towns may be preferable to big cities, no matter how appealing the tour poster might look when all the big cities are listed. Venues with a ready-made community and fanbase do exist, but these are more commonly found in towns and villages, rather than cities.

Music creators would be well advised to think how a booking agent thinks, with strategy and purpose. A keen eye for growth is perhaps more important than personal preferences or musical snobbery. For instance, a local metal band that despises tribute acts might still be far better placed supporting a Metallica tribute act for several shows rather than playing to 15 people at their own local gig. Overlooking one's values is not really a compromise of integrity if it is in the best interests of the band. Growth is key, because despondency can quickly kick in if an act is continually playing the same places to the same people. Things can soon get stale – and this is not a reflection of the music or the performance, but rather a reflection of the strategy. That same metal band could instead be researching key tastemakers in the genre by identifying YouTubers, bloggers and journalists who are keen to find the next big metal act; and these need not be people in their home town – or even in their home country. The traction they build from this can be used as press leverage to gain local and regional tour support slots – especially if they can prove they have a local following that a touring band can tap into. This local support can be driven not only by their fantastic live show, but also by their continued improvement in the studio and the good PR they build for themselves by thinking more innovatively about their social media output. Before long, the band are doing interviews about their humble beginnings in the good old days and reminiscing about places that no longer exist.

Part 3

Being a Recording Artist

11
Artist Development: The Rarely Spoken Truths of Self-discovery

If a recording artist speaks to a potential new manager, the manager will want to understand something about them. If they speak to a producer, the producer will want to understand something about them. If they speak to a record company or music publisher, they too will want to understand something about them. If they engage with a PR company, they will be met with questions which all relate to the same central subject.

"Who Are You?" and "What Are You?"

People ask these questions because they are trying to identify the place in the landscape of the music industry where the creator sits. They offer context. Questions such as "Who are your influences?" will come up. This is how people try to figure out who and what you are. It allows them to draw links between what the artist likes and what others will like about the artist.

These are simple but major questions that can stall an artist early in their career, so you should try to answer the questions for yourself before you can expect others to understand them.

Everyone is unique, that's for certain; but it is also important that artists can be placed into categories. It's rather like buying something from Amazon: it goes in a box. Music is the same if it is to be sold to the public. This doesn't mean that an artist can't be different – being different is encouraged, admired and enjoyed. There is always a balance.

Does the Creator Make the Same Music That Inspires Them?

As creators, we start out wanting to make music largely because we are inspired. We are original at our core, but we also partially emulate what we

DOI: 10.4324/9781003452119-14

have seen or heard – that is how influence works, after all. The initial step for many is to create music that is similar in style to the music that inspires us. There's nothing wrong with that. It makes perfect sense. Over time, perhaps the music that first inspired us as creators and the music we now make create a separation in distance. That distance is evolution and artist development.

Artist development is a multifaceted process of self-discovery that draws on wider influences and experiences to create a sense of balanced integrity that yields a more refined output of musical definition. It is then that an artist finds an identity that they can move forward with. It need not define them for their whole career; it just needs to define them for their introduction to a wider audience.

Interview: Karen Harding, Recording Artist and Songwriter, UK

Karen Harding is a multi-platinum-selling songwriter, vocalist and recording artist. Her debut single, 'Say Something', was co-written and produced by MNEK and released in 2014. The song reached 1 million sales in the UK and has been streamed over 100 million times since. Karen has enjoyed a successful career since and has released a huge catalogue of music – not only as an artist in her own right but also as a composer for other artists including Claire Richards, KREAM and Kaiser Chiefs. In 2023, almost a decade after her launch, Karen released her much-awaited debut album, *Take Me Somewhere*.

Label: Ultra Records
Publisher: Universal Music
Management: Upside UK

Your debut single, 'Say Something', was a hugely successful entrance to a wider audience back in the mid-2010s. What was it like to witness such monumental growth from that song?

When I think about that time, it's all hazy. It was all happening so quickly that I didn't realise how amazing it all was. I was getting into the studio with legends of the songwriting and production world and I didn't have time to take it all in. I felt like that was the time when I worked harder than I had ever done before.

Since then, you have firmly established your legacy in the landscape of dance music thanks to various successful collaborations. How best do you collaborate: in a room with other creatives or remotely in your own space?

The amazing thing is that I get to change it up and no writing session – either on my own or with others – is ever the same. I love being in the room with others, as I love the inspiration that we all get to share with each other in that moment. I do enjoy setting up on my own too – especially in moments when I feel like I need to get something heavy off my chest.

You are also active as a songwriter for other recording artists. Was this always part of your career ideal?

When I first started, I didn't realise it was even a thing! My dream when I was younger always revolved around performing and singing. I started writing songs myself at home and messing around on Garageband (music software), but I never thought I would be any good at it. To now have a publishing contract and all the songs that I have out, I feel like another hidden dream has been achieved.

In September 2023, you released your much-awaited debut album on Ultra Records. How did you go about finding your sonic identity for this project and how did you know when you had found it?

It all started with 'Undo My Heart'. I felt like this song was part of something bigger. I remember how I felt when I sang it when we recorded it, and it felt very similar to 'Say Something'. I knew it was good and I loved singing it! After that, when the album was finally coming into view, I kind of followed that same feeling. I listened to all my unreleased tracks over the years and picked the ones that gave me that same feeling. I guess this meant that maybe I had found my identity in these songs, as they truly spoke to me.

Do you have any advice for emerging music creators who are looking to build a career in the business?

Have self-belief. A lot of people out there might not 'get it', but that's just a moment in a time and a place. Move on and keep working. Rejection is a key factor in succeeding in any area of business. I've had my fair share of rejection – as have many artists – and it's only ever made me stronger and more determined.

What Defines a Recording Artist?

Genre Definition

A solid understanding of an artist's primary genre is crucial. A 'primary genre' is an umbrella term covering an array of styles. For instance, EDM is a primary genre, but inside it fall house, dubstep, euro-dance, dark ambient, drum and bass and electronic rock, among many others. Inside of R&B fall soul, disco, Motown, funk and many others.

While it could easily be argued that these are sub-genres, in the context of metadata and artist discovery, it is important for an artist to acknowledge their primary genre and then identify their secondary genres. For some, this is a relatively pain-free task; but for others, it is confusing and overwhelming. "I just do what I do" is something artists often state; but in the digital age, it is not always enough to rely on this. One of the battles artists often face is when they merge genres and then have to work out how best to categorise themselves. It is often worth asking trusted sources what their opinions are; but it's best to avoid unrecognisable categories often creatively titled by the less informed. 'Alternative' is a word which is often used; but by its raw definition, people often associate it with something that is obscure, eclectic or abstract, or that challenges the mainstream. Meanwhile, others associate it solely with alternative rock. Alt-pop is a genre which largely conforms to mainstream appeal, which negates the original definition. This kind of thing can send artists in circles, but it is worth the research. For instance, you could have a metal band that plays with a classical music influence. The band might label themselves as 'progressive metal' due to the hallmarks of their fusion style or rapid technique, when in all actuality identifying their genre as 'neoclassical' could open new doors not only in the live sector, but also in terms of digital categorisation for playlist consideration.

Also, there is nothing shameful about a country artist labelling themselves as 'pop' and then finding suitable secondary genres such as country pop and cowboy pop. Genre definition is a retrospective task for some and an intention from the off for others. In any case, an artist knowing their genre enables identification. It is therefore a hallmark of an artist's identity.

Cultural, Stylistic and Technological Traits

It is always worth considering the roles that culture, styles and technology play in an artist's sound, as these are factors that contribute to the artist's identity. Antares Auto Tune has become integral to the sound of many hip hop artists in recent years, to the point where some artists would not sound the same without it. Meanwhile, the stylistic impact of TikTok dances is influencing the texture and structure of many dance pop songs today. Styles often have scenes and cultures attached to them. For instance, Billie Eilish is a unique and influential artist with a distinctive sound; but it could be argued that no matter how unique she is, even she derived – at least in part – from the bedroom pop movement of the early 2010s.

There are also musical cultures to consider. An artist can easily identify with a culture as part of their music, even if that culture is not part of their upbringing as a person. A singer-songwriter from a city in Europe could be a country artist without having ever been to the USA, in the same way that a K-pop-inspired girl group from Australia may never have been to South Korea. These are all factors to consider, as they contribute towards an artist's identity.

Values and Message

An artist can get a message across in their music. This could be in their lyrics, the types of stories they tell or the vocabulary they use. Perhaps it is in how they use rhyming schemes or metaphors. Maybe it is in how they conduct themselves. Every great artist has some kind of message that underpins their entry point to the mainstream. It is usually a combination of artistic identity and good PR, but having a message creates a sense of values between an artist and their audience. Taylor Swift is a great example of this. She generates a great sense of inclusion and unity among her fans and encourages defiance and self-leadership through the way she conducts herself as a businesswoman; and yet she exhibits her vulnerability and authenticity in her songs. This is a message of realness and it means something to people. In the 1990s, UK rock band Oasis organically embraced 'lad culture' and made music fans out of people who were barely music fans prior to their existence. The band combined their brash outlook with working class modesty, which connected with such a large number of males in particular that you still see people with their haircuts to this day. For both Oasis and Taylor Swift, while their songwriting is undeniably outstanding, the message of their acts is also crystal clear. It is important for an artist to define their message and the values of their brand through their conduct and their music.

Sonic Identity

This can be a struggle for many artists. A sonic identity is defined by the sound of the music itself. However, it is not a fixed subject: it can and should evolve as an artist develops. For something to develop, however, it needs a starting point that can be defined, and creating a sonic identity is an important factor that defines an artist's recorded sound. The key factors that contribute towards a sonic identity include:

- music production values;
- choices of instrumentation;
- vocal delivery;

- vocal production; and
- the use of technology.

Let's take Ed Sheeran as an example. He is an artist who has shown a great deal of sonic evolution throughout his career, but at the heart of it all are his voice and his acoustic guitar. Let's go a little deeper. Sheeran's voice is soulful, beautiful and heartfelt at times, and yet it also flips quite comfortably into playful and technical rap. His guitar sound is signature. It doesn't sound as clean, deep and rich as country records do, but it doesn't need to because it sounds like him. It is his playing, and it is the tinny sound of that small acoustic that he is known for.

Let's now think about Elton John for a moment. Over the decades of his out-standing career – through all the outfits, the colours, the themes and the sounds – Elton and the sound of his piano remain ever-present, having barely changed since the 1970s. Much like Sheeran, everything can be stripped down to that one voice and one instrument and still keep its power.

Or try Googling the 'Daft Punk vocal sound'. There are countless theories and projected signal paths to recreating the sound that the electronic duo famously used in so many songs. It is a signature of their sonic identity, just as vocoders and talkboxes are for other electronic acts. As technologies de-velop and fuse together, there are a range of vocal sounds that remain to be discovered.

Some producers also possess a unique sonic fingerprint that, when paired with the right artist, can bring music alive and forge vibrant partnerships. It is interesting to think about how Michael Jackson would have sounded with-out Quincy Jones, how Drake may have sounded without 40 and how Def Leppard might have communicated their music to the world without Mutt Lange; but it is fair to say that all would have sounded rather different.

Branding and Image

Branding plays a key part in how the style of an artist is perceived. Everything from colour choices to shapes, textures and font styles contributes towards an audience's connection to an artist. Specialist fashion and style consultants can play a significant part in an artist's style, but some artists style themselves as their image is so uniquely intertwined with their artistry. While styling and branding can often slip under the conscious awareness of the public, they are always present and will have been carefully thought through. There are indie rock bands that have been styled to not look styled and flamboyant pop acts that have been styled to look self-styled.

An artist's image can offer a sense of uniqueness. It can be pioneeringly glamorous or purposely dull, but both can contribute towards the story that an artist portrays.

Interview: Laurence Hobbs, Founder, Safo Music Group, UK

Laurence Hobbs is the founder of London-based Safo Music Group, an artist development specialist and a platinum-selling producer and songwriter signed to 23rd Precinct Music/Notting Hill Music. Laurence has written hit songs and created music that has been used for a variety of television shows and is also an industry specialist when it comes to early career artist development. Having worked with the likes of Pixie Lott and Sam Smith early in their careers, Laurence has a great understanding of what makes for a successful artist.

You have seen a huge number of artists come through your studio doors over the years. What makes an artist memorable to you?

The most memorable are those with either a standout personality or an incredible voice. When I worked with Sam Smith, it was before he was famous and his voice was unforgettable. Music and musicality absolutely poured out of him, along with an intelligence about where he was heading – which is something that, in my experience, is very rare.

What can an artist do to help tap into their unique sound and artistic identity?

For most artists, if they have to ask that question, they're already struggling. Most of it comes naturally and is something that's inbuilt. Look at the big stars over the years, from Elvis to Stevie Wonder, Bowie, Eminem, Ed Sheeran . . . Their talent is something that is natural. Yes, they had the right help, advice and luck; but if they didn't have that innate something that stood out, they wouldn't be where they are. Saying that, it's just about what fits them best as a person and an artist: what sort of music they enjoy and what feels comfortable to them. Don't force it – an artist can be who they want to be.

What are the most important skills that are required for an emerging artist?

Work, work, work! And be nice to everyone. There's no such thing as a lazy successful artist! Also, network like crazy: you are possibly one meeting from a record deal, so be brave, have self-belief and know that confidence stands out. It is important to understand the music business and learn as much as you can from everyone you can.

What are the biggest mistakes you see in emerging artists?

It's a tough industry that seems unfair, with no right or wrong way to start and maintain a career. However, linking back to the last question, there's a real lack of understanding of what it takes to 'make it'. Some artists don't realise the work involved and the sacrifices they must make. I also think there's a lack of business knowledge among many artists entering the music industry. They need to understand what being a full-time recording artist looks like. It is important that they have more knowledge of the recorded music business, music publishing, what management deals look like, the purpose of collection societies and any other forms of income. It's important they have an understanding of what their expenditure should look like too. Many artists make basic mistakes regarding contracts that aren't right and money they shouldn't be spending. This is possibly the fault of the music colleges; but at the end of the day, it's down to the artist themselves to have at least a basic knowledge of these things.

Do you have any thoughts on where the future of the music industry is headed?

The music industry is ever-changing. AI seems to be the current big beast heading towards it, but – like the birth of sampling and the introduction of streaming – the industry can cope and embrace these and future changes. The one thing that hasn't changed is people's appetite for music. People will always want artists and songs to listen to – it's a human need. Therefore, I'm positive. As long as there are singers, rappers, producers and songwriters, there will be an ever-thriving music industry. Artists are adapting to the technology that surrounds them, which gives them the power to record, release and manage their careers. However, I come back to the need for them to be more business minded.

12

Being in a Band

Being in a band can be very special. Often there is a synergy between members of a band that creates something unique, whether on stage or in the studio, that can't be replicated by even the most advanced technologies. There is a sense of fraternity among a collective that experience so much together. It is a bond; it is a band; but it is also a business. For a business to operate successfully, it needs to have a market; it needs to know how to reach that market; and – even more importantly – it needs to know how to handle that market when it is reached. A band is no different. It might feel different because it does not require a formal uniform or the need to turn up at 9:00am on a Monday. It feels much more important than that. It feels, in fact, more like the exact opposite of that – and in some ways it is. However, when it comes down to making a living from the work that is done, it is actually quite comparable.

Imagine working for a company where you have no contract; the company has no boss, no rules, no agreements between staff members and no corporate structure; and you have no idea what will happen to you if the company goes into liquidation. That is no different from being in a band that has no inter-band agreement.

Inter-band Agreements

Often referred to as 'band agreements' or 'internal band contracts', inter-band agreements created early in a band's career are as crucial as there are rare. Many bands flippantly state, 'We don't need something like that' or 'Yeah, we should have something like that at some point,' but then rarely do anything about it. This could perhaps be because it is perceived as somewhat unnecessary or embarrassing to have something so formal to represent your working relationship when you are friends. It can also come down to the innocence of not really understanding the business of music and what it entails; but so very

DOI: 10.4324/9781003452119-15

often, it stems from the reluctance of band members to have a conversation about song splits. Songwriting splits are one of the biggest killers of bands. At the start of a band's life, it is not about the money; but that changes over time. It doesn't change because people get greedy but because they need to make a living. The early days are the fun times of freedom, self-expression and dreaming. Drafting an inter-band agreement is the last thing on anyone's mind; but this is the right time to draw one up. In order to succeed, you must be prepared for success, and that means knowing what the steps into professional musicianship will look like.

What Should Be Included in an Inter-band Agreement?

In a perfect world, a lawyer would draw up a contract for the band. However, this can be expensive and the agreement need not be overly formal; it just needs to be legally binding. There are also plenty of inter-band agreement templates available for free on the internet that can guide a band towards what theirs should look like. The key subjects to agree on include the following:

- Band members: The agreement should include the names and addresses of all members.
- Who owns the band name: This also covers the permission for use of the band name in the future and how many of the original members of the band must be present in the line-up for the name to be used. This aims to prevent multiple uses of the same band name, as we now see with many legacy acts.
- A collective agreement on the rights to the recorded music and the associated artwork: In most cases, there is an even split between the band members on recording rights. This relates to the income generated by the master recordings.
- An outline of how songwriting splits work in the band: Many inter-band agreements state that each individual song must have its own split sheet, as the writing credits vary from song to song. Some band agreements state that all songwriting is split evenly between band members. Others state that songwriting is the exclusive right of specific band members. There is no right or wrong here – what matters is that there is an agreement moving forward.
- Band income, expenditure and spending: Often, income relates to collective income that the band generates that sits outside of songwriting royalties. A band bank account should also be applicable here. The key things to agree on are how funds will be split once expenditure is recouped, the

percentage split between band members and the percentage that will remain in the account. It is also important to agree on how financial decisions will be made (eg, by vote between the band members). Categories of outgoing expenditure should also be agreed upon (eg, marketing, PR costs, rehearsals, bills, merchandise, travel, accommodation, insurance); as should how related decisions will be made by the band. It is important for the band to agree on what are categorised as band members' personal costs and what are categorised as band costs.

- Decision making: This partly relates to the previous point regarding financial choices, but it also relates to creative and business direction. A system should be established and agreed upon in writing for how band-related decisions will be made. This can be especially difficult for bands that have an even number of members, as there is no possibility to assign a casting vote. A system must be agreed upon by all parties.
- Band member responsibilities: A code of conduct of sorts should be in place.
- Changes to band members:

  - If the band wish to vote for a member to leave, a fair system should be agreed as to how this will be done. This often relates to the previous point about responsibilities and conduct, in addition to how decisions will be reached.
  - What happens if a band member decides to leave of their own accord? The rights to any share of the songwriting and recording royalties will still be due, but it would create a sense of transparency to acknowledge whether any other income streams should continue. If the band is signed to a record company, it is worth gaining a solid understanding of whether the agreement that is in place means that the individual members of the band are signed to the label in addition to the entity of the band.
  - What happens in the event of the death of a band member should also be agreed upon. In some cases, assets and intellectual property can be transferred according to how the band member has set up their legal beneficiaries. In other cases, a death is treated in the same way as a band member leaving. It could perhaps be stated that in the event of a band member's death, the band will vote on the suitable course of action.

- Band assets: It is important to keep a log of the assets and inventory owned by the band, such as PA equipment, lights, mutual band equipment and cash assets. An agreement should be in place as to what happens such assets if a band member leaves.

- Replacement of band members: The agreement system that has previously been established by the band could also dictate how a new member is recruited if this is needed.

An inter-band agreement has two primary aims. First, it helps the band to cement their working relationship and agree on how problems will be dealt with before they arise. Second, it helps the band to identify some of the key issues relating to the mechanics of how the music industry functions and narrow down their goals moving forward. In addition, it can help to educate band members on the workings of the business that they are getting into.

There are many bands that fall out when agreeing on terms. As heart-breaking as this may be to witness, it is far better that an unhappy band member leaves sooner rather than later. Another outcome often seen during the negotiation discussions is that non-songwriting band members become aware of their lack of song copyright royalties (if this is what is agreed by the band). Many songwriting band members are afraid of this happening, but it is far better to make non-songwriting members aware of what they are getting into from the outset. There is no right or wrong in terms of what should be agreed – that is for the band to decide as a unit. The document need not be written in legal jargon; nor need it be laminated. It just needs to make sense to all parties and be signed and dated by all band members, so that they can move forward with building their career together.

Interview: Gavin Monaghan, Music Producer, UK

UK-based Gavin Monaghan is a multi-platinum-selling music producer who owns and runs the award-winning Magic Garden recording studio. Gavin has an illustrious history of working with a range of artists such as Robert Plant, Ocean Colour Scene, Paolo Nutini, Editors, The Twang, Nizlopi, The Holloways, Scott Matthews, The Sherlocks and JAWS. Gavin has carved a reputation as someone who brings the very best out of people and understands the dynamics of bands at an advanced level.

You have worked with several bands over the years. In your experience, what are the ingredients that make for a successful band?

When it comes to bands or groups of people making music, as opposed to solo artists, the rules are slightly different. In both cases, the songs must be fantastic, whether they're written from within the band or by songwriters. The sound should be cohesive, natural and original. The aesthetic of the band should integrate seamlessly with the music to present a strong, memorable and unique image. Chemistry between the members is vital. After falling in love with the music, I look for the interplay between the members and how they interact. I'll later bring this out in every way possible in the performances that we capture when we make records together.

When the band perform or record together, everyone on stage should interact with each other in an engaging and entertaining way. They must generate energy and carry the audience along with their spirit.

Being good at your craft is not enough – there must be a sense of magic that happens when they play and sing together that is not there when they perform alone. All the best bands have this quality both offstage and on. It shines through at concerts and auditions, in studios, on the radio, in interviews and when they are just hanging out together.

When I first saw Editors play together in a small pub at the end of the 1990s, it made my jaw drop: there was something wonderful going on all over the stage. And when I met them backstage prior to us working together, I just knew they were going to be enormous.

Starting my first duo, Mama ft Antonella, last year has had a massive impact on the way I operate in the studio. I played gigs all over the world in my twenties with bands in which I wasn't particularly invested, touring with the Cult and so on, but it was never intimate. Mama has really changed the way I interact with bands and has given me a far deeper empathy for the needs of musicians. I think I could sometimes be too tough before.

There are numerous roles that a producer can play in the studio. Do you find that these roles differ from band to band – for instance, some bands may need more support in pre-production to gain a tighter structure, whereas others may need support in understanding the market for their music?

I'm often asked about my role as a music producer. To sum up, it's normally a combination of functions: part musicologist, part cheerleader, part arranger and part psychiatrist. There are no rules. People have different needs in the studio and it's my job to determine what those are quickly, so we can get on with the important business of creating their work. Some need a lot of help with their arranging and with achieving their radio-friendly intros, their insightful verses and their incendiary choruses. It's an art – creating the perfect arrangement for radio in particular. I must also keep the label's interest in being able to market the music in mind. By this point, there will normally have been several creative meetings to establish the artistic, social and commercial vision of the release and how to maximise its impact in every area. I do occasionally have to play the diplomat to get the job done and ensure everyone feels happy about the result we achieve together. It's sometimes tricky, but it's an essential part of the process. The music must be bigger than everyone involved in making it and egos should always be left at the door to serve the song.

As a producer, do you offer a buyout of the master rights to an artist or label or a percentage deal, or does it vary?

Contracts vary widely these days. Not that long ago, the 360 model where a label takes a cut of everything simply didn't exist. Now, in some cases it is offered as standard. My manager always tries to get both an advance and a points deal in place for me wherever possible. If this simply isn't an option, we will work with the management and the label for the best possible outcome for everybody.

Sometimes the creative vision of an act can differ from that of the label they are signed to. How do you handle this aspect of your work?

There will usually be some difference in opinion regarding almost every aspect of how to create a recording and present a band artistically and commercially to the public. The key thing to remember is that everyone is on the same team. A solution can almost always be reached and common ground achieved with some thought and a few interesting ideas.

At the same time, it has always baffled me why a label signs an artist and then tries to change everything about them until they are unrecognisable. This invariably ends in arguments and sometimes even chaos. Better to sign someone that you believe in and then work with them to help them become their ideal creative selves. This carries through the stages of an artist's career much better and leaves everyone feeling authentic and much happier with the process.

Do you have any advice for emerging bands that are looking to build a career in the music business?

- Stay open minded, always.
- Be grateful, be humble and don't believe all your own hype (just manifest the useful stuff).
- Develop your business as much as you can before trying to sell it to anyone else. It's much more attractive for potential investors to see a healthy understanding of the business side of music.
- Write amazing choruses that you can learn and sing while drunk in a field.
- Don't underestimate the impact of social media. It's one of the first things a manager, a publisher or a label will look at when determining whether to take you on.

The Legal Structure of the Band

One of the key aspects to consider as a band is when and how to turn profes-sional. For some, this is when they sign a recording deal, a publishing deal or a management deal. For others, it's when they gain their first sync deal or do their first tour. It is difficult to pinpoint a particular time when this starts to happen, because it is usually more of a gradual process than a sudden one.

One common observation is that many bands are geared up for the professional pursuit in terms of mentality and ambition, prepared to work hard and ready to put in the time. However, this is not the same thing as being prepared for it from a business perspective. It is important to consider the legal structure of the band when it is a business. What this looks like in terms of legal structure and company formation will depend on where the band is located in the world. It is advisable to seek the support and advice of an accountant when taking these steps; but let's explore a basic overview using the UK as an example.

A band can choose from the following company structures in the UK.

Limited Company

A limited company (Ltd) is often the most suitable choice for bands. There are running costs involved with being a limited company and there are costs involved with setting up so that the company formation is correctly registered under the recognised legal framework with Companies House and HMRC. A limited company needs at least one director in its initial incorporation, but band members will become shareholders of the company and a shareholders' agreement must be put in place to govern the system for making major deci-sions together with the splits between shareholders. In many cases, there is an even split of company shares between band members, but there needn't be. It could be that all members of the band are directors, but again this is optional if there is one director in place. The shareholders own the company and the directors are responsible for running the company. There are also running costs involved with having a business bank account and it is also worth considering that corporation tax will be due by the company. The upside is reduced respon-sibility for business debts. Salaries can be paid by the company to the band members and directors' dividends can also be paid out as bonuses. Legislation will dictate changes to the thresholds for taxable income over time; and once a variable threshold of company income has been met, the company will need to be registered for value added tax, which has both advantages and disadvantages that should be considered.

Partnership

Instead of running the band business as a legal structure with directors and share-holders, it could operate under a partnership agreement, which effectively means that the partners both own and run the business. A partnership requires multiple owners, which is a factor that makes it suitable for bands. However, a partnership is suitable only for a watertight group, which can be difficult to ascertain in the context of bands and the music industry. This is because if one partner incurs debts and makes bad financial decisions on behalf of the company, all of the partners will be liable and not just that one partner who caused the problems.

Limited Liability Partnership

This is rather like a hybrid of a limited company and a partnership. Limited liability partnerships (LLPs) don't have shareholders or directors, but instead have an unlimited number of members. The members of an LLP can all take part in the management of the company, but they also have reduced personal responsibility for business debts. Members must all be appointed at the point of formation, but other members can be appointed at a later date, which makes this a strong and flexible model for bands that change their line-up further into their careers. This issue may not be at the forefront of band members' minds when they start their venture together, but the implications of a change in line-up must nonetheless be considered.

The Transition to Being a Full-time Band

Setting up a band as a business is a big step, but it is a necessary one in many (although not all) cases. It is worth noting that individuals can be self-employed (known as 'sole traders' in the UK) and remain responsible for their own tax payments until the band is ready to become a company. It is also worth remembering that band members may have other non-music jobs before, during or even after the transition is made. Within a band, it is more than likely that band members will each have their own circumstances to consider.

Interview: Chris Clark, Bassist, Daytime TV and Session Musician, UK

Daytime TV is not the first incarnation of your band. Like many other successful bands, you previously went under a different name. What was it like to go through a rebrand and what has the impact been?

The band did indeed have a previous life, known as Hunter & The Bear. The band originally started as a duo, Jimmy and Will. They then recruited Gareth on drums and me as bassist. The band had a string of releases, EPs and albums; we were very active live. One of the main reasons for the name change to Daytime TV was that one of the original members, Jimmy, decided to leave the band and was replaced with a new guitar player, John. We decided to operate under the previous band name for a little while, but we came across several issues that led to the name change and rebrand.

The music developed in such a forward-thinking way because of the combined personalities due to the addition of our new guitar player. I personally felt it may have been a slight disservice to the band's original fan base to release music that sounded so different from Hunter & The Bear. So we decided to draw a line in the sand and almost start over again as Daytime TV. We did, however, make sure to keep the older music on streaming platforms etc for the original fanbase to enjoy. That music meant a lot to us – and, I'm sure, to the fanbase that supported us during that time – so we wanted to keep it findable.

In terms of rationalising the rebrand/name change, we were advised that the continuation of the project was difficult in the eyes of various industry execs and press due to the evolution of our sound, writing style and image. I personally think a lot of institutions within the music industry build very quick notions and understandings of how a project operates and therefore how it can be represented. If there is any ambiguity to this representation or concept of understanding, it can lead to confusion and dissonance, which causes those institutions to disengage; and the incline of the trajectory will ultimately be increased. I feel the band experienced this a few times – for example, some people who had previously engaged and worked with the band suddenly because a little disinterested. For context, the band had started with acoustic-led folk structures and were now writing fully electric, mainstream commercial rock-leaning songs with pop structures. So I can understand how that journey can feel difficult to represent. The ultimate outcome of the rebrand has been overwhelmingly successful! The music and rebrand really consolidated the correct image and thus the project identity in a completely new way. I feel this has reinvigorated and rejuvenated industry interest. For example, we now get some great editorial playlist support on Apple Music and Spotify, including being on the cover of the official rock chart.

The rebrand has allowed our music to be understood and presented in the correct way, which has really stirred the fanbase and led to a lot of newer fans following us. This has also massively affected the types of support we are being offered – bands like The Amazons, Kaiser Chiefs, Circa Waves and Two Door Cinema Club. A big part of the band's recent development has been emphasised or is partly due to the response to the rebrand – but also due to the wider team who work around the project.

What key professional relationships does the band have that you feel have been important is driving your growth?

There are some amazing things you can achieve when working 'DIY', while establishing the growth and size of a project. However, there are a few important roles and responsibilities which function better when done outside of the project members.

I once heard a bizarre analogy about it being like the columns on a tiered cake: you need a specific number of columns to share the load which all work together to hold the layers above correctly. For some reason, this resonated with me! I would categorise these additional roles and relationships as follows.

- Booking agent/promoter: Booking agents and promoters should be passionate about a project from the off, as they need to have the time to invest in finding the appropriate opportunities for its development and growth. On paper, it may appear to be super-beneficial to have a major artist's booking agent because of the level and scale of show that they regularly deal with. But quite often, this may translate to them being incredibly busy and therefore not having enough time to focus on developing your live potential. It may be more productive to find a young agent at an established booking agency who is looking to find projects to make their own name with. Agents need ammunition to contact promoters and festivals. These people need to know what is planned to happen around the timeframe of their event to make booking your project an exciting prospect for their event. This means talking about things such as release strategy, which leads to the next point . . .
- Recording/producer: With the ease and affordability of music technologies, most bands can achieve great recordings. But it takes a producer to provide a different approach and point of view to take the songs into a sonic realm which the band may not have considered before. Many bands work with different producers, but having one or two producers you really trust to record and represent your songs in the best way possible is really important, in my opinion. This also subtly impacts the writing and forms a more cohesive body of work.
- Label/DIY servicing entity: The next step to release the music. We have partnered with a small but excellent label called Kartel to help with this. The release of music can vary depending on your own project's intended outcome. For example, some independent artists love the online communities created by platforms such as Bandcamp and Soundcloud. We like to have physical products for sale online and at shows, but we also hit all the main digital service providers, as we feel these will target more mainstream music consumers. This will also hopefully get the band on some editorial playlists along the way, massively increasing brand awareness and influencing other areas of interest such as press.

- Pluggers/PR: Press is a big part of building the story and informs other areas of the industry that the project is exciting and viable. This can involve a financial outlay for the band, unless it's bundled in with your label deal. But it is crucial to build awareness of the project and the story gives the booking agent the ammunition they need to grab exciting opportunities. A good example is if you can get some radio play on the main stations – for example, in the UK, BBC Radio 1 has some very good shows. If you can get on those, this can become a much wider talking point and affect many other aspects of the process.
- Management: In an ideal scenario, a manager would oversee all of the above and be the conduit between all the parties, ensuring that things are consistently happening and moving forward. If you don't have a manager, it is important to have personal connections with all the above entities, who can regularly check in with you and offer support or assistance as required. For example, if the PR asks for a specific piece of content or asset to influence a publication, this in turn may influence the plugger's ability to get a track heard by a certain radio producer; which may then cause a spike of listens in a territory; which can then be a talking point for the booking agent to confirm a show in that region.

An important mention should go to two other very important figures in the band's development: a music lawyer and a music accountant. Both will ensure that moneys are fairly agreed and collected on your behalf.

What aspects of band life have surprised you that you did not foresee or expect?

When starting out, all young musicians see being in a band as just playing music they love with (hopefully) their best friends. I am very lucky that this is the case for me; but there is an incredible amount of work and understanding that goes on behind the scenes to ensure you are involved in important decisions and developments. The music industry evolves so rapidly and revenue streams change, so it's about seeing the bigger picture, trying to forecast where you should position yourself in 12 months' time and working now to make that a focus.

There is a current trend of bands having to become content creators who also make music. I understand this is due to consumer media trends, but the balancing act can be difficult unless you have found your viral video 'niche' from the off.

I'm very lucky in the band, as two of the guys are really into filming and video, so we can shoot content such as music videos cheaply. Some of those have even made it onto MTV, so it does prove it's possible! I do think a band's output may not connect with certain social media platforms such as TikTok and this may feel disheartening for the band at first. But there is a way to connect with fans on those platforms – it's just about finding a way to portray your personalities, as well as the music.

What do your creative and recording processes look like, from pre-production and rehearsal to the end product of a new single, and do you use remote recording as a part of your process?

The creative process usually starts with one of us bringing an idea to a writing session, which we will then demo up together. We can send bits around to record individually if needed, but we try not to be too final with the choices in the demo. The demo is there to portray the song in a pure form, so it's okay for things to change in the studio when you record it properly.

This can feel awkward, though – especially if you have laboured over the demo too much and are stuck on certain ideas. We like to try songs live before we record them in the studio, to see how they feel and how audiences react to them. We also have the ability to record our live shows, which is cool to listen to and get ideas from.

It's important to see the demo as a stepping stone in the recording process. We as a band may have some stripped demos, but we all know how big it will sound when recorded in the studio with great mics and maybe some cool hardware that we don't own.

What advice would you give to emerging rock bands just starting out now?

Being in a band is still the coolest thing ever! My top advice is to explore the musical elements of your group that make you tick and how those elements can leak into the music you create. In Daytime, we all come from different musical backgrounds. I've played a lot of heavier types of music; Gareth (drums) is mad on jazz; John (guitar) plays everything and is a classically trained trombonist; Will (vocals) is obsessed with melodies and lyricism. But somehow, we all meet in one place and create music we all truly love. When it comes to owning your station (playing), that must be a given if you're serious. But it sure does feel like an industry built on personal and professional relationships. Be true to yourself and find likeminded individuals who share the same vibe and you won't go too wrong.

Becoming Members of Collection Societies

It is crucial that band members are registered with the correct collection societies. Just to be clear, you generally do not register as a band, but as individuals with the names on your passports rather than your stage or professional names.

Songwriting band members must be members of the performing rights organisation (PRO) for the country in which they are resident. The PRO will collect and distribute royalties to songwriting band members for their percentage split of their song copyrights. In most countries, you do not have a choice of which PRO to sign up with, unless you are located in North America.

In most cases, all band members must be registered members of the society that collects neighbouring rights, which are royalties due to the copyright holders of the master recording when song recordings are used in public. This applies to both performers and rights holders.

It is strongly advised to research the organisations that are relevant to you and your geographical location. Also note that there are some key differences between the organisations in terms of what they collect. The important differences are between the collection of song copyright royalties and the collection of sound recording royalties for performers on the recordings.

Band Names and Trademarks

Coming up with a name for a band can be fun or can be arduous and lengthy. While it may be argued that simplicity is often key, it could also be said that this doesn't matter as much as we might think. It is, after all, something that the public become accustomed to in due course, without questioning it. There is no set or standard global solution to picking and protecting a band name. There are, however, some logical steps that can be taken in doing so.

Searching through Spotify and Apple Music to see whether another band has already taken your name is a simple but effective initial step. The next step is to trademark your name and logo. Applying for a trademark involves a few steps and it is strongly advised to ensure that you are contacting the correct organisation to help you. Your government will almost certainly have a trade and industry department, which is usually the place to look to. If your trademark is to be protected by law, it will need to conform to a jurisdiction and have some form of government authorisation. In the UK, the Intellectual Property Office (UKIPO) is the only official body that registers trademarks. There are plenty of companies in existence that will gladly take your money for trademark applications and may even give you a nice-looking certificate that looks formal and official, but is actually meaningless. Trademarking is a business that involves many scams – you need only do a quick Google search on the subject to see how true that is. Obtaining a trademark for a band is also not necessarily something you need to hire a lawyer for. Always look for the official government body that registers trademarks. The application process in the UK is relatively straightforward and the UKIPO is available to handle questions relating to the process. In other geographical locations, there will usually be a subsidiary department of a government that handles the administration of trademark applications.

The key steps in this process are as follows:

- Decide on your category of business (a trademark does not generally cover you to trade under every sector).
- Categorise your goods and services (known as 'classes' and 'terms').
- Check to see whether anyone else has registered a similar trademark.
- Apply to register the trademark (the application should include the details you want to register, such as the band name and any associated logo, and the personal or company details of the registered applicant).
- Pay the fee (roughly £200, with a further £25 for extra 'classes' if necessary – but for bands, this usually isn't).

You can then either run the full application or pay an initial fee to receive feedback before completing the process (feedback usually projects the likelihood of success).

If successful, the trademark is then published in the trademarks journal for three months. If it is not challenged by any party during that period, the trademark is then officially registered.

This process will vary depending on where you are based, so it is always best to research the correct protocol for trademark applications in your country.

Interview: Jonas Ekdahl, Songwriter, Producer and Drummer, Evergrey, Sweden

Jonas Ekdahl is known to many in the rock and metal world as the drummer of Swedish progressive metal band Evergrey. In other areas of the music industry, he is known as the creator of songs of many styles. Jonas is a multifaceted artist who is in hot demand due to his immense skill set and genre versatility.

What does the creative process look like in Evergrey, from starting a new song in rehearsal and pre-production through to end product, and how much of that process is done remotely?

We usually start writing ideas individually; then we sit down together and present whatever we've come up with to each other. We go through and listen to everybody's ideas, and every band member says which they find the most inspiring. Then we write some sort of list or order of the ideas that we want to start working on.

We start by getting the basic song structure done – sometimes with vocals and sometimes without. In the past, we could write and finish a lot of songs without having any vocals on them and our singer, Tom, would put them on afterwards. But on our most recent album, we incorporated the vocals from the beginning and sometimes we used a vocal melody or chorus to build the rest of the song around – which makes more sense in a way, when you think about it, since the vocal is the key element in a song unless you play instrumental music. When the vocals are done, we go back and finalise and finetune the song to see what can be improved. Small things always happen along the way when we record the instruments and it's always cool to see how these small improvements lift the song.

During pre-production, a lot of keyboard and synth parts get finished, as well as a lot of guitar tracks. We never rehearse the new songs as a full band; we write them and record as many instruments as possible on the spot, so that we don't have to go back and re-record them again just for the sake of it. We always pro-gram MIDI drums when writing because it's easier and faster. Once the songs are done, I have to learn them and practise them on my drumkit before I record my tracks. I usually do some rehearsing with our bass player, Johan, before en-tering the studio, and that is always a good thing.

What considerations do you have regarding the evolution of the band and challenging genre boundaries?

We've never been afraid to push the boundaries in our songwriting. The only limit we have is that it must sound and feel right without losing the Evergrey vibe. We have incorporated everything from 808s and drum loops and samples to real string quartets and choirs. So our span is pretty wide – and that's an awesome feeling to have when it's time to write and create a new song. If you can tie the knot together at the end of the song and make it sound complete and natural, you can take many different routes and turns within it.

Which key professional relationships play an important role in the continued growth of the band?

Find yourself a dedicated and ambitious booking agent – someone who not only gets your shows, but who can get you the right types of shows in order to get your band exposure. Having someone to help out on social media is also a good idea.

You are also a very active songwriter and producer and create music for a range of territories, including the K-pop market. How did you get into this?

It hit me a couple of months ago that I've been writing songs since I was 12 years old. And even back then, I liked to try writing in different genres. I wasn't aware of what I was doing and I didn't pay attention to the fact that I was trying out different styles of music; it just felt like a natural thing. But once I hit my teens and became a 'serious' hard rocker, I started rejecting everything in music that didn't include distorted guitars. I narrowed my musical field of vision radically for a while and became what certain people in the metal scene call 'true'. When I think of it, it actually sounds like the total opposite, at least to me. I remember when the Backstreet Boys had their break and released singles like 'Everybody (Backstreet's Back)' and 'Larger Than Life', something within me said, 'Wow, this is so good! And it has a rock vibe!' But I just pushed that feeling away because it wasn't 'true' like Metallica, KISS or Testament. But once I woke up from my 'true metal' phase, I started listening to a lot of different types of music again and I have done ever since. I wrote some pop music on and off through the years, but in 2016 I decided to take songwriting and producing to a more serious level, so I started to reach out to different songwriters and producers for writing sessions. And this is where my passion for different genres of music started to play a big role for me. I love to challenge myself and sometimes jump into new and deep waters. K-pop is one of those things. Sometimes it's so weird and complex – like a different musical language from Western music. So far, I've done country music, rock, pop, R&B, industrial metal, instrumental music, K-pop, singer-songwriter songs and Christmas songs. A good song is a good song and if the project speaks to me, count me in!

What advice would you have given to yourself 15 years ago?

I would have loved to have given myself three pieces of advice:

- Follow your heart – it always knows what is right for you.
- Let go of the things holding you back.
- You are good enough.

13
The Art of Negotiation

The first thing to acknowledge here is the simple fact that it is possible to negotiate. Often, many of us tend to define our understanding of a subject when we see it written down. When a contract is put in front of us, it feels final; but it is not. Negotiation need not be awkward, tense or confrontational. It's just business and all parties need to be comfortable with the terms that are being agreed. If a creator queries a clause in a contract, this does not mean that they are jeopardising their chance of seeing the contract move towards signing. Often, one of the most important aspects involves understanding the contract's terms and why they work for the opposing party.

On a basic human level, if two parties disagree on a subject, it is usually because they are unwilling to understand each other's perspectives. It is only when each party can fully absorb and understand the other's perspective that conflict can be avoided or resolved. Negotiating on contracts is no different. It is therefore not only useful but crucial for a creator to understand why a specific term or clause exists. After all, it is impossible to negotiate on a subject that you don't understand.

Negotiation Scenarios

Scenario 1

A songwriter receives a single song assignment from a music publisher. This is a contract for only one song and the songwriter is assigning the rights to that song to the music publisher for a three-year term. The fundamental gains on both sides are clear:

- The music publisher gains control of the copyright of a particular song for a fixed period so that it can try to monetise a song in which it sees potential.

DOI: 10.4324/9781003452119-16

- The songwriter gains the services, time, expertise and connections of the music publisher for their song.

The songwriter cannot afford a music lawyer, so they are trying to gain an understanding of the contract's key terms through self-education in the form of a music business book and some online videos. They come across a term that they are uncomfortable with:

> Publisher holds creative control and therefore may enter into sub-publishing or collection agreements and license or assign the rights within this agreement and delegate any of its obligations to a third party, firm, or person within the agreed territory without the consent of the writer.

The songwriter wishes to negotiate on this term because they don't feel the following points are fair:

- giving creative control to a music publisher; and
- having an additional company or person that is unknown to the songwriter take a stake in the rights to their song.

The songwriter has some options here:

- Option 1: They could sit on the subject and dwell on it. This could lead to anxious thoughts and feelings, which could possibly dent the music publisher's enthusiasm and trust in the project.
- Option 2: They could try to negotiate on the term with the music publisher.
- Option 3: They could try to understand why the publisher needs to include this clause in the contract from the publisher's perspective.

It is at this point that the input of a music lawyer could be very useful. The lawyer could provide some impartial advice together with some definitions of key terminology. The lawyer could also negotiate with the music publisher – although the need for negotiation here is perhaps not as important as the need for the songwriter to understand the publisher's perspective. It is not necessarily the role of the music publisher to educate the songwriter.

Solution

The songwriter chooses Option 3 and reaches out to the music publisher. The songwriter politely asks the music publisher to expand on the term and explain its importance. This will give the songwriter a better understanding of the music publisher's perspective. The publisher emails back the same day and provides the following clarifications on the two concerns raised by the songwriter:

- There are two elements that make up copyright ownership. There is the writer and the control. You are the writer, and you are assigning control of the rights of the song in exchange for the services we offer to your song, which are things such as where we pitch it to, how we make money for the song, how we collect money and how we distribute the money to you. Creative control does not mean we have the right to change the song in anyway; it merely gives us the creativity to pitch the song to opportunities that we think it may work for.
- We have other music publishers in our global network that we partner with. They will help the song to gain opportunities in further networks and help with collection methods. For instance, if we thought that your song could be a good fit for the German market, we may wish to partner with our sub-publishing partner in that territory. The royalty split that the sub-publisher gains is from our share, not yours. By the way, in both cases we will report to you on any successes that we find for you! I hope this helps you but please do feel free to ask further questions.

We can see here that this music publisher is kind, helpful and informative. These are questions that it gets asked a lot and, on this occasion, it is quite happy to help the songwriter to understand the issues so that they feel more comfortable. The songwriter is now at ease with the term and goes ahead and signs the contract, and the songwriter and music publisher begin their working relationship. The key here was the clarification of the terms rather than the need to negotiate.

Scenario 2

A rock band receives a recording contract from an independent record company. The record company wishes to acquire the exclusive recording rights of the band for a set term. The band have obtained legal advice and fully understand every aspect of the contract. However, there is a section in the contract that the band would like to negotiate on. The section in question outlines the commitment of the initial term together with a first option period, a second option period and a third option period. There is also a breakdown of the proposed advance payments made to the band:

- **Commitment:**
    - One single containing a newly recorded, original and previously unreleased studio master recording by the artist ('Initial Period').

- One single containing a newly recorded, original and previously unreleased studio master recording by the artist ('Option Period 1').
- One single containing a newly recorded, original and previously unreleased studio master recording by the artist ('Option Period 2').
- Four additional newly recorded, original and previously unreleased studio master recordings by the artist ('Option Period 3').

- **Advance:**

  - Two Thousand Pounds (£2,000.00) shall be non-returnable but recoupable from the artist's royalty rate as outlined in the agreement ('Initial Period').
  - Two Thousand Pounds (£2,000.00) shall be non-returnable but recoupable from the artist's royalty rate as outlined in the agreement ('Option Period 1').
  - Two Thousand Pounds (£2,000.00) shall be non-returnable but recoupable from the artist's royalty rate as outlined in the agreement ('Option Period 2').
  - Six Thousand Pounds (£6,000.00) shall be non-returnable but recoupable from the artist's royalty rate as outlined in the agreement ('Option Period 3').

Every aspect of the contract is agreed in principle between the band and the label, but the contract is not yet signed because the band wish to negotiate. The contract outlines a three-month option in each option period and this they can agree to. However, they want the initial option period to be two singles, not one. They also wish to ask for a larger advance for the recording of the EP in the event of this taking place: £8,000 rather than the proposed £6,000. These are very much negotiable items in the contract. This contract is more than likely a draft contract which the record company uses with many bands, but this does not necessarily mean that all of the bands on its roster have agreed to the same terms. The band discuss recording budgets with the label and justify why they would need a higher advance should Option 3 be taken by the record company. The band also state a fair case as to why the record company should commit to two singles in the initial period rather than just one. The band also ask for their legal fees to be paid by the record company, which will cover the advice they obtained from the lawyer that they hired. Through negotiations between the band and the label, they find solutions moving forward that work well for both parties and exclude a lawyer from the negotiations in order to save money.

Why are Contracts So Hard to Read?

It is the job of a music lawyer to draw up a draft contract. This means that the music publisher, management company, record company, promoter, booking agent or any other party that is issuing a contract to a music creator pays a lawyer to draft a contract that is both legally binding and adjustable to specifics which are negotiable, such as length of term, advance and so on.

The wording of the contract is chosen by the lawyer. The ideas in the contract are not always overly complex, but often the wording can be intimidating for some music creators. The terminology can be hard to read, technical and perhaps somewhat difficult to follow, as the style of writing is not always aligned with everyday vocabulary. At times, this can be because some of the terminology is music industry specific; but mostly it is because lawyers are experts in their fields and choose to use ironclad wording that leaves nothing open to interpretation, to ensure they cannot be sued by the party that hired them to draw up the contact. A music industry professional may not always necessarily understand every single aspect of the wording of a particular legal clause because it is not they that drew up the contract. However, that same professional will always understand the idea behind the clause. This can lead to many contracts being more formal than they really need to be, because every potential outcome of the contract is explored within it in a formal manner. The everyday practices within a music company can be far less scary than the contracts themselves. The contracts exist to formally bind an agreement under a recognised jurisdiction; but there are many instances in which the protocols of a music company will be far more lenient than what a contract might suggest. Scenario 1 in this chapter explored a single song assignment being issued by a music publisher to a songwriter. The contract states:

> The writer shall during the term deliver to the publishers at the expense of the writer a copy and recording of every lyric or musical composition which they may compose or create during the term by themselves or in collaboration with any other person.

However, when the writer queries this with the publisher, the response may well be something far more informal, such as:

> Yeah, don't worry about that. The wording is a little dated as the original draft of the contract has not changed in years. Just send Word docs for your lyrics and MP3s of each song together with a list of your collaborators and their publishers' details.

Key Considerations for Recording Artists in Recording Contracts

- 'Master recording' refers to the original studio recording of a song. The 'title master' is the copy of the recording from which all other copies are made. For instance, a nine-track album will have nine masters.
- 'Master rights' refers to the ownership of the rights to the master recording. These are usually owned by the record company because it financed the recordings.
- 'Published price to dealer' (PPD) is the wholesale unit price of a recording. It is often used as a basic figure in the context of royalties within contracts and yet a contract rarely explains what this means. If a digital store retails a track at 79p, the label will receive 45p as the PPD. The artist royalty is calculated against this PPD.
- A 'key person clause' in a contract reflects the importance of one or more key people in an agreement. It could relate to a key creative person in a band whose presence is viewed as essential by the record company. If this 'key person' were to leave the band, the record company would have the right to end the contract. Alternatively, the key person clause could relate to a specific manager being involved with the act. It could also relate to the A&R who signed the act: the artist may wish to have a clause in place stating that they can terminate the contract should the A&R who signed them depart from the company. It often happens that A&Rs sign artists but then move on to a different company, and their replacement may not believe in the artist in the same way or have the same relationship with the artist as their predecessor.
- Advance and recoupment must always be carefully considered in contracts. Generally, the higher the advance, the worse the royalty rate is for the artist. It is a simple risk/reward ratio for both parties. When negotiating on an artist's advance, the label will consider the costs associated with the number of releases being contracted for. Other factors which may affect the size of the advance include the artist's previous accomplishments; existing artist data in the form of streaming figures and social media engagement; and an informed projection of how well the artist may fare in the marketplace. If other labels are bidding on the artist, this may also increase the advance being offered. The process of repaying an advance from sales is called 'recoupment'. Costs that the label pays for which are not generally recouped through royalty rates include manufacturing, shipping, promotion and advertising.
- The 'term' refers to the duration of the contractual period, which is usually measured in years, or the number of products being agreed upon – for

instance, two EPs which include a total of six singles followed by one album over a three-year cycle.

- 'Options' are flexible clauses which allow the record company to build in an immediate follow-on should an unexpected wave of success arise. For example, the record company may wish to have an option on follow-up releases once the term has ended.
- 'Territories' relate to the countries and continents in which the record company plans to make the recordings available. In almost all cases, a record company will want exclusive access to the entire world. The word 'universe' is becoming quite normal in contracts now, due to the potential for the expansion of recorded copyrights beyond Earth in the future.
- 'Royalty rate' refers to the revenue splits that the label and artist agree on between them. It may be subject to change based on the level of recoupment from the original advance. It is always worth negotiating on the breakdown of revenue. For instance, master sync fees will go directly to the record company, so it could perhaps be agreed that any such fees could be reflected in the scale of the advance repayment. Another factor to consider is whether the record company is willing to offer a higher artist royalty rate once the advance has been recouped.

Key Considerations for Songwriters in Music Publishing Contracts

- The negotiation on territory is important. Most publishers will want writers to sign on a worldwide level. However, it may be that a writer wishes to sign to different publishers in different territories if they have sectioned off different areas of their catalogue that relate to different projects and different countries. For instance, a writer could have a deal in Asia with one publisher and a deal for the rest of the world with another. This will usually be because the writer writes for or plans to write for countries in Asia. Perhaps translation and specialised local collection methods that are offered by that publisher are key here. Imagine that a writer plays in a touring metal band and also wishes to write for Western artists in addition to their exploits in the Asian market. The writer signs to a different publisher that covers the rest of the world outside of Asia. This allows them to collect on their songwriting royalties from their role in the metal band while also helping them to connect with European writers, producers and artists in the hope of composing for other artists.
- It is crucial to gain a thorough understanding of the difference between the 'term', the 'retention period' and the 'collection period'. The 'term'

is the length of time for which the writer is contracted to the publisher; while the 'retention period' is the length of time for which the writer is assigning to the publisher their rights to the songs they compose during the term. For instance, the contract could specify a three-year term and a 10-year retention period. This means that the songwriter can sign to a different music publisher after the three-year term has ended, but the rights to all songs written during that three-year term will still be assigned to the publisher for a further seven years. The 'collection period' is a period after the retention period has elapsed which allows the music publisher to mop up its final royalty collections from that period. Collection periods are usually between one and two years. These are all negotiable items in a music publishing contract, but it is always important to understand why a music publisher has retention periods in its contracts with songwriters.

Scenario

Imagine you are a music publisher. You have signed a young writer who has no previous track record of success, but you believe in them and think that they could do well with the right mentoring, the right opportunities and a wider network. You sign them on an exclusive three-year term with no retention. In the first year, you introduce them to other writers, producers and artists to collaborate with them. In the second year, you get them places on songwriting camps and they also start to learn how to produce music to a more professional standard. In the third year, they begin writing with and for numerous artists and composing for TV and film projects. Towards the end of the three-year deal, you get them a big cut with a major label artist, two song placements on a new TV show on Disney+ and a song on a new Netflix show that is in development. Then the deal ends; a major music publisher offers them a big advance and they leave you immediately. All the work you have done has brought you no financial rewards thus far. This is why retention periods exist.

It is always worth considering how things work for both sides when negotiating:

- The minimum commitment is another negotiable item which is worth considering. This relates to the number of songs that the music publisher expects you to submit to it throughout the agreed term – for example, one song per month. It is important to consider whether the minimum commitment is achievable for you; if not, it is a good idea to negotiate with the publisher on what would be achievable. It is also worth exploring whether the songs should be finished masters that can be licensed or whether a simple demo recording of a song that can later be fully produced is the accepted standard.

- Are you licensing or assigning rights? Most traditional music publishing contracts will relate to a songwriter assigning their rights to a music publisher, which then gains 'control', as mentioned previously in this chapter. However, there is another option, whereby the writer retains their rights and merely licenses them to the music publisher for specific tasks such as collection and synchronisation. In most cases, the assignment of rights to a music publisher is the most common route; but it is always worth understanding this when signing a contract and possibly even negotiating on this if you feel that would be suitable.

- Consider whether the music publisher is taking any upfront splits on sync placements in relation to the licensing of master recordings. This is a growing trend for many independent music publishers.

- Another notable item of negotiation is the royalty rate that you are splitting with the music publisher. This could be 50:50, 60:40 in the writer's favour or perhaps 75:25 in the writer's favour. While many music publishers have their own expectations of what they feel their time and services are worth, you will also have your own expectations as to what you think is the right deal for you.

- There are also other considerations that writers should consider when working with a music publisher – and these may be issues which are not typically addressed in a music publishing contract. Examples could include:

  - how active the publisher is in gaining sync placements;
  - how connected it is in gaining leads from record companies, music managers and sync agents;
  - its strategic set-up with regard to sub-publishing partnerships;
  - the territories it is strongest in; and
  - its overall track record.

- It is also worth considering what type of music publisher it is – for instance:

  - whether it offers feedback on songs; and
  - whether it is on top of the latest technologies and trends in the music industry.

- These are important considerations which will not be reflected in the contract.

Don't Be Afraid of Contracts

One of the key things to remember when signing a contract is that it is incredibly unlikely that the company is trying to trick or deceive you. It is trying to do business with you in the best way possible for its interests. This is no different from what happens in any other trade. It is more likely that the contract will sit in a drawer or be scanned on a hard drive after it is signed and then never really be looked at again. It's seldom a case of the 'big bad record company' trying to get the artist to sign a 'bad deal'. This is far more common in movies and books from bygone times, before the transparency of the internet era. Any fears often relate to the complexity of the wording of contracts rather than the day-to-day practices of the music business. As mentioned already, contracts often use complex legal jargon, but this is not intended to be deliberately awkward or to mislead the creator. Contracts allow business to happen.

14
Rights Management and Collection Societies

What Collectable Rights Exist?

Copyright

Creators have rights over how their music is used by people and companies. If a third party uses a song without permission, this is an infringement of copyright. A copyright is defined by the creator's decision-making process which led to the composition of lyrics, melody and harmony of a song. A songwriter is often referred to as the first owner of the copyright. However, if there are multiple creators of a copyright, ownership is split between all parties. Control of copyrights can be assigned to a music publisher.

Neighbouring Rights

Neighbouring rights relate to the public performance of a master sound recording. When a recording of a song is broadcast or played in a public place, neighbouring rights royalties are collected by collective management organisations (CMOs) and distributed to master rights owners and performing musicians. The processes used to collect master rights royalties vary depending on the CMO and the country which it is based in or collects for; but to put it as simply as possible, CMOs identify and track the use of sound recordings, negotiate fees with music users and collect and distribute royalties to rights holders and performers. The term 'neighbouring' relates to how the rights 'neighbour' those of a compositional copyright holder when a song is used in public. Compositional copyright royalties are collected by a performing rights organisation (PRO). It might be fair to say that this subject is one of the least understood areas of royalty collection. It is also currently the fastest-growing area of global rights management.

DOI: 10.4324/9781003452119-17

There are various CMOs in the world, such as:

- Phonographic Performance Limited (PPL) in the UK;
- the German Organisation for the Management of Neighbouring Rights (GVL) in Germany; and
- Phonographic Performance Company of Australia Ltd (PPCA) in Australia.

In some countries, neighbouring rights are often referred to as 'related rights'. There is a breakdown further in this chapter which outlines which PROs and CMOs are responsible for each major country in the world.

Neighbouring rights can be broken down as follows:

- Rights holder's share: 50%.
- Performers' share: 50%. This relates to both:
  - featured artists (ie, the recording artist(s) releasing the record); and
  - non-featured performers (ie, musicians who performed on the recording)

In the case of an independent artist (not signed to a record company), both categories of shares will be distributed to the artist. In the UK, PPL collects what is referred to as 'equitable remuneration' for performers when their re-corded music is performed in public spaces or broadcast on radio. This is a statutory right that, in theory, cannot be governed by a recording agreement. PPL revenue for performers is not the same as a royalty.

The primary reason why neighbouring rights are often uncollected in many countries is the difficulty of identifying and claiming the royalties due to the lack of information exchange between countries and their CMOs. Another issue concerns differences in neighbouring rights policies and protocols in specific territories. For instance, there is currently no reciprocal agreement in place between PPL in the UK and PPCA in Australia because PPCA does not recognise the rights of international performers for ongoing royalties, as it only collects on domestic performers' shares. This works both ways, as Australian artists will not see any performance share of their rights collected in the UK. The reasons for this lie in complex jurisdictional issues which one can only hope will be resolved in the future.

Digital Performance Royalties

Neighbouring rights are not recognised in the USA in the same way as they are in many other countries. This stems from a historical stance that many US-based record labels adopted in the 20th century whereby they did not wish to charge broadcasters for the use of recorded music, as they saw more benefit in the free promotion to be gained from their recorded works being used on radio and television. To this day, no royalties are paid out for the use of recorded music. Performance royalties are collected for the underlying copyright of the songs, but not for the use of recordings.

There are, however, digital performance royalties that are paid to rights holders for the use of recordings on non-interactive platforms such as satellite radio and internet radio, and by digital service providers that stream recordings to the public. Digital performance royalties are collected by CMOs and distributed to rights holders and performers. The primary CMOs for digital performance royalties are SoundExchange in the USA and Re:Sound in Canada. By contrast, PPL in the UK distributes royalties to UK performers and rights holders for both neighbouring rights and digital performance royalties.

Mechanical Rights

Mechanical rights relate to the reproduction and distribution of songs in:

- traditional physical formats such as DVDs, CDs, cassette and vinyl;
- digital formats such as downloads; and
- digital fixed formats such as streaming.

The rights are owned not by the performers, artists or record companies but by the composers, songwriters and music publishers, as they relate only to the compositional copyright and not to the copyright of the sound recording. Users of the compositions – such as record labels, streaming services and online music stores – must obtain a mechanical licence from the rights holder(s) to reproduce and distribute the recorded product of the songs. Mechanical rights have no link to the public performance or broadcast of a song. They relate to the units of sales, downloads and streams. The statutory rate for mechanical royalties often fluctuates. To simplify the understanding of these rights, here is an example.

A commercial songwriter composes a song for an artist in South Korea. The artist is including the song on an album which is being released on a major label. The songwriter will receive their performance royalties through their designated PRO and will receive their mechanical royalties from their CMO. The mechanical royalties will relate not only to streams and downloads, but also to the song being reproduced and distributed in physical formats as it is released on a CD and then, later in the year, on a live DVD release.

Mechanical rights for music compositions are typically collected by CMOs, which are also responsible for licensing the mechanical rights to users. In certain countries, specific organisations collect and distribute mechanical rights royalties. For example, in the UK, the Mechanical Copyright Protection Society (MCPS) collects and distributes mechanical royalties to its members, who are songwriters, composers and music publishers. The MCPS works together with the Performing Rights Society, which collects on broadcast and performance royalties. Collectively, they operate as a joint venture CMO called PRS for Music that administrates both performance and mechanical rights under the same umbrella organisation; but they collect and distribute as different entities.

Case Study: BMG (Germany)

A good example of an organisation that functions to serve both recording artists and songwriters is BMG, which is based in Berlin, Germany.

BMG functions not only as a record label, but also as a music publisher and a rights management company. As a label, it signs, develops, releases and markets music for recording artists. As a music publisher, it administers the rights to a wide range of songs; and as a rights management company, it offers a range of services that cover royalty collection, distribution, licensing and sync, with the aim of striving for fair compensation for music creators across a range of media platforms.

Collection Societies and Collection Management Organisations

Collection societies manage the rights to music and collect and distribute royalties to rights holders. They don't control the rights (the control belongs to the right holders), but they do enforce the rights of rights holders and issue non-exclusive licences for the use of music.

Below is a list of collection societies and CMOs around the world. It is always worth exploring the organisations that relate to your country of residence, as there are notable differences between the rights that they license and the types of rights holders on whose behalf they collect.

North America

- Canada:
  - SOCAN
  - CMRRA

- CPCC
- Re:Sound
- Costa Rica:
  - ACAM
- Dominican Republic:
  - SGACEDOM
- Eastern Caribbean:
  - ECCO
- El Salvador:
  - SACIM
- Guatemala:
  - AEI
- Honduras:
  - AACIMH
- Jamaica:
  - JACAP
- Mexico:
  - SACM
- Panama:
  - SPAC
- USA:
  - ASCAP
  - BMI
  - SESAC
  - Harry Fox Agency
  - Sound Exchange
  - Pro Music Rights

South America

- Argentina:
  - SADAIC

- Bolivia:
  - Sobodycom
- Brazil:
  - Abramus
  - AMAR
  - ECAD
  - UBC
  - Sadembra
  - Socinpro
  - Sbacem
- Chile:
  - SCD
- Colombia:
  - SAYCO
- Ecuador:
  - SAYCE
- Paraguay:
  - APA
- Peru:
  - APDAYC
- Suriname:
  - SASUR
- Trinidad and Tobago:
  - COTT
- Uruguay:
  - AGADU
- Venezuela:
  - SACVEN

Europe

- Albania:
  - Albautor
- Armenia:
  - Armauthor
- Austria:
  - AKM
- Belgium:
  - SABAM
- Bosnia & Herzegovina:
  - AMUS
- Bulgaria:
  - Musicautor
- Croatia:
  - HDS
- Cyprus:
  - GRAMMO
  - PRS for Music
- Czech Republic:
  - OSA Collective Rights Management Society for Musical Works
- Denmark:
  - KODA
- Estonia:
  - EEL
  - EAU
- Finland:
  - Teosto

- France:
  - SACEM
  - SNEP
- Georgia:
  - GCA
- Germany:
  - GEMA
  - GVL
- Greece:
  - AUTODIA
  - ERATO
  - APOLLON
  - EDEM
- Hungary:
  - ARTISJUS
- Iceland:
  - STEF
- Ireland:
  - IMRO
- Italy:
  - SIAE
  - RASI
- Kazakhstan:
  - KazAK
- Latvia:
  - AKKA/LAA
  - LAIPA
- Lithuania:
  - LATGA
  - AGATA
- Macedonia:
  - ZAMP

- Montenegro:
  - PAM CG
- Netherlands:
  - BUMA/STEMRA
- Norway:
  - TONO
- Poland:
  - ZAiKS
  - ZPAV
- Portugal:
  - SPA
- Romania:
  - UCMR-ADA
- Russia:
  - VOIS
  - RAO
- Serbia:
  - SOKOJ
- Slovak Republic:
  - SOZA
- Slovenia:
  - AIPA
  - IPF
  - SAZAS
- Spain:
  - EKKI
  - SGAE
- Sweden:
  - STIM
- Switzerland:
  - SUISA
  - SwissPerform

- Turkey:
  - MSG
  - MUYORBIR
- UK:
  - PRS for Music
  - MCPS
  - PPL
- Ukraine:
  - UACRR

Middle East

- Israel:
  - ACUM
- Lebanon:
  - SACEM

Asia

- Azerbaijan:
  - ASS
- China:
  - MCSC
- Hong Kong:
  - CASH
- India:
  - IPRS
  - IRRO
- Indonesia:
  - WAMI
- Japan:
  - JASRAC
  - NexTone

- Macau:
  - MACA
- Malaysia:
  - MACP
  - PPM
- Nepal:
  - MRCSN
- Pakistan:
  - COMP
- Philippines:
  - FILSCAP
- Singapore:
  - COMPASS
- South Korea:
  - KOMCA
- Taiwan:
  - MUST
- Thailand:
  - MCT
- Vietnam:
  - VCPMC

Africa

- Burkina Faso:
  - BBDA
- Democratic Republic of Congo:
  - SONECA
- Ghana:
  - GHAMRO

- Kenya:
  - MCSK
- Malawi:
  - COSOMA
- Mauritius:
  - MASA
- Mozambique:
  - SOMAS
- Nigeria:
  - COSON
- South Africa:
  - SAMRO
- Uganda:
  - UPRS
- Zambia:
  - ZAMCOPS

Australasia

- APRA AMCOS
- PPCA

If you do not see your country of origin in this list, it does not necessarily mean that you do not have a PRO or CMO that you can sign up to. It could also be that one of the abovementioned companies covers your territory. For instance, SACEM in France also extends to French Polynesia; and the PRS for Music in the UK extends to Malta, Bermuda, Gibraltar, and The Bahamas, among others. So, be sure to do your research on which organisation covers your geographic location and what rights are covered. It is worth noting that many of the major collection societies cater only for residents of the country that they are based in. For instance, BMI can collect through ZAMCOPS in Zambia, COSON in Nigeria and KODA in Denmark, but will only pay out the collections to US residents who are BMI members. However, many of the collection societies listed have entered into strategic partnerships with each other to facilitate much wider collection. In theory, these could extend further over time, to the point where they could eventually allow for full global collection for anyone from anywhere in the world as technologies continue to develop.

15
Song and Recording Registration

The Registration Process

If a song is not registered with a performing rights organisation (PRO), song-writing royalties cannot be collected and distributed. If a recording is not registered with a collective management organisation (CMO), recording royalties cannot be collected.

It is therefore crucial that the correct steps are taken to register songs and recordings with the correct organisations. The first step is to become a member of the correct organisations. The list in Chapter 14 will help you to locate the right organisations depending on your geographic location.

The specific process for registering the identity of a song and a recording will vary depending on the processes of the specific PRO or CMO.

The general information required when registering a song copyright is as follows:

- the song title;
- the names of the songwriters;
- the percentage splits of each songwriter's ownership;
- information on the music publisher (if applicable) and its split of the ownership;
- the duration of the song;
- the type of work (eg, song, instrumental);
- the language of the song; and
- the known usage of the song (if applicable).

The general information required when registering a recording is as follows:

- the recording title;
- the name of the recording artist;

DOI: 10.4324/9781003452119-18

- the label (if applicable);
- the release date;
- the International Standard Recording Code (ISRC) (see below);
- the duration of the recording;
- the percentage ownership and names of all rights holders;
- contribution information (ie, the names and the roles of everyone who performed on the recording); and
- the name of the distributor.

Song and Recording Codes

International Standard Recording Code

The ISRC represents the unique identification of a sound recording: an individual 12-character alphanumeric code that is assigned to each single song recording. The tracks on an EP or album cannot have a collective ISRC – each unique song recording needs its own ISRC. An ISRC allows for the tracking of a unique recording. The codes are typically embedded in the sound recording, which makes it much easier to track usage. It also enables streaming services to read the metadata attached to a recording to understand how to categorise it. One song can have various ISRC codes because the ISRC relates to the identity of the recording rather than the song itself. ISRCs can be obtained through your country's national ISRC agency or by contacting the International Federation of the Phonographic Industry. The UK's national ISRC agency is the PPL, which offers free membership to rights holders. Once the membership process is complete, an applicant become a registrant with their own prefix to create their own ISRC codes.

An ISRC code is a composite code that is dictated by three separate elements. For example, in the IRSC code 'GB-6Q7–24–00001':

- **GB-6Q7** is the prefix code;
- **24** are the two digits that represent the year of release (2024); and
- **00001** is the five-digit designation code.

Perhaps an easier and quicker option for creators wishing to release their music with an independent music distributor such as Distrokid, TuneCore, CD Baby or another similar service is to have the distributor provide the ISRC. This is an option that most digital distributors will offer to independent creators.

It is also worth mentioning that an ISRC code works as an identifier for both music and video recordings.

International Standard Work Code

An International Standard Work Code (ISWC) is an international 10-digit code which is assigned to the identity of a song copyright (rather than a recording). Only a music publisher or a PRO can create and assign ISWC codes to the registration of a work.

Catalogue Codes

European Article Number

A European Article Number (EAN) is a 13-digit product code which helps to identify releases. An EAN can be used as barcode and consists of a country-code prefix, a label code and an internally assigned code (as set by the label). An EAN is primarily used to account for product sales rather than to signify rights ownership.

Unique Product Code

A Unique Product Code (UPC) is primarily used in the USA and Canada. It is a code that is compatible with an EAN. EANs and UPCs can also often be referred to as 'media catalogue numbers'.

Label Code

The Label Code (LC) is a system that is governed by the German Organisation for the Management of Neighbouring Rights in Germany. It is used for radio and TV in relation to broadcast rights and is not required for online music distribution. Royalties are paid to the label and not directly to the rights holders.

Performing Rights Organisation Codes

Many PROs often have their own internal registration codes. These codes are less relevant when it comes to international recognition but are useful on a domestic level. For instance, PRS for Music uses the following two additional codes for song registration:

- **Electronic Joint Notification of Work (EJNW):** An EJNW code is auto-generated by the PRS database to help track a song's identity before it is formally accepted onto the PRS database. This code is superseded by a tunecode once the process is complete.
- **Tunecode:** This is a unique eight-digit code that helps PRS for Music to identify a song in relation to queries regarding royalty payments.

It is always worth checking to see which internal code system is used by your relevant PRO.

Part 4

Releasing Music

16
Releasing Music Without a Record Company

It could be strongly argued that we have entered a golden era for releasing independent music. Anyone anywhere can do it anytime they like. It's never been as inclusive. On the other hand, however, it has never been as hard to get noticed as it is right now. The digital sphere is a place where music can survive and thrive in an age of instant discovery and organic growth with minimal spend.

There are many ways of releasing music, but navigating how best to do so can be a puzzle, solved perhaps only through observation and experience. Let's start with some basics.

Why Release Music?

Why do you want to release music? It's a seemingly simple question that can be quite difficult to answer. However, it is important to know the answer because this will dictate everything that comes next:

- Are you looking to establish a digital foundation of what your musical offer is to the world?
- Are you hoping to launch an artist?
- Maybe you have already done that and you are looking to expand?
- Perhaps you are seeking to determine who your fans might be?
- Is the goal to expand into new markets?
- Maybe you are looking to experiment with where you sit best in terms of genre and style?
- Perhaps you want to get a major record deal and the only way you see yourself achieving that is by having success independently first?

DOI: 10.4324/9781003452119-20

- Perhaps you want to get music into the public domain so that you can pitch yourself to the festival circuit?
- Are you looking to build your artist data so you can use it as leverage to get a manager, a booking agent and a sponsorship deal to take your show on the road?

Once you know why you are doing it, you can then start to consider your strategy.

Campaign Structure and Philosophy

Understanding the algorithmic nature of the digital space is critical to gaining traction and growth. You want your music to create impact and to do that, the algorithms need to understand where you best fit. One of the important facets to this is through regular releases in periodic release cycles. In short, there is more than enough evidence to suggest that for most artists in most genres, singles are the way to go in the 2020s.

An understandably common concern for many emerging artists is that their songs are part of a larger story – perhaps an album or EP – and should be kept as a collective body of work. It could perhaps be said that artists need to get used to the idea of telling that same story over an extended period of time in order to gain greater visibility in a crowded marketplace. This takes us to the subject of strategic purpose. We are back to the *why*. If the aim is to launch the artist or build on past releases, you can start building an understanding of what feeds this approach. Let's consider the following scenarios.

Scenario 1

An emerging artist has five songs. Two are recorded and ready for release. The artist wants to start releasing music. They release one song followed by another and then release nothing for an entire year because they no longer like the music they previously created. They lose momentum before they've even started because they were too eager. This artist was not ready.

Scenario 2

The same artist records all five songs with three different producers. One of the producers is someone they have built a great working relationship with. The artist has started to find their sound. The five recordings are whittled down to the three made with the producer they like. Before they start releasing any music, the artist hones their craft by playing gigs; experimenting with branding, fonts and logos; and developing an understanding of their position in the landscape of the music industry. They are inspired. They write and record more songs. Before long, they have nine songs recorded and a good understanding of their genre, the moods associated with the music and what similar artists exist in the marketplace; and they have also become familiar with the kinds of playlists and bloggers that might align with what they do. The artist is slowly turning their hobby into a viable career route through patience, strategy and purpose. They release seven singles over the next 12 months with the aim of establishing a foothold in the music industry as an independent artist. This gets them press features, festival slots and some good playlist places.

Now they move into the next phase. They want to release an album. They know there's no point in one big marketing punt on a 12-track project, so they drip-feed the songs to the public by releasing six singles over a nine-month period, with the remaining six released on the album one month after the multi-single campaign has run its course. The artist receives great reviews. They gain a sync on a big TV show and a manager comes into the picture who they build a great relationship with. They gain a sponsorship deal and a music publishing deal, with leads to further opportunities in the sync world; and their first major main support tour is confirmed after landing a deal with a booking agent which their manager helps to broker. This all takes place over a 20-month period.

Strategy is Everything

Regardless of the specific number of releases over a projected amount of time, it is important to build a sense of purpose and expectation around a wider campaign. It is advisable to look ahead and think about the next year and the year after that. That is, after all, what a record company would be doing. This will make any artist a far more appealing business prospect. So, the first step is to establish a campaign structure and philosophy.

Interview: Erik Nielsen, Director/Consultant, Wingnut Music, UK

Erik Nielsen is a music professional who works across multiple sectors of the business. A true pioneer of the industry, Erik launched a direct-to-consumer (D2C) business model for British rock legends Marillion which went on to become the basis for modern-day crowdfunding – a model now widely used throughout the world. Erik is an artist manager and music industry consultant who has worked with Elton John, James Blunt, Bryan Ferry, The Hoosiers, Grace Jones and many more. Erik is a co-author of *The Music Management Bible*, a business adviser for UK music charity Help Musicians, a music business lecturer, a music producer and director of Wingnut Music.

What advice would you give to emerging artists without an established fan-base who struggle to know what kind of content to post on their social media channels?

Try everything once! There are as many opinions about what to post as there are people, myself included. When working with artists, I usually suggest starting with what they're comfortable with. See what happens. This will usually not be enough, but it will give them a good idea of their natural talents and skills to focus on moving forward (eg, video editing, AI video generation, great art skills, a natural sense of humour). Rather than forcing artists to do things they don't have the skill, ability or inclination to do, they should start with what they're good at.

The next step is to steal from other people. Internet memes are about appropriating pop culture using familiar products/images/videos. So, with that in mind, check out what other bands in your genre are doing – preferably the more successful ones. If it works for them, it will likely work for you. But also check out other genres and other things that interest you – related festivals, clothing brands, movies, literature . . . What do the most successful ones have in common? (Probably a video of a cat!)

It's good to try to be original; but in music, so many people identify and react to what's comfortable and familiar that we need to make sure we're ticking that box, too.

For independent artists who are looking to release their music into the digital sphere, what is a good timespan between singles in a campaign involving the release of four singles prior to an EP or album?

The general industry view on that these days is about six weeks. But really, it's about maintaining attention more than timeline. You can talk about anything from four weeks if you break it down into constituent parts (eg, lyrics, inspirations, recording, songwriting, production, themes, live versions, lip syncs). If you have a music video or lyric video or visualiser, that can extend the conversation even longer. But there is a limit.

If you look at a major label, which includes behind-the-scenes videos, acoustic versions, remixes . . . They are trying to extend the attention on that same song for as long as possible before switching to the next one. On that lever, you can see the timeframe stretch from eight to ten weeks; but that requires a budget for content generation and marketing that may not exist at a grassroots level.

I'd say there should be an absolute minimum of four weeks between singles – ideally no less than six; but eight is about the limit for holding attention on the same subject.

But much more important than that is to have all four tracks finished, and to have a plan and a calendar for them, before you even release the first one. Then there are no surprises, which leaves you time to be responsive and interactive with fans, reviews, radio etc.

Do you think that a D2C strategy works more effectively for specific genres?

Definitely. Frontline pop music is largely about that 'maintaining attention' approach and the way music is consumed by the mass market is primarily through streaming and social media, rather than through physical formats. That's not to say fans won't want merchandise. I largely put vinyl into this category these days – many vinyl purchasers don't even own a turntable. Pop is very much about the 'latest thing', which is streaming from playlists, getting the next new track and streaming that.

Hip hop, trap, grime, to some extent R&B – the artists I've worked with in these genres are less about merchandise and D2C offerings and more about business-to-business sponsorships and endorsements. As a result, D2C has never really been a part of that strategy – although there are certainly examples of artists in those genres who have been very successful with it.

The D2C market for pretty much any genre with a guitar in the band is different. Those bands in many genres tend to have a much slower growth cycle, largely on the live music, small club circuit, gradually building loyalty over time and largely in physical spaces. Selling t-shirts and tote bags is a high-markup endeavour that a fair number of fans of small acts will happily buy into the knowledge that they're helping the band directly (and this is the usual 'indie band' sales language!).

If those guitar bands are legacy acts or if their fanbase is comprised of 40-plus-year-olds, you have the perfect storm of a history of buying physical medial plus disposable income (and I should know a thing or two about that market!).

The same holds true for the non-guitar genres such as jazz and classical; although the younger demographics in those genres are often looking for quality over physical product, so the D2C approach of 'studio-quality audio' as a download sale is becoming more prevalent.

Do you think there is a strong link between an act's online presence through blogs and forums and the visibility they gain on streaming platforms?

That's always a difficult one to pin down, because it's hard to track the cause and effect of messaging if a lot is happening at the same time. If it's a comment or discussion in isolation, you can use that to see a bounce in streaming; that's great, but it's rare.

Obviously, the more people that are talking about you, the bigger the percentage of those that will convert; but as digital service providers (DSPs) are a locked box, it is usually impossible to identify traffic sources in the same way that you can with detailed website analytics (YouTube stats are still strong in this regard for the most part, though). If the online blogs/zines are also providing playlisting on the DSPs, that makes things a bit easier to track and attribute to a single source; but often that is not the case.

Starting out, you'll often only have your own social media to point people to your music/streaming. That's a good time to start looking at your baseline: when I say, 'Go there and listen,' how many people actually do?! Once you then start getting external coverage, reviews and playlisting, there are ways to measure whether they are having an effect.

It's important to pay attention and measure to see whether what you're doing is working, rather than blindly just 'doing'.

Do you ever see a misalignment between the branding of an act and the style of their music?

Quite a lot, yes. A lot of acts will broadly – albeit unconsciously – understand what a genre expectation is in terms of branding and will naturally fit into that broad neighbourhood of visual aesthetic and social media language without even realising it. But I also think that most people equate the word 'branding' with the word 'logo', which is why they tend to stop at that superficial level.

Without descending into an analysis of branding theory, the core of it is not really about a logo at all; it's about how that brand makes people feel, or whether it provides something that fans want. If you can find a way to effectively communicate both of those – a rational connection and an emotional connection – and ensure you are clear in what those are as values, you're finally talking branding. That then forms the basis for the visual aesthetic and social media language and – going back to your first question – should help guide what you should be posting on social media (or, more broadly, how you should communicate your brand).

With all that said, that misalignment between brand and music is usually because most people haven't really considered what their brand actually is and are simply relying on genre conventions that have no emotional or rational depth.

17
Ten Key Steps When Releasing Music

Let's now cycle through a potential single release and explore what the steps involved might look like.

Step 1: Distribution

Once your campaign structure has been identified, you are likely to have some idea of what the next 12 to 18 months might look like. Ideally, this will be a breakdown of how many singles you plan to release and whether any of the singles will become a part of an EP or album. You will then need to choose an appropriate and suitable partner for release. Chapter 19 of this book focuses on how to go about choosing a suitable distribution partner, but let's summarise it as follows:

- Do you want to work with a distributor that will partner with you for the entirety of your 12 to 18-month strategy?
- Would you be happy to relinquish 10%–15% of your master rights in exchange for working with a distributor that can monitor your growth and offer strategic support and editorial playlist pitching?
- Maybe you would rather keep the entire 100% of your master rights for yourself or your act and instead pay for a fee-based distributor where you retain all of your rights?

You should perhaps consider what your expectations are from a distributor:

- Are detailed analytics important to you or will you look elsewhere for this kind of information?
- How quickly does the distributor deliver to the stores and can they guarantee release dates?

DOI: 10.4324/9781003452119-21

- Do you need them to generate the International Standard Recording Code (ISRC) for you?
- Can your distributor offer unlimited releases per year?
- Do you want to be able to customise your release plans?
- Do you expect to see access to other services, such as distribution to additional media platforms for licensing opportunities?
- Maybe you want your distributor to deliver your songs to social media platforms and create Content IDs for Facebook and YouTube?
- Do you need to check whether they deliver to Shazam?

There are a few factors to consider here; but once you have decided who your distributor should be, sign up with them and prepare for Step 2.

Step 2: Upload Release and Import Metadata

This seems like a simple step, but it is so easy to get wrong. The goal is to upload a WAV file of your song together with the artwork and choose a release date. The release date will ideally be six weeks after the moment you upload. Your distributor will ask you some questions about your song. Don't rush this – it's a crucial step. They are extracting metadata about the song so that they can paint an accurate picture of how your music will be recognised and categorised by digital service platforms (DSPs) such as Spotify, Apple Music and Deezer. Ultimately, what you input here will need to align with what your music represents in terms of genre and mood once the WAV file of the song is analysed by the DSPs. If it doesn't, your music will have to work much harder to survive the rigidity of the digital environment. If you plan to release an alternative version of your song – perhaps an acoustic or stripped version – and you want it to drop a week or two after your single, this is the time to upload it. It will need a separate upload with its own ISRC code even though it's the same song.

Step 3: Establish an Electronic Press Kit and Creative Asset Bank

You will need a range of creative assets both for social media content and for tastemakers to use when promoting your music. These should ideally be made available in the form of an electronic press kit (EPK) through a downloadable link on Google Drive, Dropbox, OneDrive or similar. Make it easy for taste-makers to access a range of assets that promote your release, together with some assets that you can use yourself for the same purpose. Ideally, creative assets will include:

- a range of high-resolution images;
- video content (music videos, lyric videos, behind the scenes, documentary or storytelling content that aids your release);
- a biography (written in the third person);
- a PDF copy of the press release (see Step 5);
- artist logos in various shapes;
- contact details; and
- MP3 or WAV files of the song and instrumental.

Try to be creative when writing the biography. Steer away from unnecessary detail about how much music means to you or when you started to sing. Focus instead on the following aspects:

- who you are;
- what genre of music you make;
- where you are from;
- what you have done recently with your music (live performances, previous releases); and
- what you plan to achieve moving forward.

Step 4: Prepare Your Channels

Tastemakers will need to be able to hear your song, but it has not yet been released. Make this easier for them by allowing access to your unreleased music in two ways. First, put your song and an instrumental version in your EPK so that they can be downloaded by the users you are trying to engage with. Second, upload a private link of the song on a platform which can be streamed. Soundcloud is a good fit for this because it is a trusted source for many radio stations and bloggers, and because an upload on that platform can be changed to public once the track is released. Create a private link of the song and place it in your press release (see Step 5).

Prepare your social media channels for your release. This can be achieved by using banners and squares to generate awareness of your release. These should be sized appropriately for the various platforms you are using. For instance, the size of a YouTube banner is unique to that platform, as is the size of a Facebook banner. Be sure to create a visualiser for Spotify's canvas. This will need to be a three to seven-second video that works well when placed on a loop. It needs a veridical 9:16 ratio and it will need to be between 720px-1080px tall. Once your release has been delivered by your distributor to Spotify, you will be able to upload this asset. To find out whether your release has been delivered to

Spotify, you can check on the Spotify for Artists app. If you are signed up to Spotify for Artists, Spotify will also send an email to you and your team with a notification of delivery of your song.

Step 5: Creating a Press Release

You now have a release date and a range of assets, which means that the PR campaign on you as an artist and your release can begin. You will need to send your press release to tastemakers such as bloggers, journalists, playlist curators, YouTubers, influencers, media outlets, radio stations and anyone else you can think of or research that could be useful in helping you to market your release. This all starts with a press release: the official statement that you issue to the media to inform them of your release, in the hope that media outlets will want to write about it in order to generate momentum around your release date. A press release will contain information on the artist and the release details, and ideally some kind of narrative that supports either the artist or the release. The release will generally gain more press attention if the press release is written in a journalistic style. This not only makes it more professional but also allows tastemakers to use the descriptions in the press release when sharing information about the artist and the release. Chapter 18 goes into more detail on how to build a press release. A template for creating your own press release can be downloaded from the music industry resources tab available at www. jonnyamos.com.

Step 6: Engage with Taste Makers

Arguably the most important step in this list is researching and targeting key tastemakers in your genre. Tastemakers are individuals or entities that have significant influence on the direction and popularity of music. Often, they are key gatekeepers to a much wider audience than you could reach yourself, as they have a readymade audience and are trusted voices in their community. Tastemakers could be journalists, radio hosts/presenters, radio producers, social media influencers, promoters, YouTubers, bloggers, streamers or playlist curators. Many of these players have the power to introduce music to their audiences. A positive recommendation can often break an artist to a much wider audience. One of the key attributes of many tastemakers is their ability to spot emerging talent before others do. They need artists and artists need them. Research here is crucial. There is very little point in bombarding every single tastemaker out there. Instead, research those who are aligned with your genre, style or values. We are now in an age when it is possible to make connections with people who were previously inaccessible. Spending the time to research the tastemakers who are best suited to you is critical. Centralised platforms such as SubmitHub, Groover, DropTrack and MusoSoup can be used to pitch to various tastemakers. Pitching approximately five weeks ahead of the release date is advised, but this can vary depending on the preferences of the tastemaker. Offering premieres to specific platforms can also be a great idea; as can doing interviews with bloggers, podcasters, radio and other media outlets.

Step 7: Social Media Release Ramp – Sell Without Selling

Researching, planning and scheduling social media content is a crucial part of the release preparation process. This begins by understanding the platforms that you think will best serve your promotional assets. Once these have been identified, you can start thinking aboZut the types of content you wish to use to promote your music. The evolution of many social media platforms in recent years has seen changes to what works well for artists, and it could be argued that this loosely boils down to the fact that PR is now more effective than marketing. Direct, in-your-face marketing posts about pending releases and subsequent countdowns to releases are no longer as effective as they once were, due to the saturation of this technique. Instead, the artists who are gaining more success are those offering better PR through insights into their daily lives and activities. Three goals are achieved here: enhanced transparency on the artist and their values; a higher level of engagement with users; and stronger preparation for the way in which the algorithmic nature of social media informs users. For example, a storytelling build-up of what the artist is doing from day to day creates a micro community that can then be sold to, as opposed to merely selling from the outset. This also mirrors the business model of how visibility is successfully bought on Facebook and Instagram through likes and traffic, which are then followed by product. A common mistake is often to spend more on marketing rather than putting the time into PR and telling a longer story. It is important to think about how an artist tells their story and how good they are at it. Key collaborative posts in which businesses and organisations are tagged can often help to feed further visibility. Something as simple as a band complimenting the coffee in a local café is a good basic story post that can be reshared and become good PR. The band doesn't even really need to like the coffee! Better yet is a video reel of something comical but not defamatory that happens while the band is there. It is important to think ahead and schedule posts and social media activities. Stack up the content and post it over an extended period of weeks.

This is showbusiness. Not everything needs to be real. Get creative and hustle your way into algorithmic visibility. It will serve your music well if you are polite and professional.

Step 8: Pitch to Spotify Editorials

Pitching your song through the Spotify for Artists app is strongly advised. This is a short process that gives Spotify's editorial departments the opportunity to curate your new single into one of their editorial playlists, which are generally focused on mood and genre. The pitch must be made at least seven days prior to the release of the song. After this, it is too late to be considered. The pitch includes questions about the mood and genre of the song, together with some other questions relating to the culture and instrumentation of the song and the artist's home city. This is an opportunity to consolidate the metadata that is aligned with the song which has been sent to the distributor ready for release. There is value in pitching through this tool every time you have a new song, even if Spotify doesn't playlist it straight away, as you are allowing for further data entry on the song, which in turns feeds how visibility works on the platform. Extended projects such as EPs and albums cannot be pitched, only songs; so if you have an EP or album being released, pick the strongest song for the pitch. It is worth noting that some distributors can pitch to editorial departments in addition to an artist pitching their song themselves.

Step 9: Work Your Old Songs

If you have previous releases, it is worth pitching them to as many audio streaming platform playlist curators as possible in the run-up to a release. There is a great deal to be gained from this, as it feeds data to the DSPs on who is listening to your old music and what else they listen to. The more data that is available on your old songs, the better for your visibility when releasing new music. This process will ensure your new music is deemed lower risk for platforms and will ultimately enhance the chances of your new single being introduced to a wider audience through algorithmic functionality. Pushing existing catalogue as part of the build-up to a release is an approach used by many music industry professionals. This process has become easier with the introduction of Spotify's 'Discovery Mode', which allows artists and their teams to use the Spotify for Artists app to achieve a higher discovery rate through autoplay or radio functionality by using specific songs to target growth. This has become a popular tool in campaign preparation by using older catalogue to drive awareness of a new release.

Step 10: Plan Release Day Activities

The release day is a celebration. It's also a busy day for administration, as live track links need to be shared with the tastemakers you've prepared for engagement. The curators and bloggers will be waiting to receive the news that the song has finally been released, and there should be a buzz on social media about the release. It is worth looking ahead to this day and preparing some special content to market your release through your social media channels. While it may be tempting to create multiple posts, reels and stories on release day, it could be argued that patience is also helpful here. Perhaps there is a piece of video content about the behind-the-scenes recording process or a talking-to-camera video on what the song is about. Perhaps these pieces of content could wait for a few days, to extend the marketing campaign. Release day is also about the excitement of something new and people will want to hear the song straight away, so let that be the priority. It is also worth looking ahead to release day several weeks in advance and thinking about how a live performance could contribute to the launch of the new release and what that event might look like.

Post-release Pitching

It is arguable that a great deal more can be achieved in the post-release period than in the pre-release period. As the digital sphere has evolved further in the 2020s, there has been a notable shift towards third-party playlist curators not wanting to have songs pitched to them until the links to the song are live. Once the song has been released, many playlists that your song could be pitched to can now be considered. There are a wide variety of methods for pitching to influential third-party curators, especially on Spotify. Centralised platforms that might be useful include DailyPlaylists, SoundPlate, SubmitHub and PlaylistPush; and many publications – such as *The Spotify Indie Bible* – also have the contact details of numerous playlist curators across a wide variety of musical genres and cultures. The ideal way to move forward here is to build your own database of curators who your music is suitable for and forge relationships with them so that you can pitch your new releases to them as and when these are ready.

The key here is to do your research. It takes time. As a recording artist, it is important to remember that each release should always be aimed at bolstering your data and reach. This can truly happen only when your music reaches the appropriate audiences; and one of the key steps in making this a reality is for new audiences to hear it on playlists that they listen to.

18
Writing a Press Release

A press release ultimately enables people to become aware of a release. How a press release communicates its influence has evolved in recent times due to the decrease in printed media and the increase in online media. However, the core purpose of a press release remains the same. Gaining the support of online press outlets is about far more than winning new fans; it is about building a web presence which is then scanned by numerous forms of natural language processing (NLP) and used for data to gauge metrics on a range of information about an artist. This is why it is important for emerging artists to gain press coverage: to use the digital sphere to inform the world of their work.

In the resources that accompany this book, you will find a template which can be used to create your own press release. This is available to download from the music industry resources tab on www.jonnyamos.com.

The Ten Elements of a Press Release

Element 1: Headline

A strong headline that creates a narrative is key. Although the subject of the press release is your new music, it is not always a strong enough story on its own to gain multiple features. Think about your backstory: is there something about you that would make for compelling reading? Perhaps a human-interest story? Maybe there is something in your past which links to the meaning of the song you are releasing? Perhaps there is something topical right now that supports the narrative of your song theme? Build a story to sell your song. It doesn't even need to be true; it just needs to be interesting. Don't let the truth get in the way of a good story.

DOI: 10.4324/9781003452119-22

Element 2: Photos and Artwork

Embed a photo of the artist and the song artwork towards the top of the press release but below the headline. This affords immediate understanding and context to the recipient. Crop them to fit the piece so that they don't overwhelm the scale of the press release.

Element 3: FFO

'FFO' stands for 'for fans of . . .' Journalists will appreciate you telling them which artists your music can be compared to. If someone mentions a well-known artist in the feature alongside your artist name, this contributes towards meaningful data through NLP scans. In addition, it is useful for any tastemaker who needs help in categorising your music. Many blog writers write for numerous blogs and it may well be that the one you're pitching to is not suitable for your music, but another blog that the writer works for is a better option. By using FFO, you can help the writer to find a suitable placement.

Element 4: Opening Paragraph

This section should cover only the release details. It should state:

- the name of the artist;
- the name of the song;
- the release format; and
- the release date.

This section need not link with Element 1.

Element 5: Song Details

Identify the genre, the sound, the significant instruments and the feel of the song for its audience. Try to limit this section to three sentences. Refrain from talking about how you wrote the song and instead talk about what the song is. This section should help the reader to understand how the song sounds without hearing it. Use descriptive text that tastemakers can copy or paraphrase (eg, 'thunderous drums', 'heart-melting lyrics', 'ambient guitars').

Element 6: Narrative

Return to the title from Element 1 and explain the meaning of the headline. This is where you can expand on the story you started telling earlier.

Element 7: Quotes

Collect some quotes about your music. The higher the profile of the person giving the quote, the better. It could be a music producer, a radio presenter, a journalist or somebody working in the music industry. The quote should refer to the artist, not the song.

Element 8: Contact Details

This section should include the contact name for the press release and their contact details. It should also include all links to social media and streaming platforms that the artist is on.

Element 9: Song

Provide a link to the song so that tastemakers can easily access it. As mentioned previously, a Soundcloud link set to private works well here.

Element 10: Electronic Press Kit

Include a link to your electronic press kit, so that tastemakers can download the assets they need when writing a feature on you.

Preparing a press release can feel like an arduous task for many music creators, but it is key in creating momentum. It doesn't need to be long; it just needs to be informative, useful and engaging. If writing a press release feels too difficult, hiring a press release creator, a copywriter or a journalist is an option – although bear in mind that they will ask you the same questions that are encompassed in the ten elements above.

The Public Actions versus the Real Actions
of an Emerging Artist

When it comes to releasing music to the public, not all of the jobs that an emerging recording artist has to do are exciting. The artform of social media is often to make the day-to-day look and feel engaging even when it's not. The reality is that an artist might spend two solid days on research, collecting the details of suitable playlist curators and pitching music to them. This is perhaps not as exciting as playing a show, but arguably it will do far more for the growth of the artist's reach. This is a job that many emerging artists struggle with, but it's the cold, hard reality needed to achieve the desired outcome.

19
Understanding Digital Distribution

Music distribution has never been as accessible as it is today. However, understanding everything that creators need to know to maximise and futureproof their releases can be a little more complex.

The first thing to ask yourself is what your expectations are from a distributor. Knowing what they do and don't do is crucial in building an understanding of who the most suitable distribution partner might be for your project and your budget. The primary goal is to make the music available to the public by getting into the right digital stores; but in a rapidly evolving marketplace, there are also other factors to consider.

What Kind of Price Plan Works Best for Your Project?

Budget is an all-important part of any business model and an independent artist's career is no different. It is advisable to gain an understanding of what distribution will cost and what you will get in return. An annual upfront payment plan is a popular choice for many independent artists because the cost is manageable for those on a tight budget. There is an annual fee for this type of distribution service, which works well for those wishing to distribute numerous releases inside a calendar year. However, something crucial to consider with an annual plan is whether the distributor will require you to pay that same fee every year. This is a business model that many companies are now moving towards. The downside is that the distributor may remove your tracks if the annual fee is not paid each year. However, not all distributors adopt this approach: some companies with upfront costs in the same price bracket only expect artists to pay once to upload their music, and not yearly. Some distributors also expect artists to pay commission on sales and streams, and an even higher commission on optional add-ons which cover YouTube monetisation, sync licensing and music publishing administration. Other distributors provide

DOI: 10.4324/9781003452119-23

both free and premium plans, offering a risk-free approach for early career artists to test their music on an audience without any spend and then switch to a premium plan if their plans work out and they start earning.

The digital distribution landscape is changing rapidly – not only due to ongoing technological advancements, but also because of the growing demand and intense competition between distribution services.

Genre-Specific Factors

It might be worth considering whether your music could benefit from you working with a distributor that can put it into genre-specific stores. For instance, some distributors deliver to stores such as Beatport, which is significant for creators of certain genres of electronic music.

What Is the Difference Between a Distributor and an Aggregator?

- **Distributor:** Focuses on the delivery of both physical and digital releases and uses a commissionable model together with additional fees.
- **Aggregator:** Focuses only on digital releases and primarily charges an upfront fee.

The above is a generalisation and there are some exceptions.

Delivery to Stores

Speed of delivery and notification of delivery are important aspects to consider. Knowing when Spotify has received your track, for example, is important because you are then given the chance to submit your track for its editorial playlist review. If you don't know that Spotify has received your track, you might miss the small window of time that you have in order to make this submission. This window opens the moment your song is delivered to the store and the cut-off is seven days prior to release. The speed of delivery is also useful to know when considering your release date. For instance, if a distributor states that it takes seven to ten days to deliver your release to the digital stores, it is worth considering whether this will give you enough time to prepare the Spotify submission and promote your pre-save link prior to your release. Knowing how quickly your distributor works and how it will notify you of which stores have received your music is very beneficial to a release plan.

Social Media Delivery and Content IDs

It is important to consider whether you would like your music to be distributed to social media channels. This enables social media users to use your track as part of a reel, story or similar post. In most cases, this is both advisable and desirable – especially when you consider that social media shares of a song are a crucial metric for establishing growth. It is also worth considering whether you would like your distributor to attach platform-specific Content IDs to your music. A Content ID is a digital content identification system that is used by a growing number of platforms. Its core function is to protect copyrighted recordings; and it works by scanning the stereo waveform of a recording and analysing its use when that recording is uploaded by users, shared or perhaps even included as part of a live stream. In essence, this allows creators to manage and enforce their rights. In many cases, the level of restriction can be dictated by you and your distributor. For instance, it could be that you are happy for video content creators to use your music in their video. This could be good promotion, after all. Alternatively, perhaps you would like the video creator to seek your permission in advance. However, the reality is often that a video creator will not want to wait and instead will look for music that is not subject to a Content ID restriction.

In theory, Content IDs are a step in the right direction for rights holders, as they enable content creators to monetise their work through revenue-sharing agreements with copyright owners. There are some downsides, however: for example, the algorithms are early in their evolution and often generate false results. And there is another downside. Imagine gaining an upload from a hugely influential tastemaker who wants to upload your new single to their YouTube channel, which results in you gaining a six-figure stream on your song on their channel overnight. If you have a Content ID in place, they may be far less likely to want to use your song if they can't monetise their upload in full. In other words, gaining big data and potentially new fans is the payoff for not getting any royalties for that particular upload. In a rapidly evolving landscape, a good understanding of how to handle Content IDs and social media accessibility is vital. While it might seem appealing in the early career stages to gain as much exposure as possible, you may regret this in future if you see millions of streams that can't be monetised because of how you set up the distribution and access.

Aiding Discovery and Futureproofing Releases

Setting up your music to be delivered to discovery applications such as Shazam is an added extra for some distributors but is included in many packages by others. It is strongly advised to make your music discoverable on such applications. Think of this as a form of futureproofing. For instance, the song you are uploading for distribution might have potential mass appeal and may end up in a film or a TV show. If that happens and it connects with its audience, people will get their phones out and use apps to identify the song in order to save, stream and maybe share it. If that song is not distributed to the right platforms for discovery, it might miss out on a crucial form of traction and visibility. Creators can access details of how often and where their songs are being discovered on Shazam through the Apple Music for Artists app.

Playlist Pitching

Some upper-tier distributors offer playlist pitching as part of their package. While this is usually offered by distributors that have a gateway to creators in the form of an application process, it is possible that some of the streaming platforms may start working more closely with key distributors by giving them access to their editorial teams. In addition, many distributors have a network of playlist curators who sit outside the realm of editorial playlist curators. These could include record label playlist curators and influential third-party curators who the distributor could pitch your song to if it falls within the parameters of their distribution package.

The Process of Waterfalling Singles

A sequence of singles that is released prior to or becoming a part of an EP or album release is most commonly referred to as a 'waterfall release'. This is a popular approach to releasing music – due in part to modern consumer habits, but mostly because it creates organic growth through how it feeds the algorithmic nature of many streaming platforms. However, it is very easy to get this wrong. For instance, imagine you want to release three singles and then follow them up with a five-track EP which includes the three singles. For the streams of the singles to carry over to the EP, most distributors will require the entirety of the EP to be uploaded and delivered to the stores in advance. The common problem for many creators is that they release singles and then wish the streams to be carried over once the EP is ready. Despite some hacks that can make this happen, it is not advisable. There are signs in the digital sphere that perhaps this process may become simpler in time; but for now, it is strongly recommended to complete an entire project (EP, album or mixtape), upload it in full and schedule the release of the singles and the subsequent larger collection in advance. It is most certainly worth checking what this process would look like with your distributor of choice, as some are more flexible than others in this regard.

Support Service

It is always worth considering what the distributor's help and support options look like. Some distributors are criticised for their approach to support, which may involve being bounced around from one country to another for the same query. However, others have a much more personal touch. You may well need the support of your distributor at some point, so this is worth considering and balancing in line with your budget.

Making Changes to Releases

It might be the case that some details of the release need to be changed after it has already been uploaded. This can be an inconvenience for distributors – so much so that many don't allow for changes once a music product has been uploaded for release. However, others offer the flexibility to make changes without the need for re-uploading.

Code Generation

A distributor will generate a Universal Product Code (UPC) for your release. A UPC is a barcode that acts as a unique identifier for a recording and is associated with a song's metadata, which includes information such as the product title, artist name, release format etc. A UPC helps to track and monitor streams, downloads and overall usage of a recording. Each individual song needs its own UPC.

An International Article Number (EAN) is an additional type of barcode which offers further clarification on tracking and usage. EANs are widely used in Europe.

A distributor will also issue a catalogue number, which is a referencing system that is typically used internally within the distributor's catalogue to further identify a music product.

A distributor will always ask whether you would like it to create your International Standard Recording Code (ISRC) for you. Every single song recording needs an ISRC to track global usage. Generating the ISRC for your release is something that all distributors can do at no extra cost.

Once you have created an account with a distributor and uploaded your releases, you will be able to access all the codes once they have been generated and deposited into your online account.

Data Analysis

A standard expectation of a digital distributor is the reporting of sales analytics. This can range from simple reporting to a deeply informative study of data which you can use to inform future choices in strategy. Spotify for Artists, Apple Music for Artists and YouTube Studio have detailed data analysis systems that are accessible through their own applications; but a distributor can look at all or many platforms in a single report. If detailed analytics are important to you, then perhaps consider a distributor's approach to data analysis reporting.

Meta Tagging

Meta tagging is the process of tagging metadata to music releases. This usually covers details such as the name of the release, artist(s), genre, release date, artwork, composers, producers and more. It is crucial that this information is as accurate as possible, because the information is shared with and displayed by various media players, streaming platforms and download sites. Metatags are typically embedded within a file, but also exist in files and databases that contribute towards a piece of digital content.

One of the most common problems in the context of music distribution is inaccurate meta tagging of artist names and song titles. We are now in an age when you can quite easily release a song with the wrong artist profile. In fact, this happens a lot. Many distributors try to avoid this problem by asking artists to locate their Spotify Artist ID and Apple Music ID during the upload process by tagging a previous release as a referenceable anchor point to ensure accuracy on delivery. Some distributors really seem to struggle in this area and create needless confusion. Others have solid protocols and solutions in place to address this growing problem.

Additional Tools and Features

Some distributors will offer additional features such as video distribution; while others might offer some technical analysis of your files and loudness normalisation which aims to level out volume dynamics in a track and create a more consistent listening experience. The latter can be useful when pitching to curators because it enables your song to sit comfortably within the context of a playlist alongside other songs of the same genre. While this can also be achieved beforehand with the assistance of professional-level mixing and mastering engineers, it could be an asset for self-produced artists.

An additional facet to consider is that some distributors are more proactive than others when it comes to generating promotional and pre-save links which can help to generate excitement and social media content in the pre-release period. Some distributors also offer label functionality for use with multiple artists and opportunities for partnership with brands.

Marketing Services

An expanding area of music distribution is in the marketing services that many distributors are now starting to offer to artists. While distribution and marketing are fundamentally different subjects on a traditional level, in the digital landscape the two are increasingly intertwined and distributors are now offering a range of marketing services to artists as a result. These can encompass anything from a set of tools built into the distributor's platform along with guidelines on release tactics through small, budget-friendly packages on social media marketing to more advanced, customised options tailored to fit a specific strategy and budget.

Commission

For many creators, paying commission on royalties to a distributor might seem like something to avoid. While this is indeed avoidable (it's a choice, like any other), there are advantages too – especially when you consider the circulation and collection methods that some distributors can offer.

Just to make you aware of how streaming revenues work: a distributor collects 80% of your streaming royalties. This is because the distributor collects on the master recording, not the songwriting. The other 20% relates to the songwriting and composition. Some distributors now offer music publishing collection in relation to that 20%, which effectively means that artists who write their own songs need not sign up with a performing rights organisation (PRO) to collect their streaming income, as the distributor can do it on their behalf. This notwithstanding, it is most definitely recommended to always sign up with your PRO, because streaming royalties account for only a portion of what a song's copyright can generate in income. Moreover, only some distributors offer this service, and only in certain countries.

When considering the commissionable options that exist when it comes to digital distribution, it is worth remembering that there are different streams of income that are commissionable, and the rate of commission can and usually does vary depending on the area of distribution. For instance, some distributors will collect and distribute revenue splits on YouTube monetisation and sync licensing, but this is usually at a higher rate of commission compared to audio streaming.

Splitting Revenue with Co-creators

While the option to set up collaborator splits should be expected as standard, many distributors struggle with this facility and therefore don't offer it. It is thus important to consider whether a distributor can offer multiple collaborator splits and royalty distribution to all parties if this is something that you may need. Otherwise, accounting can become disorganised and lack transparency.

Sync Licensing Options

Many distributors now provide a tiered system of services that offer variable benefits to users. One of the fastest-growing areas in tiered distribution services is in sync licensing. This allows creators who use an upper-tier service to pitch for sync licensing opportunities in TV and film. Although still in its infancy for some distributors, this may increase in popularity in the years to come – especially if the process yields positive results for independent creators.

Working with a Serviced Distributor

It is important to try to work out the ideal duration of your partnership with a distributor. Many of the distributors that dominate the marketplace serve a short-term purpose for creators who wish to release their music quickly. However, there can be advantages to working with a distributor on a longer-term basis where the distributor is committed to achieving the goals of an artist's wider campaign. For instance, AWAL, Ingrooves and Believe Digital are examples of serviced distributors that operate for both artists and small labels. Typically, companies such as this work well for both established artists with a track record and emerging artists with a longer-term business plan and a clear understanding of their marketplace. There is usually an application process and the serviced distributor will want to gain an understanding of how the creator will promote the work themselves, so having a team around the artist is key. It will also want to see a strategic outline of the creator's plans and hear about the campaign timeline, budget, live plans and what the next few releases sound like. It is always worth exploring companies of this nature if this is aligned with your vision for progression as an artist. Many artists who have been on the rosters of major or large independent labels often take this route once they have gained a clearer understanding of how music distribution operates.

Interview: Emily Jackson, Assistant Head of Distribution and Quality Control, Horus Music, UK

Horus Music has several services that are available to independent artists and labels. What are the most popular services you offer?

The primary and most popular service that Horus Music offers is digital audio distribution, which is available to artists, labels and as a white label service for companies wishing to act as their own distributor. We have direct partnerships with the digital service providers (DSPs) and constantly work on negotiating deals with any new platforms as and when they appear in the market. In addition to the audio distribution we offer, we provide video distribution and physical distribution of CDs to Amazon UK, which are also popular. Our marketing packages are also very popular.

As a team, our customer service is also integral to our offerings. Our team all either were once musicians themselves or have worked in the music industry from a business perspective, giving us broad expertise in all areas, not just distribution. This is why a lot of our clients choose to work with us, along with the accessibility of our support by email and by phone.

What role can Horus play in distributing music videos?

We currently offer different music video distribution packages, with our most popular being VEVO distribution. Our partnership with VEVO creates a channel on YouTube with the official VEVO watermark. Our clients can customise this channel with a profile image and banner or have the VEVO channel merged with their own to create an official artist channel that YouTube offers.

We also offer video distribution to several other platforms – such as Tidal, iTunes, Netease, Joox and Vibe – which will sit alongside audio releases if an artist already has these on their profile.

Distribution of music videos is beneficial because it enhances an artist's brand, with imagery and official video channels reducing imitations or copycats. It can also help in promoting to socials or DSPs and vice versa, providing more content for social media posts. Probably the key point for artists is that video distribution through a distributor such as Horus Music means that they can monetise their videos. Each view of the video will generate a royalty that is owed to the artist, whereas uploads to their own channel may not earn anything if the channel does not meet YouTube's monetisation requirements. With our distribution to the VEVO channel, there is no minimum monthly watch time or subscriber count, and therefore every view is instantly monetised.

What considerations do you have when considering working with an independent artist?

When it comes to distribution, we have no specific genre criteria and are open to artists at all levels of their career who can distribute their music and earn 100% of the royalties. However, we follow guidelines set out by each store, so we do have to ensure that the music and metadata comply. This includes ensuring that the audio is mixed and mastered to industry standard; is submitted in a WAV file; and is 16-bit, 44.1 kilohertz (kHz) or 24-bit, 44.1 kHz to 96 kHz. Artists and labels will also need to ensure that they have the relevant rights/ownership before submitting to us.

For some artists who are already established and have a larger following, we can offer a slightly different business model where we take a small percentage of their royalties in return for free marketing and artist showcases. Some artists may even be eligible for a financial advance. With this model, the criteria depend on monthly listeners across several DSPs and the marketing they plan on carrying out; but we do sometimes offer this to other artists if we really like their music.

For marketing, we are slightly more selective and ask that clients apply for these services. We offer free basic playlist pitching to all; but a full global campaign or other services such as PR or radio plugging are paid services. For this reason, we assess each submission to ensure that we think we can provide results, since – while nothing is guaranteed from legitimate marketing – we don't see the point in charging clients for a service if we don't think it will be successful. Our criteria for the marketing services are usually twofold:

- What our campaign leaders are looking for at the time: If our contacts are stronger in the pop/rock field at that moment, then we may not see as much success with classical or jazz pieces.
- Our campaign leaders' schedules: We don't want to take on a campaign if we cannot provide the time and attention it deserves.

What role can you play in the marketing of an artist's release campaign?

We have so many marketing services available to suit different aims and budgets, including playlist pitching, radio plugging, PR and social media. We also have tailored services to suit different territories.

We invite our clients to submit their music for marketing consideration. Our team will then reach out to discuss their goals and what we can offer in more detail. This means we can offer a bespoke service with the human touch we pride ourselves on.

Our global approach means that clients can see better results than they could have imagined possible themselves. For example, we previously had a client based in the UK who had a track that was influenced by their Indian heritage, so our Horus Music India team saw great success with playlist pitching. In addition, the track had afro-beat elements to it, so our teams shared resources and we also saw success from our Horus Music Africa team pitching for the same release.

What changes do you foresee in the coming years?

The industry is so fast paced and ever changing that this is hard to predict. However, looking at recent developments, I expect to see more territory-specific growth in the industry. This includes Africa, South America and even France and Spain. As dominant markets such as the UK and the USA become saturated, it only makes sense that big players (eg, DSPs, marketing opportunities) move to where there is more room to grow and make money. This could provide opportunities for certain types of music – for example, the growth of amapiano or Latin music styles and other regional genres. This is an opportunity both in terms of the creation of music and from a marketing perspective, with growth mirrored in the number of playlists focusing on these genres.

Another hot topic in the industry is artificial intelligence (AI) and the opportunities and challenges it brings. AI could increase creativity and provide opportunities for artists to offer up their own work in order for AI tools to learn from it. However, this also poses lots of questions. Who owns a piece of work created by AI? Where does the owner of any work the AI learns from stand in terms of ownership or copyright, and how does licensing work in this scenario? Talking again of saturation, will the use of AI add to an already saturated pool of music uploaded to DSPs every single day? There is the possibility that this could be a fad – a bit like blockchain and non-fungible tokens, which seem to have fallen off the bandwagon; although, depending on who you ask, they may still be considered relevant. It just shows that, as with most industries, things come and go out of fashion and move in cycles.

Finally, another issue that faces the recorded music sector – and one that Horus Music is currently trying to fight, along with many other companies and distributors – is fraudulent streaming. The manipulation of streams and the subsequent payment of illegitimate royalties are problematic for the whole industry, but particularly for real artists who ultimately lose out financially and creatively through altered algorithms. Our artists deserve to be paid fairly, and therefore we work hard with stores such as Spotify, which have their own anti-manipulation procedures. For us, this includes offering legitimate, organic marketing campaigns; and we would advise artists and labels to approach any company offering 'guaranteed' success cautiously, as it could be that this is achieved through bots. Similarly, with technology such as Content IDs, some artists have learned to game the system; therefore, we take it upon ourselves to educate our clients on what is and what is not eligible for these services, in order to make the environment fairer for all.

20

Releasing Cover Songs and Remixes

Cover Songs

It is possible to release a brand-new recorded version of a cover of a song in digital format on multiple streaming platforms without the need for any copyright clearance. However, there are some factors to bear in mind. First, this does not extend to sampling an original recording – not even a tiny snippet, no matter how seemingly insignificant it may be. To use any part of a recording, creators must obtain clearance from the rights holder of the recording, which in many cases is a record company. Second, if a newly composed song features even a fraction of a composition that is a recognised and previously released song, it could be classified by the digital service platforms as a cover. Third, it is not possible to release a cover of a song on all platforms in all countries – for example, the USA, Canada, Mexico, Pakistan and India have policies that prevent this on many platforms. However, a growing number of digital service platforms (DSPs) no longer have any global restrictions in place for releasing cover songs. It is possible to release a cover in all countries on Spotify, Tidal, Deezer and KKBox; and as times goes by, it might be realistic to expect that more DSPs will go this way. The reason why it is possible for just about anyone to release their own version of a cover song on these platforms is because most DSPs pay for the required mechanical release themselves.

The term 'mechanical release' is still widely used, even in the digital context, despite its original definition being linked to physical formats. It is possible to gain your own mechanical release for all platforms in all countries. This is purchasable through services such as the Harry Fox Agency and Easy Song Licensing.

DOI: 10.4324/9781003452119-24

Remixes

For a remix of a song to be deemed an official remix, it requires the approval of the rights holder of the original recording, which will usually be a record company. A remix that does not have the approval of the rights holder is often referred to as a 'bootleg remix'.

Unlike a cover song, where an artist records a new version of a song, a remix relies on the use of some or all of the original stems of a recording, especially a vocal recording. It is illegal to release a remix on streaming platforms without the written approval of the rights holders, so don't expect a distributor to be able to deliver an unofficial remix of a song to the major platforms. That said, electronic music creators should not be deterred from creating remixes as part of their artform. One element of the artform of electronic producers and DJs is their ability to reinterpret different elements of songs when fused together. A mixtape of such examples to promote a DJ's work is an effective way to show-case their unique style. The aim for many remixers is not always to officially distribute their mixes. It is also worth mentioning that record companies with dormant catalogue are always keen to hear how a song has been reinvented by an electronic creator of the next generation. This is a great way to gain that all-important clearance for distribution.

Just to clarify: if all the instrument stems and vocals are re-recorded, it then becomes a cover, not a remix.

21

Costing and Budgeting for Artists Releasing Music

Much as for any business, there is often an outlay of costs involved in getting a music project off the ground. Understanding what things should cost enables creators to take an informed approach and make good decisions that are aligned with their strategy. It also allows them to budget more effectively. This is, after all, what a record company would do with an artist. Many artists who go on to gain the investment and support of a record company initially succeed in getting their project off the ground on their own. This is what makes them an appealing prospect to an investor.

Who is more appealing to a record company:

- The artist who has potential but is yet to test the marketplace?
- The artist who has tested the marketplace and has found a proven audience?

The answer is somewhat obvious: the former is an idea, while the latter is evidence; the former is higher risk, while the latter is lower risk. One of the key aspects that underpins this is the knowledge that expenditure is inevitable, so it is useful to for creators of original music to understand what this might look like.

Recording Songs

Artists who retain their own master rights are in a more favourable and investable position. Artists who own their own master rights have the flexibility and power to trade differently. This can apply to sync and branding deals and a host of other options. Owning the master rights is of paramount importance if part of an artist's strategy is to license their recordings to a record company. By paying professional producers and engineers and asking them to sign a master release document (which you can find on the accompanying website to this

DOI: 10.4324/9781003452119-25

book), artists create a watertight pathway to doing business with their recordings without other parties being involved in the recording process. If the artist has a producer working speculatively alongside them on a recording project, be clear about the working relationship and use a song split sheet (an additional document which you can also find on the accompanying website to this book). Involving a friend, a family friend or some other form of acquaintance in the recording process is entirely feasible if they are good and can deliver. It may be that this party is happy to work for free, but even this must be put in writing. It safeguards the artist's intellectual property and it may affect their future if handled carelessly. Unfortunately, problems such as this are quite common. Artists need to start their project with a professional intention and therefore a professional mindset. If artists want to work with professionals, they should be professional themselves – and that starts from day one.

Costs per track can and do vary significantly, depending on the status of the producer and whether they charge by the day, the hour or for the project as a flat fee. It is important to understand how a producer breaks down their costs so that there are no surprises at the end of the project. The fee will also be dictated by the contribution time of the producer. A producer creating tracks from scratch involves a different level of commitment compared to recording a band and mixing their music. By contrast, merely recording vocals over a track involves less work for a producer.

If artists are using a track that has been leased or purchased from an online store, be sure to check the terms of the licensing agreement very carefully. While only a micro payment may be needed to buy a track, it could cost considerably more to buy the track exclusively. If possible, it is also worth understanding how many licences to the track have been sold. The last thing an artist needs, after pouring their heart and soul into a new record, is to discover that 400 other people are using the same track.

Costs per track can range from £100 to £1,000 on a grassroots level.

Distribution

It is very much worth the effort to research the subject of distribution further. There is an array of options for independent artists, which vary depending on a wide range of factors (as discussed in Chapter 19). Key considerations include, among others, the artist's expectations; support and advice; marketing and playlist options; and willingness to split revenue shares compared to paying flat fees.

Fees vary from free to £750 per annum.

Artwork and Branding

Artwork can be as expensive or as inexpensive as the artist wishes it to be. Approaches to artwork can vary from self-creating pieces to hiring photographers, paying graphic designers through online platforms, leasing assets from library stock images and more. It is key to understand what rights the artist is acquiring when working with the creative assets of others. When using a library stock image with an artist's own branding placed over the top, for instance, it is important that the artist is aware that they have obtained a non-exclusive licence for commercial purposes. The result can be used as artwork for the artist's digital release, but the artist will not own the image. If you are hiring a photographer, be sure to discuss and put in writing the mechanics of the business transaction for the image:

- Is it exclusive?
- Can the photographer submit your artwork that they created to an award show on their own behalf?
- Perhaps the photographer will halve their fee if they can use the image elsewhere online to promote their work?

Never make assumptions.

Artists should be cautious of their egos getting in the way of artwork. Artwork is incredibly important. Often artists feel very proud of themselves for creating their own artwork and perhaps don't realise that this work does nothing to represent their brand and their music.

Branding works much the same way. Imagine that an artist has paid a third party for a font style on InDesign because it fits perfectly with their brand. Does the artist have the commercial right to use that font for a release? It is always worth exploring the terms of the licence. The chances are that the use of the font for commercial purposes is perfectly acceptable upon receipt of the purchase or rental. This will not be the case, however, if the artist uses the font style in a logo that they try to trademark. Customised graphic design can be a little easier to handle, as this is commissionable work that is unique to the artist; but it is important again to clear the purpose of the use with the creator, as the price may change depending on the intention. This might surprise some artists, but in many ways, it is logical that prices differ depending on context. It's rather like beat leasers who lease their beats for £10 but sell exclusively for £450.

It is always advisable to use a simple written agreement to establish clarity about ownership when it comes to logo design and artwork. Having the

Video

A music video is a great creative asset for an artist who is looking to scale up their marketability and growth. If there is the budget to create one, it may well stand the artist in good stead for further discovery – especially if it tells a good story that is aligned with the artistic message and value of the artist.

However, music videos can be quite expensive and perhaps don't always yield a substantial return on investment. Music has become a very visual artform in the 2020s and there are other more cost-effective options to create visual content in the form of lyric videos or animation videos. Even an artist uploading their music to YouTube through their distributor is still a good idea – even if only accompanied by the song's artwork – because it allows for discovery, free access and visibility.

It is the artist who is in charge of managing creative and marketing spend, and this is still true to an extent even if the artist is signed to a major record company. When building a release strategy, it is important to think about the goal of the campaign and then budget around this to see what is and what is not possible.

The costs of music videos can range from £200 to £10,000.
The costs of lyrics videos can range from £20 to £500.

Does an Artist Need a Website?

Ten or 20 years ago, the answer to this question would have been a resounding 'yes'. However, the landscape has changed. It is perhaps now more important for an artist to have a web presence than a website – at least early on in their career. This is due in part to the various different profiles that an artist has online through social media channels, streaming platforms and other websites. These are online locations where anyone can seek information and access media on the artist. If budget can stretch to a solid, open-source website with an impressive design, that is a bonus; but it is healthy to ask what the purpose of that website would be. If there is a call to action from social media for people to visit an artist's website for a specific reason, it might be worthwhile. Perhaps there is built-in e-commerce functionality on the website that the artist can use as a direct-to-fan tool for product downloads, ticket sales and merchandise. This would make a website a useful investment. But the reality is that for many artists, their websites are merely landing pages that offer a professional presentation of their work and that signpost to other web-based sales and streaming options.

22
Understanding Organic Growth on Streaming Platforms

Once the music has been created, it's time for it to find its way into people's lives. Songs can trigger memories of people, events and moments, so introducing the right songs to the right people at the right time is crucial. Understanding how this happens in the context of digital discovery is of paramount importance to the creators of those songs.

To understand of how growth works in the digital world, it is important to understand that data is being crowdsourced from us all and for us all, so that our choices become quicker and easier – whether we approve of this approach or not.

Systems of Recommendation

Most platforms use machine-based learning to generate recommendations for users. User data such as listening history, playlists, likes, saves, skips and behavioural preferences is all considered when recommendations are generated. This is one of the most technologically competitive areas of the digital sphere in the 2020s, as platforms test out new and innovative ways of generating recommendations to keep users consistently engaged. The more we engage as users, the more data we send and the more suitable the recommendations become for us. This is similar to how Netflix, Amazon, Disney+ and other visual streaming platforms operate: the longer you have your Netflix account and the more movies you watch, the more likely you are to benefit from the suitability of the recommendations because you are sending more data about your likes and dislikes to the platform. It could be argued, however, that audio streaming platforms are far more aggressive in their tactics when it comes to recommendations. Where Netflix might suggest, Spotify will simply force a new song into your life, which creates an abundance of opportunities for listeners and creators alike.

DOI: 10.4324/9781003452119-26

Collaborative Filtering

Collaborative filtering is a technique that identifies similar users based on listening behaviours. The aim is to introduce listeners to music that they will probably like based on what similar users have enjoyed. This involves a deep analysis of listener histories; the algorithms will look to detect patterns which can subsequently inform on suitability. Simply put, if User X and User Y have similar listening histories and User X saves a particular song, User Y may be served up that same song.

Content-based Filtering

This focuses not on the users but on the actual music itself. If you've ever looked at the shape of a waveform of a song, you might be able to tell when the chorus comes in or when the pre-chorus starts; but the limitations of human capability prevent us from understanding anything more about the song without hearing it. This is where machine-based learning has an insightful edge, as it can analyse the characteristics of a song and categorise its key elements. Information such as tempo, genre, mood, instrumentation, vocal style and even danceability can be examined through advanced content-based filtering. This form of machine-based learning removes human interpretation of music. Once again, patterns are analysed, and these play an important role in assessing the suitability of suggestions to users. This data is often combined with the metadata that the creator sends to their distributor, and if it is all aligned, the recommendation is considered to be less risky by many streaming platforms in the context of introducing music to new listeners.

Contextual Factors

Algorithms sometimes consider additional contextual factors when it comes to generating recommendations. These can range from the time of the day or week through location, recent releases, popular trends and specific playlists right up to whether listeners are using desktop or mobile devices to stream at particular times of the day.

Algorithms evolve over time and are often refined and enhanced based on user data and technological changes. Each platform has its own proprietary methods to enhance the listener experience and offers music discovery in its own unique way. While social media algorithms evolve rapidly, the fundamental mechanics behind streaming algorithms are arguably fairly set in their structure. The future will no doubt see fine tuning and new advancements added along the way, but these will mostly be built within the framework of the current digital landscape.

23
The Algorithmic Scaffold of Spotify and Its Playlists

An 'engine' is defined as a machine with moving parts that converts power into motion. This is a good metaphor for the role that Spotify can play for music creators. While it could be argued that YouTube is the global monster of music discovery, its algorithmic nature caters more for content creators than it does for musical introductions.

In terms of music discovery, Spotify has become the most influential audio streaming platform in the world. It serves a wide demographic of users, whose unique tastes are individually catered to through the concept of crowd-sourced data. Spotify aims to offer a customised listener experience that blends familiarity with fresh music. A consistent flow of new songs is therefore crucial to the company's fundamental values.

The Complexity of the Spotify Algorithm

Understanding how Spotify's algorithm is built is somewhat comparable to understanding the recipe for McDonald's famous Big Mac sauce: it's a secret. It is an undisclosed and proprietary piece of information that nobody has the legal right to publish. There is not a book in existence (including this one) that can fully explain it. However, through studies, research and testing, we can come closer to understanding how it is pieced together by exploring some of its key elements. It is not possible for music creators to hack or cheat their way to growth with such a sophisticated algorithm. However, there are ways in which music creators can feed the algorithm, and this starts with gaining an understanding of its probable fundamental operations.

DOI: 10.4324/9781003452119-27

Six Fundamental Elements of the Algorithm

Disclaimer: The following is an educated guess designed to support the careers of music creators and is not a factually accurate depiction of Spotify's proprietary information.

Element 1: Natural Language Processing

Natural language processing (NLP) enables technology to understand text and speech, and Spotify uses the findings to inform its understanding of a song. NLP will scan the internet to find all the information it can on a song. This could include what people are saying in forums, what music reviewers are saying in publications, what bloggers are writing about the song and more. Spotify seeks to understand how the song is being heard and understood outside of its platform. NLP also aids Spotify in analysing a song's lyrics, which can help inform as to key themes and moods – something which is very useful in the context of creating recommendations. NLP is also used for song categorisation and metadata tracking.

Element 2: Collaborative Filtering

This is where the platform analyses the listening history of a user and searches for other users with similar tastes. Once patterns have been identified among listeners, comparisons are drawn between them. Preferences are based on songs, artists and playlists. Once Spotify has a greater understanding of a listener's profile, that listener is introduced to music that they have not yet heard on the platform but that has already been enjoyed by listeners with similar tastes.

Element 3: Contextual Information

Spotify tries to build in context to the suggestions it serves to listeners to curate experiences that cater to different lifestyles. The time of the day, week and year can play a part in its offerings. A listener's geographical location also influences this, to offer a more advanced level of suitability for the right song at the right moment.

Element 4: Audio Features

Each song is analysed to extract its key features. While the mood of a song can perhaps be open to human interpretation, Spotify can scan the waveform of a song and assess factors such as danceability, energy, speechiness, rhythm and loudness, among other factors. This process helps Spotify to categorise songs into primary and secondary genres from a technical perspective, rather than from a human perspective. This process provides a deeper level of accuracy when it comes to recommendations and can also assist with playlist curation.

Element 5: Machine Learning Models

Machine learning (ML) is at the heart of what Spotify is. Spotify uses a host of ML techniques to analyse various factors based on user data. This is possibly the most crucial aspect of what makes Spotify so popular, as the platform has been designed to offer hyper-personalised recommendations to users. It is assumed that Spotify uses a highly sophisticated form of reinforcement learning to analyse user behaviour while listening. This in turn generates predictions on what listeners may like in the future. If the algorithm gets a suggestion wrong, the user will unknowingly inform Spotify of this crucial piece of data, which in turn will help refine future recommendations. The profile of the listener builds over time and the recommendations become increasingly attuned to their tastes. Spotify uses ML to assess a listener's preferences across a variety of factors, such as genre, sub-genre, mood, tempo and instrumentation.

Element 6: User Feedback

User feedback is another crucial aspect of Spotify, especially as it aims to provide a smooth listening experience with the primary aim of pleasing the listener. Spotify gathers user feedback based on various interactions, including whether and how quickly a specific song is skipped, song likes, saves to playlists and whole album likes. Social media shares constitute further interaction data. This all feeds into ML and informs future recommendations.

Feeding the Algorithm as a Consumer

It is worth considering your behaviour as a user. Stop and think about how you consume music yourself and what effect this could be having on your generated recommendations. To understand how growth is gained through platforms such as Spotify, it is important to understand how they work. A great place to start this off is by understanding how you use streaming platforms – not as a creator, but as a consumer.

If you share your streaming account with a family member or friend, the recommendations that are being generated will be significantly distorted and confusing. Different users using the same account will compromise the experience if their tastes vary. However, if the person you are sharing with has very similar tastes, this could make for a useful collaboration!

It is worth considering how you find new music and how music is introduced to you. As a music creator, it's important to listen to music. Being a fan of music is almost certainly what inspired you to make music in the first place. Perhaps you are using algorithmic playlists to listen to new music; or perhaps you are consuming home-screen mood-based playlists curated by Spotify's editorial teams. If so, you are helping Spotify to source data on you, which in turn feeds into an enhanced experience for you and others with similar tastes. Perhaps you are saving songs to your own playlists. If so, the outcome is equally desirable for Spotify: you are helping it to understand you and your habits on a greater scale. Perhaps those playlists that you self-curate can be enjoyed by others with similar tastes – in which case, perhaps there is an influential tastemaker inside of you who is ready to curate for others? This can be a useful marketing tool as an artist, as it allows you to build playlists that have followers, which are then readily available to you when you have new music to release. Plenty of artists and labels all over the world are doing that now – and are doing a very good job of it.

Just pause for a moment and consider your own behaviour in the context of streaming platforms. It can be useful.

Playlist Categories

There are three categories of playlists on Spotify and they all play a crucial role in the discovery of new music. The multi-dimensional processes which curate the listening experience are part machine and part human.

Editorial Playlists

Editorial playlists are created and managed by Spotify and are predominantly based on genres, moods, trends, cultural moments, activities, regions, countries, eras and more. Seen as the Holy Grail by many artists and labels, editorial playlists have tremendous influence and can play a vital role in boosting a song's awareness. Since 2018, anyone with a verified Spotify profile can pitch their soon-to-be-released song to Spotify's editorial team, provided that this happens at least seven days in advance of the release date. This can be done through the editorial pitch tool in the Spotify for Artists app in either mobile or desktop format.

Some genre-specific playlists can have an undeniable impact on a song's visibility: for instance, Rap Caviar has over 15 million followers, while Rock Classics has in the region of 12 million. (The more universally appealing Today's Top Hits, by contrast, has closer to 35 million followers.) Other editorial playlists focus on a specific geographical location and its associated musical style. Examples include the predominantly era-based Made in Manchester, which boasts around 300,000 followers; and I Love NYC, which has closer to the 120,000 followers – although this focuses on songs that are themed on the city, rather than music from the city. Spotify has numerous editorial teams based in various global locations who are widely acknowledged as being more approachable than those of other major streaming platforms. This is perhaps due in part to the transparency of their app-based pitch platform, which is accessible to anyone; although Spotify also has many key relationships with record labels and distributors, which have access to its influential editorial teams. It is important to accept that there is nothing fundamentally wrong or unfair about this either. It is comparable to any other trade that sees companies working in partnership with other trusted sources that can help to filter useful information on their behalf.

Editorial playlists can give valuable data boosts to artists, yielding benefits beyond added exposure and the kudos gained from the placement. Inclusion on a large playlist not only guarantees a song a higher stream count, but also boosts the artist's profile by adding a range of new collected data, which in turn feeds further visibility through algorithmic growth. This is especially true if the save rate reaches a particular threshold. While Spotify knows that many of the streams on an editorial playlist can be deemed as passive listens, this deepens the crowdsourced data on a song's suitability for additional audiences. For some artists, the big boost of streams disappears as quickly as it appeared; but this is still useful for the reasons mentioned above.

According to data from Music-Tomorrow.com (www.music-tomorrow.com/blog/is-spotify-editorial-playlist-landscape-fair-to-emerging-artists), an analysis of the hugely influential New Music Friday editorial playlist reveals that in April 2022, its global playlist featured 63% non-major tracks. This figure was significantly higher than in past years, which should make pleasing reading for independent artists and labels. By contrast, Rap Caviar was also studied in the same research, alongside the Get Turnt editorial playlist. A dataset of 2,000 songs that featured on either playlist showed that major label releases accounted for 86% of the songs listed. The inference we can perhaps draw from these studies is that when it comes to global dominance of pop culture, the major labels hold significant sway in the landscape of editorial playlists; but there is still enough space and opportunity for independent artists and labels to break through with editorial support and visibility. If, as a music creator, your desired genre or mood is a little more niche than the wider commercial playing field, it is both fair and accurate to think that editorial support from Spotify is more achievable. If, on the other hand, your goal is to impact popular culture in a mainstream genre with your music, the support of Spotify editorial playlists will be crucial; but that will be difficult to achieve without the backing of a major label.

So, how does an independent artist build traction – and ultimately visibility – on a platform such as Spotify without significant editorial support? Let's study the following two types of playlists.

Algorithmic Playlists

Algorithmic playlists are a crucial part of the Spotify engine. They are unique to each listener and introduce new music to listeners every single day in some form or another.

Discover Weekly is served up to listeners every Monday morning and comes in the form of a 25-song digital mixtape. These are songs which Spotify knows that listeners have not heard before (at least not on this platform). Release Radar is refreshed every Friday and predominantly features artists that listeners follow alongside some additional options which the algorithm deems to be of interest to the listener. Other forms of algorithmic playlists are compilations based on what listeners have already enjoyed. Examples include On Repeat, Songs of the Year, Time Capsule and Summer Rewind. It is worth noting that even these types of playlists introduce new songs to the listener. For instance, Summer Rewind will curate an experience that allows the listener to reminisce about a specific season; but songs that the listener did not hear during that season will still be placed in this unique playlist due to the power of collaborative filtering (explained earlier in this chapter). In many cases, the new songs blend so seamlessly with the rest of the playlist that listeners may not even notice the new music being piped into their lives.

Spotify also recognises that listeners have eclectic interests and caters to this through what it calls a listener's Daily Mixes. There are usually between four and nine different daily mixes available to each unique listener, numbered Daily Mix 1, Daily Mix 2 and so forth, with a summary of the artists featured on the playlist underneath. The Daily Mixes are not named by genre, but the style of music is clearly indicated by the acts listed in the description. Daily Mixes feature a blend of familiarity and fresh music. These are all excellent gateways for new music to break through to new listeners.

While many creators regard editorial playlists as the Holy Grail of Spotify playlists, it is perhaps the algorithmic playlists that prove a slower but more effective route to organic growth. A certain threshold of streams may need to be reached before a song can secure a spot in an algorithmic playlist. Rumours suggest that 20,000 streams are needed for Discover Weekly; but further research reveals that songs with far fewer streams have also found their way onto this lucrative discovery tool, while other songs with higher stream figures have not. We can therefore assume that other factors also play a part in the selection process. One thing that we know for sure about Discover Weekly is that it usually starts with a low-risk process. A song is perhaps (but not always) served to five listeners on a Monday, 50 listeners the following Monday, 200 the Monday after that and 1,000 the Monday after that. Spotify is testing the song and assessing its skip and save rates – not only to see how well the song is performing, but also to see whether the song is being served to the right audience. The algorithm ultimately wants to understand the audience for the song and the artist so it can understand listeners' sonic profiles in greater detail. The by-product is that this can also help to softly break an artist's song.

User-Curated Playlists

User-curated playlists can be created and managed by anyone and therefore can vary significantly in terms of influence. They include everything from privately curated fan playlists through artist playlists right up to the playlists of influential third-party curators with a large audience. Many independent record companies have their own playlists which would fall under this category, and even major labels curate their own playlists. There are now independent companies that manage their own playlist range; and there are other playlists that started out life as fan pages and have since grown into something influential in a way that is somewhat comparable to YouTube. A placement on an influential tastemaker's playlist can sometimes generate more streams and traction than a placement on an editorial list.

24
Pitching for Playlists

As mentioned in Chapter 23, Spotify has only one official method of pitching for its editorial playlists: through the Spotify for Artists app. There are other routes through solicited sources, such as record companies and music distributors, if you have a deal in place with them; but not a soul on this planet can guarantee any kind of placement on one of the major playlists in advance. Algorithmic playlists cannot be pitched for; they are compiled by an algorithm, not curated by humans. However, there are ways in which creators can gain traction by pitching to the wide variety of user-curated playlists.

Pitching Methods

The ways in which creators can pitch for user-curated playlists vary from informal private messages to following the playlist, pitching on the website, emailing and social media. However, perhaps the most convenient way is by using centralised platforms such as www.submithub.com, www.playlistpush.com, www.dailyplaylists.com and www.groover.co, where creators can identify playlists that they feel that their music is suitable for and pitch to them via the platform. This has an advantage over pitching directly, as it comes with certain assurances such as guaranteed listens and word count standards for feedback. However, it also comes at a cost, which will need to be budgeted for – just like any other part of a promotional campaign. It's worth mentioning that it's not just independent music creators that find growth and traction through these platforms, but independent labels too. Some creators are reluctant to spend on this type of service, while others see it as a great investment. One thing is for certain, though: a song's growth through user-curated playlists leads to a much wider pool of data and ultimately further visibility on Spotify for the artist.

DOI: 10.4324/9781003452119-28

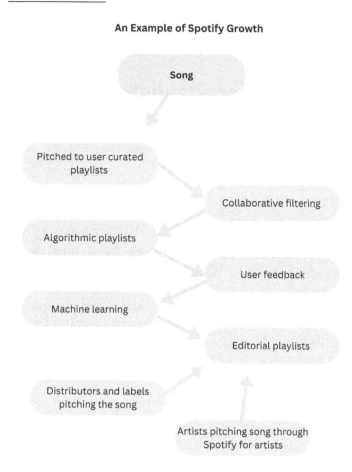

Figure 24.1 An Example of Spotify Growth

The Key Cultural and Stylistic Traits of a Song

It is important to try to identify some of the key stylistic and cultural elements of a song, as this may result in a wider pitch potential. This could be as simple as a song that has a seasonal message to it, such as Christmas, making it more relevant to a specific type of playlist. Or a song could incorporate elements of a specific culture, which would immediately align it with some key playlists in overseas territories.

In Chapter 19, Emily Jackson from Horus Music mentioned a release that gained significant editorial support precisely for these reasons:

> We previously had a client based in the UK who had a track that was in-
> fluenced by their Indian heritage, so our Horus Music India team saw great

success with playlist pitching. In addition, the track had afrobeats elements
to it, so our teams shared resources and we also saw success from our Horus
Music Africa team pitching for the same release.

This is a great example of identifying key traits of a song's production, arrangement or story that make it highly suitable for specific playlisting.

Songs featuring instruments which are less common also often offer specific
playlist potential.

This type of consideration could be something which is studied after a song is
composed and recorded, but before it is pitched. It could also be a factor that
informs creative decisions prior to recording a song.

Key Things to Avoid When It Comes to Playlist Pitching

It is against Spotify's values and its terms and conditions to charge creators a
fee for placing their music on a playlist. However, there are third-party service
providers that charge creators for the opportunity to pitch their music to curators. This is a very grey area – it has been for a few years now and will probably
continue to be so for a few years to come. While Spotify's terms and conditions
forbid curators from charging a fee, there are a couple of things to bear in mind.
The first is how closely Spotify can regulate such practices. Much like police and
international intelligence services, it can't have eyes everywhere and it needs
evidence to act upon on the suspicion of a breach. This can be quite difficult,
especially in light of technological advancements. Second, while curators themselves cannot charge, there appears to be a grey area whereby third-party service
providers that act as a broker between curators and creators can charge. This is
a very complex subject to fully understand, but it's useful to know that it exists.

What make matters more confusing for creators is that on some of the centralised playlist platforms, there are certain very reputable, respectable and
influential curators who can and do make a big difference to the songs of independent music creators. This is because they have legitimate playlists with a
large organic following which can generate streams, saves, shares and an overall sense of organic growth for creators if their song is featured on them. The
difficulty for music creators lies in being able to differentiate between these
types of curators and those that are fraudulent.

In theory, there is nothing to stop anyone from starting a playlist today and using some software (or hiring someone with the software) that can bot-generate
1,000 fake followers on the playlist. They can then give the playlist a neat logo
and a cool name, and curate a list of songs. This will gain them access to some

of the centralised platforms, which may well accept them as a curator because they meet the threshold of 1,000 followers, enabling them to start accepting submissions and monetising their playlist. This happens. A lot. Fortunately, it is becoming easier to spot those that have done this; and it's getting harder for them to survive, because the centralised platforms are changing for the better by conducting tougher checks and introducing stricter regulations. Still, it doesn't mean that independent music creators don't get tricked, so this is certainly something to beware of.

Streaming Farms

Spotify is also trying to do as much as it can to clamp down on artificial streaming. Artificial streaming is largely carried out by streaming farms, which are locations with many digital devices, each of which uses its own independent login to stream a particular song.

In Chapter 19, Emily Jackson of Horus Music stated: 'The manipulation of streams and the subsequent payment of illegitimate royalties is a problem for the whole industry, but particularly for real artists who ultimately lose out financially and creatively through altered algorithms.'

Farm creators offer package deals to those who wish to give their songs an added boost of streams. These can easily be spotted in the form of ads that 'guarantee a specific number of streams'. The reality is that there is no legitimate way for anyone to guarantee a specific number of streams, except through artificial streaming. If Spotify suspects that artificial streaming has taken place, it will not issue a warning to the creator; it will remove the track instantly and notify the distributor as to why it has done so. The creator can then submit their case for reinstatement of the track along with evidence of organic growth, which must be submitted via their distributor. There is no doubt that there are some very clever and mischievous computer wizards at work who realise how many music creators are eager to give their music a 'streaming boost'. The advice is never to do this, for two reasons. It not only brands the artist as risky to the distributor and the streaming platform, but also creates some very distorted data which is hard to recover from, as it infiltrates and dilutes statistics on listeners, locations, save rates and a host of other useful data.

Scenario 1

An indie rock band have released two singles. Thanks to their pitching process, their first single gained some local radio support, a headline show in their hometown and 16,000 streams on Spotify. Their second single was accompanied by a video which they premiered on the channel of an influential tastemaker who they pitched to through SubmitHub. This secured 190,000 streams on You-Tube; and the song also did well on Spotify by gaining a range of placements on user-curated playlists and an algorithmic boost on both Release Radar and Spotify Radio.

The band now release their third single. They believe it is their strongest song and they want to do everything they can to grow the reputation of the band even further. They are on the brink of gaining some great traction on Spotify; but the guitarist gets impatient and sees an ad on social media that offers 30,000 streams for $30. He pays it, thinking that he is helping the band. All these 30,000 streams are traced to a small town in Europe. Spotify detects this and takes the track down. This is a disaster for the growth of the band.

Friends and Family Sharing and Streaming Your Music

There is a natural and understandable inclination for family and friends to want to support their loved ones when they create and release music. On a basic human level, this is lovely. In terms of algorithmic growth, it is a problem. Often a creator's family are sharing and streaming the music because they love the person, more so than their actual music. It goes without saying that this is not always the case, of course; but the problem is often that the friends and family of the creators are not always the natural fans of the music, which can lead to distortion in terms of crucial data. Spotify, like other streaming platforms, is keen to try to understand who is listening to your music by building a profile of each listener's interests. Collaborative filtering enables a more accurate understanding of how to present new music to listeners.

Scenario 2

If a creator has a new release that is enjoying an initial boost on or just after release day due to support from friends and family, it can feel rewarding; but it's not always useful if the target audience is not the natural audience for the music. That said, it could still be argued that as many social shares as possible can help a track to grow if it is still filtering its way through to people who like it and save it. This is perhaps comparable to a new band starting out who need to pull in 20 paying members of the public to secure a rebooking from a promoter. In theory, if the band keep doing this, it will help them to play more and more shows in more and more towns, which in turn will introduce them to a wider and more natural fanbase. As a consequence, the band start to attract fans who enjoy their music without knowing them personally.

However, the landscape of machine-based learning is a little different and a little less forgiving.

Scenario 3

Here's another comparison. Imagine that you are a marketing executive trying to enhance your reputation in the corporate world. You have a good position in the company you are working for, but you are also trying to widen your network by building your profile online through a platform such as LinkedIn. You are making good connections, learning, networking and having useful conversations with people in your future working world. Then your aunt, your grandad and your nephew all ask to connect with you on the same platform. This will change how the algorithm works. Your family just wish the best for you and want to be aware of what you're doing because they love you. There is a difference between their intention and their action.

For music creators in the digital landscape, there is a balance between these scenarios to consider.

25
Sonic Virality: When the Listeners Speak

We are now in an age when music can speak for itself, to a certain extent. This is perhaps a golden era for organic growth, when great songs by independent artists can become popular without major backing. On the flipside, in an age of huge passive listenership, some big-name artists with major label backing do not always achieve the hits that are expected of them. This is the listeners speaking. Marketing has its limitations and today only the strongest songs can survive the toughest of all tests: the opinion of the listeners. This is sonic virality.

The algorithmic nature of digital platforms works in favour of songs that are proving popular with a wide audience. For instance, Australian recording artist Tones and I had one of Spotify's mostly highly streamed songs of 2019 with her hit 'Dance Monkey'. It has been widely reported that the song grew organically because of Spotify's editorial playlist ecosystem. Spotify's editorial team in Australia first heard the song when it was submitted through the pitch tool on the Spotify for Artists app. This resulted in the song being added to a domestic editorial playlist, where it was received well by listeners, resulting in a high save rate. It was then heard by someone in the editorial department in Scandinavia, who added it to one of their domestic playlists; within a few weeks, the momentum had grown further through the platform and after a few months, the song was charting in the Billboard Hot 100. It is believed that this was achieved without a traditional fanbase or any form of major backing. This is an example of what can happen in the modern landscape: high-quality music is surviving and thriving in today's competitive global market.

It could perhaps be said that some listeners are more influential than others, although they may not be aware of it. Spotify has a highly sophisticated understanding of its engaged premium-tier listeners and can analyse patterns in early adopters of new music. This enables the platform to track which listeners are good at spotting recording growing and emerging artists and songs. By analysing

DOI: 10.4324/9781003452119-29

the listening behaviours of these early adopters, the platform can identify artists who are on the rise.

The Key Performance Indicators for Growth on a Spotify Profile

The goal for music creators on Spotify is clear: growth. Creators can develop a deeper appreciation of how growth is being charted by understanding a series of key steps in this process.

There are several aspects of an artist's profile which are populated by default when they release music. Examples include a discography section, an artist's own playlists and a 'Discovered on', section which lists some of the playlists that listeners have found the artist music on.

Other key steps include the following.

Profile Verification

This is a straightforward identification step that enables blue-tick status on the platform. It also gives an artist and their team access to their Spotify for Artists data. Once a release is live on the platform, an artist can claim their profile. Some distributors can enable activation of the verification process in advance of a release.

Radio

Studying an artist's radio is a sure-fire way of understanding how well Spotify understands their music and their listener base. A quick listen to some of the songs on an artist's radio will instantly offer insights. If the songs are similar in style and are consistent throughout the list, this is a strong indicator that Spotify understands the artist's audience. If the songs are quite varied from style to style, this means that Spotify is yet to fully understand the artist's listener base. A song's radio might be different from the artist's radio. This is an indication that Spotify might understand the audience of a particular song by the artist rather than the audience of the artist in general. Radio is a key factor in Spotify's 'Discovery Mode', which at the time of writing is available in over 90 countries and allows artists and labels to build data when preparing for a new release, in addition to promoting catalogue that falls either inside or outside of a campaign period.

'Fans Also Like'

As an artist's listener base grows, the 'Fans Also Like' section will begin to populate. This is a strong indication that Spotify is starting to understand the artist's audience – particularly if it is accurate. There is nothing that an artist or label can do at an operational level to assist this aspect of an artist's profile, although consistent releases with a coherent and cohesive genre will certainly help. It is controlled algorithmically and cannot be manipulated. As time passes, the 'Fans Also Like' section will repopulate and refine itself further by changing the artists to ones that are more similar in style and sound to the mentioned artist.

'This Is . . .'

Gaining a 'This Is . . .' page (eg, 'This Is Illennium'; 'This Is Oasis') on a Spotify profile is rather like a digital badge of honour. It is widely regarded as an indication that the artist has triggered the Spotify algorithm to such a degree that the algorithm is finally working in favour of the artist. 'This Is . . .' falls under the 'Featured on' section. Significant editorial support and consistent algorithmic playlist introductions are the hallmarks of this status.

Old Is the New New

This is a subject that is often overlooked by many music creators. It is all too easy for creators to consider their past music releases as less exciting than their new releases. There is a natural excitement to something that is new. However, it could also be argued that old is the new new.

Every time a new song is released into the digital sphere, it is competing not just with the songs that are released at the same time, but also with all the songs that have come before it. Legacy acts are enjoying a great deal of streams among the younger generations because of how their catalogues are being pushed. There is great music from across the decades and every day it is 'new' to someone.

Releasing music in the 2020s is often much more about playing the long game. Generation Z listeners have become accustomed to shorter songs and expect instant gratification, through no fault of their own. For creators, it is different. Releasing music requires patience. There are many different discovery methods for music and song discovery may not necessary fall inside of what a creator considers to be their release campaign period. It can be a mistake to try to push a song for a set amount of time only. Digital service providers consider any song that a listener has yet to hear but might like as 'new', and so should creators. In an age when listeners are constantly being introduced to new music through crowdsourced data, it is entirely possible that your 'old' song will appear as 'new' on an algorithmic playlist for thousands of listeners several years after its release. Creators should become mindful of this in their journey of releasing new music. If songs are good and they find their audience, the word 'old' is barely relevant.

26
Top Tips for Gaining Growth on Audio Streaming Platforms

- **Identify your lead song.** This is the song that is gaining the most growth of all your releases. It might not be the song that you think is the best. Pitch the song to as many third-party playlists as possible. Work the song for several months, even if this runs throughout a sequence of other releases. It will aid discovery of the song and subsequently future releases. Spotify's 'Discovery Mode' can also be engaged with. Identifying a lead song can sometimes be difficult, so some considerations to bear in mind in this regard are the listener-to-stream ratio and the save rate, which can be studied the Spotify for Artists app.
- Listen to your lead song's radio on Spotify and **examine which artists** are on the list. Make a note of the artists who sound like your style (disregard those who don't) and the names of their songs. Create a playlist that features those artists and the songs listed on your radio. It could be called 'Sounds that Inspire Me/Us', 'Songs with Our Vibe' or something of this nature. These artists can help you to align your music with an audience through collaborative filtering.
- Once you have created the playlist, **post it on social media and tag each act** that you have playlisted.
- Undertake the above activities regularly. It is **good PR** and a positive step to take in your social media channels; this can also aid algorithmic alignment.
- Create a **playlist that only features your music**. In due course, the digital streaming platforms will identify songs that are similar. Apply the tips above to those artists.
- Use social media to encourage your listeners to **listen to the playlists that feature your music** rather than visiting your profile to listen to your music. Share any playlists that you are featured on through your social media channels.
- Get your music into as many **blogs and forums** as possible. Use centralised platforms such as SubmitHub or Musosoup. This is often a more time-efficient process and yields quicker results for many artists. Also,

DOI: 10.4324/9781003452119-30

pitch for internet radio stations. It doesn't matter if people are not tuning in or reading. It matters that a **web presence is being created and scanned.**

- Understand with pinpoint precision **what your primary genre is** and then **identify two secondary genres.** Ask others for their opinions on this subject. Try to avoid unrecognisable creative names for genres, such as 'jazzy pop' or 'gritty rock'. Identify the correct genres and use them in your metadata. A helpful exercise to understand genre alignment more effectively is by using Google to better understand categorisation. For instance, it could be hard to define Post Malone's genre, but a quick Google search for 'What genre is Post Malone?' will tell you that he is widely recognised as sitting in two genres: hip hop/rap and country.

- Try to build an understanding of **which other artists are like you.** This helps you to understand how to feed the right data to your distributor. An effective way of doing this is to allow Spotify to help you to understand your marketplace. Click on the profile of an artist who is like you in style. Then click on 'Fans Also Like'. Identify which artists are similar to you in that list and then repeat this process on their profiles. This will help you to refine your understanding of where you best sit and who you align with. You might be surprised by the results or you might find yourself nodding along in agreement – it depends on how well you know your own genre.

- **Fill out your bio** with sufficient detail on streaming platform profiles. However mysterious and cool it might look to have an empty bio, it could be damaging your discovery if it's empty. Try to be professional and polite, and fill it out in the third person. Focus on who you are, where you're from, what music you make and what plans you have moving forward.

27
Sampling and Being Sampled: The Culture of Permission

Sampling Recordings

If a producer takes a sample of a copywritten recording and uses it in their work, there is nothing morally or legally flawed about this, provided that permission is sought and granted. Creative sampling is an artform and the ability to re-interpret and repurpose sections of a song has long been a respected outlet of creativity. However, there is not a single exception where permission can be ignored. There is often a misunderstanding among some creators that if a sample of a recording is used but is barely recognisable, this use is acceptable. That is not the case. With advancements in software – particularly in analytical technologies – it is perfectly possible to trace the origins of one piece of audio inside another, so historical sampling is now easier to identify.

Certain types of software can take the waveform of a song and split it into separate categories, which allows for the isolation of vocals, drums and musical instrument parts. Some creators may think that because this is technically possible, they can reinterpret a song in part or whole and gain commercial or underground notoriety for it. This is unfair to both the rights holders of the recording and the copyright controllers of the composition. Even if an original recording is sampled and warped or re-pitched in such a way that the original recording is less recognisable, it is still an infringement against the rights holder of the recording if it is used for commercial gain.

As technologies advance further in the future, it is important that music creators respect the copyrights of others in the same way that they would expect others to respect theirs. Obtaining permission and even understanding who the correct rights holders are can be a difficult task; therefore, some creators tend to put off dealing with these issues unless and until problems arise further down the line. This is a mistake. It is comparable to writing a song with someone and not obtaining their permission for its use. It could be argued that in an era of continual advancements in internet technologies and data access, it is

DOI: 10.4324/9781003452119-31

becoming easier for creators who wish to sample recordings use search engines and databases to identify and communicate with rights holders.

A much easier and cleaner way for music creators to use samples in their work is through the use of royalty-free samples which are cleared for commercial use upon receipt of a licence and created solely for the purpose of using them in song projects. These can be accessed in a variety of ways, ranging from genre and mood theme packs to single sounds that relate to a specific need. A range of digital stores and platforms cater to this market. However, many producers and DJs prefer to listen to complete songs in order to identify specific sounds and expressions that can be reinterpreted for new and original song projects. This is the same artform as 'crate digging': when DJs and producers search through vinyl records from various genres to hunt for hooks, musical passages and grooves in rare tracks by lesser-known artists. It is perhaps a form of talent scouting, it could be suggested. Web-based platforms such as www.Tracklib. com offer a monthly subscription to a growing catalogue of records that are all available with instant clearance. The business model used respects the rights holders of the recordings in addition to the compositional rights, which is evidenced by their approach to micro-licence payments for the recordings and a partial copyright split to the original creators. It is often the case that music creators who sample recordings are not directly looking to infringe copyrights but simply do not know the protocols for sample clearance, so platforms such as www.Tracklib.com are the perfect option.

Incorporating Parts of Known Songs into Yours Without Using the Original Recording

The term 'sample' is sometimes used inaccurately. It is often used to describe a song that incorporates a portion of another song but which does not include the original recording. The term 'sample' is relevant only if the new recording uses a section of an original recording. If a new song is composed that includes a portion of a different song which is a newly recorded version, this does not infringe the rights of the original artist because the original recording was not used. However, it does infringe the copyright of the song. The steps for clearance of the use of the original composition will depend on your geographic location, as this is something which varies from territory to territory. The key thing to identify is how significant the portion of the original song is in the new song. Some territories have fair dealing exceptions to copyright infringements while others have a zero-tolerance policy. In the USA, a mechanical licence can be purchased from the Harry Fox Agency in order to cover a song that is released on digital stores. In some countries, digital service providers (DSPs) (eg, Spotify, Apple Music) have their own mechanical copyright protocols in place which offer clearance. Some digital distributors also have access to mechanical clearance. However, a global release for a song that incorporates the copyright to a portion of a different song can be problematic, due to jurisdictional differences from country to country. Communicating with the controller of the song copyright is often advisable. Most commonly, this will be a music publisher or a songwriter. If this correct protocol is not adhered to, the creator of the new song may find that the DSPs credit the song to the original creator, even though their creative work represents only a portion of the new song. In time, this is an issue which will perhaps be standardised around the world; but until then, research and actionable steps will be needed.

Sampling Sonic Artefacts for Sound Design

Some composers and producers use recorded sounds as raw sound to create new music. There is nothing particularly new about this. The concept of *musique concrète*, which does exactly this, dates back to the 1940s. When sounds are mangled through sonic manipulation and creative audio signal processes, it could be strongly argued that the audio takes a new form – rather like melting down old gold to make new jewellery. The same rules apply where the permission of rights holders of original recording materials is required. However, this is a much more complex subject to try to regulate. If we add the concept of wavetable synthesis to the mix, it becomes even more complex. Wavetable synthesis is an approach which is used widely by numerous chart-topping music creators all over the world. A wavetable synthesiser is in essence a sample-based synthesiser that uses a recorded piece of audio (a waveform) inside an oscillator to drive a sound. The sound can be manipulated and modified in a variety of ways and periodic pieces of the waveform are repeated in a cycle. The sound is then blended with other aspects of a synthesiser to create a new and unique sound. In theory, it is possible to import a sample of a vocal from a song by major label recording artist and use it to start a sound design pursuit. The copyright on something like this is a grey area, because there is no real way of detecting this capability. The advice to music creators is to tread carefully in this rapidly evolving field of music creation. While creative software capabilities often lead the way, the analytical capabilities are never far behind.

Being Sampled by Others

Let's now flip our view on the subject. Instead of looking through the lens of those who sample, let's explore the position of those who are sampled. Once again, the two areas of intellectual property that need to be explored are the rights of the recording copyright and the rights of the compositional copyright. One metric that is often used to try to calculate a measurement of fairness is the length of the sample being used. Another is the sample's significance within the arrangement of the song. A one-second snippet of a sample that appears only once in a song in the background would perhaps be considered to be quite different from an eight-second sample that is used consistently and prominently as a hook in three choruses of a song. Time can be manipulated if sped up. An eight-second sample could become a five-second sample if its speed is increased. In some music creative processes, this may also affect the pitch of the sample and, to some extent, the identity and the compositional use. A line from a verse could be reimagined to become a prominent hook in a chorus. Cases like this can involve creativity on the part of both the original creator and the edited creator, with an amicable approach to fairness being the goal. The trouble is, of course, that it is somewhat subjective. Cases vary significantly and it is difficult to establish a standardised approach to unity and understanding on a subject that is so heavily customisable. What is clear, though, is that this is a subject which always needs to be explored, and that starts with a culture of permission and good etiquette. The rights of the rights holder of the recording and the rights of the rights holders of the composition always need clearance.

Part 5

An Exploration of Income Streams for Music Creators

28
Paths of Profit for Music Creators

These are exciting and enterprising times for performers, songwriters, composers, producers, bands, DJs and sound designers. This book has already explored the traditional income streams that relate to the intellectual property of music creation; so let's explore the additional income streams that are available and the roles that creators can play in relation to the songs of other creators.

Licensing Unique Content in the Context of Songs Created by Others

Perhaps there are songwriters who don't quite know what to do with their songs? Perhaps some of the songs they create just don't sit right in their own artist project? Perhaps they have ideas for hooks and choruses that could be used by others in their songs?

Perhaps there are performers who have mastered their instrument of choice and have no idea of how useful this could be on other people's records? Perhaps their ability to find the right musicians around them limits their understanding of how they could 'put themselves out there'?

Perhaps there are beat makers and producers with a keen interest in unique sound design, sample manipulation, loop creation and track creation? Perhaps those producers could be creating the building blocks for the songs of others?

Sample Packs

The sample pack marketplace has boomed over the last 15 years. For those less familiar with the concept, a sample pack is a digital pack of sounds that are copyright free and can be purchased and used by anyone without the need for copyright clearance. Packs can range from vocals to guitar, bass, genre-specific

DOI: 10.4324/9781003452119-33

construction kits of chopped-up song segments, culturally specific percussion sounds and much more. There are a host of labels that deal solely with the distribution, marketing and collection of sample packs, in the same way as a regular record company does. Also similarly to regular music distribution methods, creators can always self-release their content through their own e-commerce and social media channels without the need for a label or distributor. Sample packs can be a useful source of income for creators and can double up as a marketing asset, especially if the creator is an artist. Many sample labels have their own stores where their packs can be purchased and downloaded for a fee; but in recent years, there has been a market shift towards centralised platforms such as Splice, where producers can dig through thousands of packets for a monthly fee.

Beat Leasing and Licensing

Beat licensing has become increasingly prominent over the last 20 years, perhaps closing in on the point of market saturation; and yet the need for that next big track is ever-present in the global monster genre of hip hop and its various sub-genres. The market leader for beat licensing is Beatstars, where producers can lease or license their instrumental tracks to rappers for a fee. Platforms such as Beatstars are becoming very similar to mainstream streaming platforms such as Spotify, in that traction feeds visibility and putting in the graft with regular releases reaps rewards if done correctly. Unlike Spotify, it is possible to pay premium rates to increase visibility and gain promotion, as the platform boasts tools that help producers to build more momentum. This is perhaps comparable to podcasts, in that putting in the time with regular high-quality content and continually feeding through new product without any off-season are the keys to success.

Sample Libraries and Sampled Instruments

Unlike sample packs, which are downloadable waveforms of sampled sounds, sample libraries are genre or instrument-specific playable instruments in software form. Imagine being able to play a yuequin, an oud or a blues harmonica. Now imagine having those skills at your fingertips in software form. Sampling a player's technique in the form of phrases, one shots and loops can establish the basis of a sample library that can be very useful to creators all over the world. This same philosophy can be applied to a range of performers, from guitarists to drummers to mandolin players. Imagine a vocalist with a bunch of song releases, a sample pack range and a sample library of their vowel sounds in the public domain. The stock of that singer just rose and they can now charge premium rates.

Plugin Design and the Pre-set Marketplace

Much like the world of video creation, the demand for software plugins in music is continual. There is always a need for new ideas, but what is particularly pleasing is how much easier it is becoming for emerging producers to design their own and take them to market. There are also producers who use their creativity to create new and interesting sounds within existing software synthesisers. This skill is a marketable one, as pre-set packages for plugins are always in demand as genres come in and out of fashion.

Acapella Licensing and Topline Songwriting

The skill of creating lyrics and combining them with melodies will always be sought after by composers, producers and DJs. A great number of people in this world can sing but perhaps lack an understanding of how to monetise their skills outside of the traditional routes. Creating acapella versions of original songs is a solid pathway for those who are comfortable with the idea of a producer or DJ taking their vocal stem and getting creative with it. Songwriting is something that comes easily to some creators; and if those creators can distance themselves from their creative output with enough objectivity to their craft, they will see that there is a market that is ripe for their ideas.

Collaboration

Like many other aspects of music creation, working in partnership can often be the key creating useful content for the benefit of others. If a singer or guitarist does not have their own means of recording themselves, they could go to a studio to record their samples or perhaps even work in a partnership agreement with a producer who can do the work that they can't. The performer and producer can conclude a written agreement on a revenue split, rather like how a song split works, with some or no money changing hands. On the flipside, a producer may want to talent scout for opportunities to collaborate on sample-based projects. Perhaps there is a vocalist you think would sound great in software form; or perhaps there is an amazing saxophonist that you see busking in your town. These could be the basis for sample packs or sample libraries that can benefit not only the parties involved in their creation, but also those who download and use the products in their own projects.

29
Working for Hire

Remote working was nothing new to many music creators when the Covid-19 pandemic hit in 2020. The flexibility that a creator enjoys in being able to offer their services from anywhere in the world at any point in time that is convenient for them has transformed how music creators operate. Due to advances in software, portable recording systems and the extensive knowledge readily available for free on YouTube, musicians are increasingly turning their hobby into a profession.

Much as for song submissions for blogs and playlists, centralised platforms are leading the way, providing not only sophisticated e-commerce tools but also the reassurance of a recognised system to regulate compliance, complaints and customer care. Working directly through external communication with total strangers always comes with an element of risk, which is somewhat mitigated by platforms such as www.soundbetter.com and www.airgigs.com, which allow creators to thrive in this expanding marketplace.

Key factors to consider when trading include the following.

Your Offer

It might sound rather simple, but a creator's offer should be very clear from the outset. 'I sing and write toplines for dance music,' for instance, is both genre and skill specific. 'I am open to any genre and can play lots of instruments' may struggle to make an impact on these platforms as it's a little too broad, however true it may be. Be sure to state the skill and the offer to those who may wish to book you.

A Tiered Level of Options

Those who create a tiered level of options tend to do better in this marketplace. For instance, a vocalist and topline writer could tier their services like this:

DOI: 10.4324/9781003452119-34

- Lead vocal recording: £250 per song (re-recording a provided demo vocal).
- Lead vocal recording and topline songwriting: £400 per song with 50% of the songwriting split.
- Additional double track vocals: £60.
- Additional backing/harmony vocals: £70.
- Eight-bar hook only: £100 and 25% of the songwriting split.
- Optional extras: Vocal tuning £50 per song.

A producer is capable of creating a track, but they may also have other services they could offer, such as the following:

- Full production: £600 per track (master rights buyout but named credit required).
- Mix only: £200 per track (stems provided by the creator).
- Mastering only: £100 per track (stereo interleaved WAV file required).
- Audio tuning only: £50 per audio track (vocal, guitar, etc).

Here is an example for a guitarist:

- All guitar parts (acoustic and electric) for an entire track: £300 per song.
- Electric rhythm parts only: £120 per song.
- Lead guitar only: £120 per song.
- Acoustic guitar: £150 per song.
- Custom options: Contact for pricing on specific requests such as fixed eight-bar loops.

As you can see from the above hypothetical examples, creators can break down the types of services they offer rather than simply setting a single price. This also gives the purchaser the flexibility of paying only for what they need to be done (eg, depending on whether they are starting a project from scratch or perhaps just need additional parts for an existing project).

Price Point

I have included hypothetical fees above. Creators can set whatever charges they feel are appropriate for their level of skill, experience and credentials. It is always worth researching an appropriate price point by exploring what others charge for similar services, rather like how eBay sellers operate. Market value is subjective but can often be understood by studying the wider marketplace.

Turnaround Time

How quickly creators can turn around a project is of paramount importance. This is one of the key facets that wins business. So many of the opportunities in this marketplace need fast turnarounds or deadlines that are set in advance. Having a diary and being organised are essential when managing bookings.

Rights

There are some considerations in regard to creator's rights that need to be thought through:

- **Compositional share:** If songwriting has taken place in some form or another, it is important for creators to build this into their offering in the form of an expected percentage in addition to the fee required. This is the case if lyrics, harmony or melody has been incorporated into the performance. This will affect songwriters, vocalists who contribute towards the songwriting or producers and musicians who contribute towards any of the three mentioned elements of compositions. Melodic input may need to be substantial to warrant any rights. For instance, where a guitarist or synth player provides a melodic section, in some people's eyes, this could constitute songwriting. For others, this would fall under the category of arrangement and a fee would effectively buy out any songwriting claim by the musician. In all cases, a creator's offer must be transparent regarding any expectation of songwriting splits.
- **Recorded performance:** Where a musician is paid to create a part on a recording, it is often assumed that, because their time has been covered by a fee, their rights have been bought out and therefore no other income can be generated by the musician if the song gains big success. However, it is possible that a musician could retain a portion of any neighbouring rights royalties or digital performance royalties that arise in the future if the agreement is not clear on this. It's therefore important that creators clarify this issue in their offering. In many cases, this marketplace tends to lean towards musicians and musical parts being bought out and waiving their rights by agreeing to a fee; but this is not always clear and it should be.
- **Master rights:** If a producer is being hired to create a track, it is important that the producer makes their offer clear. If their offer is to create an entire track for a buyout fee, that is clear. However, if producers charge a fee and retain 2%–5% of the master rights, this needs to be built into their offer so that purchasers understand exactly what they are investing in. Often referred to as 'points', meaning percentage points, some producers like to add

this into their offer so that they gain a piece of the profits further down the line should the production become successful. It might be fair to say that this is now moving out of fashion, particularly in the online marketplace; but it needs to be clear nevertheless.

Revisions

It may be that the purchaser comes back to the creator to ask for changes to be made to what they have recorded. These are known as 'revisions'. It's important for creators to try to limit the number of revisions that they build into their offer. Some people offer unlimited revisions, but this can be a risky business if you have a very picky customer. Others offer two or three, while others offer five or more. The risk comes if you are constantly communicating back and forth, with hardly an end in sight to the project. This can be avoided by stating a clear number of revisions and an additional fee for further revisions if necessary. This can help purchasers to be more succinct because they know they will be charged extra if they keep coming back and forth continually.

Virtual Attendance and Video Assistance

A growing trend for some creators is to offer the purchaser the chance to attend a remote session through a video call or chat facility which allows them to hear how the project is progressing. A creator that intends to provide this facility will need to have this functionality available and should list it in their offer. While many do, others don't. Also, many purchasers don't want or need this option, as they prefer simply to place their trust in the creator. A more popular option is for the creator to offer a video call before a session takes place and perhaps after completion of the project to discuss revisions. This may not always be required or necessary, but more and more creators are now offering video calls.

Building a Sense of Uniqueness

The creators who thrive in this marketplace are those with consistency and a sense of uniqueness. Uniqueness can take the form of the ability to play a specialist instrument or having a particular tonal quality or a specific sonic signature. Standing out from the crowd will always be a battle, particularly when you're new to a platform, so it's worth considering what your uniqueness is in the online marketplace.

Bio

A bio is an important component of a creator's profile for any platform, but it's particularly significant here as the space to sell a service. This is often where a creator's selling pitch is located, so quite a lot of detail is required – not only about the creator, but also about their offer. Photos are important. It's human nature for people to want to see who they're paying, if possible. What tends to work particularly well in this marketplace are action shots and photos that portray the creator as humble and approachable, rather than what you might use on a Spotify artist profile – for instance, smiles rather than a moody artistic headshot.

Showreel

It's crucial to provide evidence of your capabilities. Audio clips and songs are expected. Showreels that display a sense of both variety and cohesion tend to do well. Videos are a bonus but only if they're relevant.

Genre Specialism

It can be hard for multi-genre creators to understand the importance of genre specialism in the context of a short pitch. It's important to balance this against not wanting to undersell someone's varied capabilities. It's fair to say, however, that many of those who thrive in the remote session world are known for their style, as these become the go-to people for their genre.

It's Not About You

When assisting the creative vision of another creator, it is difficult to refrain from doing what you do in the way that you normally do it. Sometimes, this works well. However, it is also important to remember to give people what they want and not what you think they need. Providing options is often welcome, but it can be a difficult and yet essential part of the gig to suppress one's own thoughts in order to achieve the goals of others.

Seasonality

Year-round availability is not something that all creators wish to offer. For example, many creators may not wish to be booked online during the summer festival season. Building in off-seasons on most platforms is quite an easy and straightforward part of the process; bookings can be reactivated when the creator becomes available again. There may be certain points in time when a creator wishes to be busier than usual. Soundbetter is a particularly good platform for those types of creators, as premium membership allows for access to a wide array of projects that can be pitched for by creators.

Encouraging Reviews

As on any algorithmic platform in the digital age, positive reviews feed further visibility and build trust in potential customers. It is always worth trying to softly encourage a good review where possible, although perhaps without being pushy about it.

Etiquette

The way in which people conduct themselves on these platforms is of paramount importance. A bad experience can leave a bad taste and people talk. Most of the points above relate to a creator's hard skill set and their ability to sell and deliver, but the reality is that communication is critical to a successful remote project. This not only means being polite, kind and warm, but also being prompt in response times.

Much like many other aspects of the music industry, trusted relationships and networks can expand in this type of marketplace and can often lead to further projects outside of the platforms once connections are made. Many vocalists and musicians are now thriving in positions of power thanks to their presence and profiles in the online session marketplace.

Interview: Natalie Major, Singer-Songwriter, USA

Natalie Major is a USA-based singer-songwriter who has created an impressive career for herself by diversifying the range of services she offers. Natalie is a recording artist, a songwriter, a vocalist, a media composer and a sample pack contributor.

You are a fine example of a modern music professional who has used their skills to create multiple outlets for their creativity. How have your ideals evolved since you first started your career?

Songwriting and singing have created quite the journey for me professionally and personally. I moved to New York when I was 20 to pursue my career choice but I didn't have any idea of what I was going to do. I just knew that I would pursue music.

Then I moved to Los Angeles and put a lot of ads on Craigslist to be a demo singer so that singing would become my main source of income. This later evolved into me generating work on freelance websites by being hired to be a songwriter and sing for others.

Over the years, I have found that working remotely with people from all over the world is rewarding. I am currently focused on creating more content for TV, film and commercials.

Do you ever use pseudonyms or just operate under one artist name?

My name, Natalie Major, is a pseudonym because my legal last name is Ukrainian and hard to pronounce, so I changed it to my stage name in 2009.

I also have other projects under different pseudonyms, one being 'Cadence XYZ'. This was to avoid having lots of projects under my original stage name of Natalie Major.

I also have a project called 'Foxxi', which is sassy female pop music which has been successfully used in many TV shows, films and commercials.

When recording vocals remotely, do you usually deliver dry vocals or do you also offer extra services such as audio tuning and effects when delivering your stems to a client?

Often, I record from home and deliver dry vocals unless otherwise requested. I usually send all vocals tuned and if the client requests, I'll send them treated.

Do you find that you channel your songwriting differently for your own artistic projects than when toplining for other artists?

Yes – my songwriting is personal to me and that is what fulfils me creatively more than being hired to topline for others.

I try to stay balanced in that mindset, but often it is difficult to be creative towards my own projects after putting all my creative energy into another project.

My toplining process starts similarly to all my projects: I mumble melodies and words to come up with the result.

Lyrically, I fit words to the melodies that I create; but in my own projects, I am usually speaking about a deep, personal experience.

What is your approach to creating sample packs?

I've been approached by several companies to do sample packs; they can be tedious. The packs usually consist of different hooks, phrases and adlibs.

Whoever is directing me will usually give me a list of what is needed for the sample pack (eg, 10 energetic chorus hooks, 25 adlibs).

Usually for me, a sample pack is done over the course of several weeks.

30
The Self-recording Musician

Self-recording musicians require a range of skills, one of which is the ability to record and deliver their work using recording software and hardware. It is in many ways expected that music creators will know how to record themselves; but for some, this is a terrifying prospect.

The key is to understand what is required for the creator's offer. If a guitarist, for instance, needs to know how to record their parts and deliver them to the highest standard, they need only develop those particular skills. It is not the same as being the producer or mix engineer of an overall song. The basics of recording audio parts can be achieved using a wide variety of audio interfaces together with software that is more affordable today than ever.

At a time when there are fewer studios and yet more demand for music creation than ever before, it makes perfect sense for music creators to be able to record their work in a self-sustainable manner that yields a professional outcome.

Not all remote creators need the most expensive equipment. Some do not even need audio recording equipment at all. There are plenty of skilled sound designers, synth players and producers who work entirely using software.

Interview: Misstiq, Music Producer and Content Creator, Australia

Misstiq is a music producer and content creator from Melbourne, Australia. She has an impressive CV, having worked with A-list artists including Bring Me the Horizon and the Amity Affliction, as well as many other artists from diverse genres all around the globe. Misstiq specialises in content creation and session work using classical piano, choir and orchestral arrangements and modern synth/electronics, in addition to creating remixes.

DOI: 10.4324/9781003452119-35

On top of session/production work, Misstiq is known for creating promotional content for prominent music/audio software and hardware brands including Sennheiser, ROLI, DistroKid, Bandlab and many more.

You play a role whereby you 'spice up' tracks that are sent to you by an array of music creators. What kind of loops, stems or parts do you usually add to creators' projects?

When I 'spice up' artists' tracks, I can write and add orchestral instruments, piano, choir, ambiences, modern synths and industrial percussive elements. Usually, clients more or less know how they would like me to approach their songs; however, sometimes they give me very little or no guidance. Some producers can be annoyed with that, but I happen to think it's really cool that they can trust me. I feel like that trust comes from the fact that I have cultivated and curated my brand very effectively, so that clients essentially know what I can provide and expect me to do a great job.

On the other hand, there are clients that are super-picky or have low written communication skills when drafting revision notes. I'm glad that I have patience and understanding with these types of people because, after all, everyone is different in how they communicate and furthermore, client satisfaction is the foundation of my business. I always want to go above and beyond.

Do you predominantly offer a fee-based service where your intellectual property is bought out or do you take a split of rights?

I normally work as an artist for hire, so a fee-based service. People pay me 50% to lock them into my schedule. The remaining 50% is paid once they're happy with what I've written and are ready to receive their final files. Occasionally, I am given a split of rights when offered or when I request it for a bigger work, like a remix or rendition. Splits are a great incentive for me to continuing posting about and promoting the song.

How do creators usually expect you to deliver files to them and in what format?

The files I deliver for my features are WAV stems, MIDI and a full reference song (demo). The bands I work with always have their own producer. That way, all their mixes are cohesive.

Because I don't get myself bogged down in the mixing/mastering side of things, it allows me to focus my energy on writing music and creating social media content. Once I hear the final track, I often find myself pleased with how my contributions have been mixed into the song. However, occasionally there are times when I feel disappointed with aspects of the final mix.

The reality is that when I'm contributing to a song, I may have a completely different vision of how prominent or ambient a certain section is, but this comes with the territory of being an artist for hire. I can't control the quality of the finished product.

For example, I often find myself working on a feature for a band and feeling proud of how my contributions have shaped the song. Upon release, I will hear the final mix for the first time and barely be able to hear my additions. This can potentially create an uncomfortable situation for me when the band then asks me to promote the song, as I lose my enthusiasm for the collaboration when my contributions are barely audible in the mix.

If I'm doing a remix, I always get the song mixed in-house. For my remixes, I work very hard to make them perfect. They have many layers and subtle embellishments, so having control of the final mix is essential. When I create a remix, I usually insist on having a trusted colleague mix/master the final release.

How does the role of social media impact your presence and services?

Social media is a fantastic way to build a brand. It's what kicked off my career as Misstiq and it remains the number one gateway to grow my business. I ensure that all my videos are high quality and that the aesthetics of my pages (especially Instagram) are meticulously curated. I stay active and post engaging and relevant content. I believe that this effort and dedication really shines through in my work and is essential for building trust with fans and potential clients. When you're consistently delivering material that is entertaining and high quality, clients can see that you're solid and possess the skills that are necessary to take their project to the next level. When a project that I've worked on is released, I spread the news via social media, which then brings in more clients. You never know who is watching you!

My biggest collaboration/achievement to date was generated by social media. I have had the opportunity and honour to work with Bring Me the Horizon simply because Oli Sykes found me on TikTok experimenting with orchestral sounds for metal music and asked me to contribute my signature choirs to their new track. The greatest thing about social media is that I can create engaging content, which leads to clients; clients lead to income; I then spread the word and the machine continues to grow and maintain itself.

What changes have you witnessed in the session work sector since you first started?

The most prominent changes that I have noticed within the session work sector is that the bigger and more successful artists are often collaborating with several producers/session artists on their songs.

When I began in metal, collaborations were rare. There are many classic metal albums that don't even have a vocal feature. The game has changed. The bigger artists often have a dozen or more producers putting their touch to a song before the track is sent off to mix.

Some music fans/artists view having this much outside help as cheating, but I believe that collaboration and joint creation are some of the most beautiful things about making music. I'm so proud to have created a business for myself where I get to do this every day.

It is inspiring to hear Misstiq's views on her work: she offers insight into her philosophy, her values and her perspective on her output in the context of other creators' songs. She has her own sonic identity as a producer and arranger, while also impacting the music of others. While she clearly respects and loves the genres of rock and metal, she is challenging the boundaries of the traditional cultures attached to them by playing a sometimes subtle yet crucial role in the development of so many acts all over the world through the art of collaboration. She is a fine example of a music professional who has used her skills to carve a niche and shape a market around her. So much, if not all, of Misstiq's work can be achieved remotely.

Let's now see how this compares with a UK-based session drummer who has also created additional services around his primary role.

Interview: Martin 'Magic' Johnson, Freelance Drummer, UK

Martin 'Magic' Johnson is a worldwide touring and recording musician with his own recording studio, providing remote drum recording sessions for artists, labels and producers from all over the world. Touring and recording credits include Guthrie Govan, B*Witched, Jo Harman, Mike Farris (US Grammy winner), Lucky Peterson (US Grammy winner), Lee Latchford-Evans (Steps), Dennis Stratton (Iron Maiden), Connor Selby, Conor Reeves, Paul Carrack, Bay City Rollers, Praying Mantis and Sari Schorr, among others.

Think back to when you first started your career. How did it move from a hobby to a career?

I often say that I work hard at 'not having a proper job'! I put the hours in and I work hard, but it's because I want to give my best, and this career I have is basically a hobby that has got out of control! When exactly did this 'hobby' turn into a career? I can't give a moment or timespan – and it is still a 'hobby' in many ways; but fortunately, I now make a living out of it.

If you are serious about something, you'll need to be willing to study it. It's about developing the skill sets you need and the regular education that comes with that; but you also need to be able to consume and absorb everything that is related to your passion. I read every word of all the major drum and music magazines. I studied all the personnel credits of songs that inspired me and dug out as much info as I could find, and tried to copy and emulate those players. That passion and commitment meant that my hobby then went on to become a career path.

What skills did you need to transition from musician to musical director?

In my experience, there are a few things that can get you asked by management and artists to be the musical director (MD) for an artist – and they have little to do with music theory knowledge! Mostly it's down to having a big mouth and big ears!

By 'big ears', I mean attention to detail, but also the ability to see the overview of a song. As drummers, we spend years at the back of the stage, supporting the band, and we naturally get a macro/overview perspective of the sum of the parts. It also helps that we can witness audience reactions – it gives us a holistic perspective. Also, as a drummer, part of the job is 'driving the bus', as it were: helping the band to navigate song structure, form and dynamics. So, a drummer is quite well placed to be an MD. A balance needs to be struck between the ability to stay aligned to 'the common good' for the song and the ability to zone in on the detail. Serving the music and egoless playing (from myself and the band) are crucial.

By 'big mouth', I mean my ability to make decisions, voice them, not be afraid to discuss options with the artist/musicians and then offer a decision. I think it's important for an artist to know and trust that you are just wanting to make it better for the whole show/production and the balance as an MD is being supportive, partly compliant, but also not afraid to voice opinions.

Music theory, while useful, is not a requirement to be an MD. However, music knowledge is. The ability to reference other artists for comparisons and influences is often useful to those around me.

As an MD, I'm dealing with professional musicians who themselves have in-depth theory knowledge. They know what works theoretically and most of the time musically so, as an MD, I'm often suggesting or deciding on suggestions with the overarching thought not of 'Does this conform to theory?', but instead, 'Does this sound good?'

The other important thing is preparation. All serious musicians should be prepped to the following level: don't practise/prepare to where you can get the song right; practise until you can't get it wrong. There's a big difference between those two things. As an MD, you must have knowledge of all the other parts as well as your own. In my experience, any artist who I MD for, the last parts I learn or take care of are the drum parts – the parts I'm playing! This can compromise my own playing sometimes, but as an MD it's all about getting everyone else comfortable before yourself.

You are very active in the world of recorded music. When recording and sending drum tracks to clients, do you tend to hire studios or do you have your own professional recording set-up?

These days, 80% of my recording sessions are from my own studio. Many years ago, I could see how the industry – with the aid of technology – was changing, so I invested time and money in designing and building my own studio and equipping it with gear that could contend with large format studios.

All digital audio workstations pretty much do the same thing. The choice is now about your own personal preference. However, the place to make a difference is in the mic preamps. I have mic preamps from Neve, API, Audient and Trident desks in my studio. All the tonal gains from these preamps, as opposed to built-in interfaces, add up. This is especially true when sending 16-plus tracks of drum stems to producers. Having mic preamps that rival large format recording consoles, together with knowledge of microphone choice, microphone placement, drum skin tuning and awareness of how the tones sit in the mix, is important to what I do.

Having a remote recording facility enables me to provide way more instrument drum/mic choices, as I have a warehouse worth of gear at my disposal. The drawback is that this way of working can often feel like a solitary pursuit. I miss the interactions from musicians and producers 'in the moment'.

You are also a well-respected senior lecturer and a highly qualified academic. Can you give any examples of where your professional music projects have helped to provide understanding in the classroom to your students?

Everything I teach is practical and relevant. It has all been used or is used every day as part of my skillset in my career. It is difficult to provide specific examples, as there are so many. For every challenge or question that a student raises, I can not only usually provide a solution, but often also recall a real-life situation that involved the issue.

I try to get students to see the value of creating cheat sheets. Sometimes they don't see the value of this and would rather play by recall only. However, I then explain the countless times when I've been called out on a tour at the last minute and have had to 'learn' 20–40 songs. There's no way – even with the best memory – you could absolutely nail that number of songs and be the musical bus driver without the ability to make some cheat sheets. This is even more so the case if playing to a click track that is synced with visuals.

The important thing to remember is that a cheat sheet is not a transcription. You are not burying your head in a written chart. It's about having the structure, the key grooves and hits of the song in a form that enables you to glance at the page and securely navigate through the song with success. There are often no rehearsals, so it is entirely possible that the first time you might ever play that song is in front of 10,000 people or being broadcast to millions round the world!

The other important thing, which relates to my point about preparation made earlier, is to be able to get the song to a place where you cannot possibly play it incorrectly. It's about having the song so well prepped that the parts are indelibly etched on your muscle fibres. An example of how this can help is walking out on stage on an arena tour and firing the click and then realising that your whole in-ear monitor mix has gone down. You cannot hear any of the band or vocals, except the delayed slap-back echo from the PA. In this situation, knowing the song inside out and being able to hum/sing the rest of the parts in your head while performing enables you to get through it without making a fuss. On the occasions that this has happened to me, the rest of the band have had no idea of the issues and have been happily oblivious to the problem. If you want to be a professional musician, this is the level you need to be at.

What advice would you give to emerging music creators who wish to follow a similar path to you?

My honest advice is to say yes to everything and worry about it afterwards! This is especially true when starting out and trying to forge a career. Then ask yourself, 'Can I do the job?' and if you are aware of shortcomings in your skill set, address these immediately. Obviously, this doesn't work for all situations; but the important thing is to keep your eyes and ears open to new opportunities and take a risk and worry about it afterwards.

I started out just wanting to play drums as a freelance session player across multiple styles. However, I have become reactive to my surroundings and have built new skills. I am now not just a freelance drummer but also an MD, a tour manager, a producer, a mix engineer, an arranger, a musical 'fixer', a composer with my own publishing and an educator across instrumental teachings, music production and module design work.

It is clear to see Martin's evolution and his ability to show courage when he could have cowered away from opportunities for fear of not feeling ready. His philosophy towards preparation will be shared by many professional musicians; but it is also interesting that so much of his recording work has moved into the remote setting instead of traditional recording studios. It could perhaps be assumed that if Martin had not evolved as he did, he may have lost a great deal of the work that he has since gained. It is not only his ability to deliver on time that appeals to clients, but also the quality he offers – and not just at the performance level. He has effectively reverse-engineered his output from what would be achieved in a commercial recording studio and can now achieve that in his own project studio.

31
The Sync Business

An abbreviation of 'synchronisation', 'sync' relates to the business of attaching songs to TV, film, games, ads and any other use that will aid a visual source in media. Songs play a vital role in aiding visual content. This could apply to a romantic film scene that is curated by the central message of a song's chorus, a TV ad that gets a marketing message across through the emotion derived from a song's melodic riff or perhaps a videogame that uses a song as its theme. Understanding how a song aids a visual is a respected art form and it is critical for music creators to gain a good understanding of the kinds of visuals that their songs could be suitable for. This requires an understanding of the essence of a song.

The Essence of a Song

What Mood is Being Created?

Perhaps more commonly referred to as the 'vibe', the mood is the overriding emotion which attaches itself to the spirit of a song. It is one of the key factors in how the song aids a visual. Many creators may struggle to understand the key emotion of their own songwriting and may instead be more effective at judging the moods of songs that they were not involved in creating. It often takes a certain sense of objectivity and distance from a song to accurately absorb its emotional content. A songwriter could be preoccupied by the emotion they felt when they wrote the song and consider this to be its key mood, when in actuality a very different mood may be established once the song has been fully arranged, produced and mixed. Lyrics can often be a key indicator of the mood of a song, but the complexity of the chords or placement of the melody can shift the narrative quite dramatically. For instance, a romantic and melancholic lyric that talks of heartache and loss can sit inside a song that feels uplifting and hopeful if the other elements of the songwriting process

DOI: 10.4324/9781003452119-36

reflect this. A particular style of arrangement and even the music production values are also key facets that can shift how a song feels and connects with an audience.

It is crucial to understand the key mood of a song, and some are better at understanding and articulating this than others. One-word moods are important when labelling the metadata of a song, as they offer instant identity to music users who may be interested in licensing a song.

What Are the Primary and Secondary Genres of the Song?

There is a natural tendency for many music creators to pour their hearts and souls into creating a song and then figure out afterwards what style it falls under. It could be said that many music professionals do this the other way around. Neither is fundamentally right or wrong, but the latter approach generally tends to yield greater results in the sync world, as it is imperative to know which genres you are working in. This is because many music users will use search functions in music libraries to filter their approach to locating songs. If they search for 'progressive metalcore', they may be looking for an American-sounding mathematical and technical piece of music with atmospheric elements and soaring fast lead guitars to aid a documentary about extreme sports and adrenaline. Right there in that moment, that's what they need; they don't want to hear a British-sounding indie rock band who have mislabelled their song's metadata. On another day, that same music user may well want to find a British-sounding indie rock band singing about lost romance in a disco because it fits with the TV drama set in the 1990s that they're doing the music supervision on. The trouble is that same band won't be found if they have mislabelled their metadata because they didn't understand their genre definition as well as they could have. It is imperative for music creators to understand their primary and secondary genres, as these link directly to the discoverability and visibility of a song. It can be difficult to pinpoint the exact genre for some songs, but there should be a primary genre that governs a song's overall classification. If a song is a lo-fi neo-soul number with vocals and guitars, it can quite comfortably sit inside R&B as a primary genre, for instance; and then the secondary genres can be neo-soul and lo-fi. If it is a dance song with tropical-sounding marimbas and claps, the primary genre would be electronic dance music and the secondary genres would be house and dance pop. It can often be useful to use internet search engines to find out the genres of existing artists by searching for their name followed by the word 'genre'. This can lead to some interesting surprises as to how certain artists are defined in terms of genres, but it offers insight into how the digital sphere understands the styles of many music creators. It is then good to understand the key stylistic traits of your genres and the typical tempo fields that they support. This not only helps you to understand what you are selling but can also inform future creative choices.

What Songs and Artists are Similar in Style?

Many music creators have a natural inclination to be different from anyone who has come before them. This is undeniably a positive thing at a fundamental level. However, a creator's music is an incredibly tough sell if it not does not fall into a recognisable style which is at least in part comparable to other artists and songs. Being categorised by comparison is an important component of song discovery and a crucial element in sync because it is a common reference point used by music users (ie, the professionals who license music).

Typical Sync Lead Examples

Sync agents are in regular need of a specific type of sound. They get a lot of requests from various music supervisors for a range of TV shows, summarised in two short sentences – for example: 'We need **gritty rock** in the style of **The White Stripes** with a **wild** and **dangerous** attitude. Songs can be with our without vocals and should be organic in instrumentation with no electronic elements.'

A music supervisor is hired by a movie director to source songs for a film project in development. The director gives some input as to what emotional role they want and the music supervisor helps to translate this into identifiable points of reference:

> We are looking for a song that has a **quirky bedroom pop vibe** with hints of **jazz** and **boom bap**. It needs to **feel bright, youthful** and **hopeful** in the style of **Rex Orange County**. However, the movie director has also stated that the need for an **introspective** feel in the lyrics and vocals is important, as it's a coming-of-age movie that focuses on a central character. We feel that **Bruno Major** is probably a good reference point for the vocal/lyric.

This music supervision team know exactly what kind of vibe they wish to portray in this project. It's in keeping with the tone of the project that their music choices curate. They are so particular about what they want that they have referenced specific songs. You can tell by the nature of this short lead that the

TV programme is complete and the final part of the process is to find the right songs to fit within a specific timeframe.

Another example could be: 'We have a fashion show edit that needs music. It needs to be **flamboyant, edgy** and **sassy.** A hybrid between **"Girls in Bikinis" by Poppy** and **"VOID" by Melanie Martinez** would be ideal.'

Metadata in Sync

Metadata is a crucial aspect in this sector of the music business, but some of it can look a little different from the metadata that a creator would send to a digital distributor or a record company. There is a sense of urgency expected by music users when it comes to obtaining clearance for use when they wish to license a song or piece of music for a project. It is therefore important that the right data is delivered. It is a good idea for music creators to keep an Excel document of data for their song catalogue, as this provides key pieces of information that are made available to music users, who can then use web-based filters to find the type of song they are looking for together with vital information. The most commonly used pieces of metadata include the following:

- the key point of contact for clearing the rights, together with their name, email address and phone number;
- the song title;
- the artist;
- the album (if applicable);
- the copyright holders of the song, together with their full names as they appear on their passports, their Interested Party Information (IPI) numbers, their performing rights organisation (PRO) and their percentage of the split of the copyright. This should also include the names of the music publishers, their IPIs, their PROs and their percentage splits of the copyright;
- the owners of the master rights of the recording – whether an artist, a label, a manager or some other entity. If there are joint owners, their full names and their percentage of the splits are required;
- the year of release (if released);
- the song's beats per minute (BPM) and tempo field. The BPM is very helpful, as is a description field for down-tempo, mid-tempo or up-tempo;
- the lyrics. If a song contains lyrics, it is important that some of the keywords of the lyrics, story or message are entered in a specific area of the document. This is because some music users like to search by lyrics to locate specific songs. For instance, if a music supervisor is searching for a song to aid a mysterious visual of a girl holding a red balloon in a particular movie

scene that sees the introduction of a new character, a lyric that talks of mystery or perhaps even about a red balloon could be very useful to them;

- explicit lyrics. It is important to mention whether the lyrics use explicit language are clean, usually through a simple Y/N box on the document as to whether the lyrics are explicit;
- the primary genre of the song;
- at least two secondary genres that help to support the correct identification of the style of the song;
- key tags – one-word categories in hashtag style format associated with a song's identity that can quickly define the genre, mood, title or theme of the song;
- a list of one-word mood descriptors;
- the file format (eg, WAV, FLAC, MP3);
- whether the song has vocals;
- an instrument list. Some music users like to find songs by searching by instrument, so it is advisable to list as many of the prominent instruments as possible (even if they're software instruments that use either sampled or synthesised sounds); and
- samples. There is often a section asking about the use of samples. This refers to whether the song has sampled any sections of other records that have been previously released. It rarely has anything to do with the use of royalty-free sounds and loops.

Clearance

This involves clearing the use of both a song and its recording to license them for use in commercial opportunities such as TV, film, etc. A music user cannot license a song and its recording into a project until every single aspect of the song and its recording has permissions and there is transparency as to the ownership of the rights and the performances. To put it simply, a lawsuit could be filed by a rights holder against a company that uses a song without permission. This also extends to the performances on a recording. If there is a guest violinist on a recording, for instance, it is crucial that a performance release has been signed by the musician so that the recording can be used for commercial purposes.

The most important things required for clearance are the permissions of all rights holders.

The following are other key players from whom clearance is needed in the sync sector.

Figure 31.1 Rights Holders' Areas

Performers

Vocalists, musicians, programmers and anyone else who contributed to any element of a recording will need to sign a performance release. Often referred to as a 'work for hire agreement', this is a short and simple contract which outlines the agreement between the rights holders and a performer on a recording. The agreement will state:

- that the performer grants permission for their contribution to be used for commercial gain by the right holders;
- that their contribution does not include any compositional rights; and

- the fee that the performer is being paid, together with their name, address and signature.

In many cases, of course, performers do not wish to be paid for this role; perhaps they are helping a friend or trying to bolster their CV or experience. In such cases, a performance release is still required but with the fee waived or marked as zero on the performance release. When working with a licensing agent, one of the key expectations that they will have of rights holders is for them to sign off on clearance of a recording. This means that the rights holder must have a watertight agreement in place with anyone who contributed their time and expertise to the recording, no matter how minimal their role was.

Producers

Producers play a significant and often very varied role in the recording of songs. But whether the role of a producer is significant or minimal, that role must be both acknowledged and cleared through a producer release or a work for hire agreement. If a producer has been paid for their time, this does not automatically mean that they don't own any of the master rights; it all depends upon what has been agreed. In many cases, producers will be quite happy to sign off on not owning the master rights once they have been paid; but there are also many cases in which producers insist on a percentage split of the master rights in addition to their fee. This can come as a rather unwelcome surprise, especially when trying to get producers to sign a producer clearance months or even years after a recording has taken place. Therefore, it is always recommended that a written agreement be reached prior to any recording work taking place with a producer, and that they be made aware that you will expect them to sign a producer release which waives their rights upon payment. It could perhaps be that a producer works for free on a speculative basis without the need for a fee. In this case, the producer is a joint master rights holder along with the artist or act that they are working with, so a written agreement will be required for the benefit of all parties.

Engineers/Mixers

A common oversight in sync clearance is not obtaining clearance from the professionals that engineered or mixed a recording, regardless of whether they were paid a fee. In some cases, engineers and mixers are paid a flat fee or an hourly rate and are happy to sign off on clearance. However, in other cases a percentage split of the master rights may be expected. Perhaps there may even be a blend of both in other cases.

Studios/Location of Recording

This is often linked to producer or engineer clearance. Some sync agents refer to this as a 'studio release' because it can relate to both the production and location of a studio, although it is more than likely that many sync agents will be satisfied as long as the engineers' and producers' roles are cleared. It is worth noting that some colleges and universities that have music studios often expect a 5%–10% ownership stake of any recordings that take place in their facilities. This can often be in the small print of a student contract at a university. Cases such as this are rare but still need factoring in if you record in a studio that's part of an educational setting.

Additional Contributors

Any other contributors to either the recording or the composition will need to be involved in the clearance process. These could be a co-writer who didn't feature on the recording (this would be a partial rights holder); a musician who recorded a one-off part; or even groups of people who contributed to a recording, such as a choir or orchestra. Clearance is generally not required for any royalty-free loops, samples or third-party software instruments.

Preparing Your Pitch

To be ready to start pitching songs and instrumentals, it is important to consider three initial steps:

- Be ready – I mean actually ready! – if you get some interest. If you stall or panic, you might lose the interest of the music user. They need speed and efficiency. Ensure that you have all your clearances in place and that your final mix is ready.
- Prepare your files. It may well be that your song needs to be edited for specific cue points and scenes that have a specific time length constraint. It is always recommended to have shorter versions of your song and instrumental prepared. A 60-second, 30-second and even 15-second edit may be required. It may well be that the company you are dealing with is willing

and able to edit your audio as per their needs, but it is always good to be ready with the edits they need ahead of time.

- Research who you want to work with, what your offer is and what kinds of visuals your music aids. To aid further understanding, you could research what songs were used in specific TV programmes and films. www.tunefind.com is a great resource for finding out what songs were used in projects. If you know your genre, your mood and your similar artists, your next step is to understand what kinds of visuals could be aided by your music.

How to Pitch for Sync Opportunities

It is important to consider which professionals music creators should connect with when pitching music for sync. Let's explore who music creators should be working with.

Sync Agents

Possibly the most accessible professionals in this list for independent music creators are sync agents. It is their job to build a library of music that can be accessed by music users, who then identify the songs they wish to license. Sync agents are always keen to explore new creative talent that can help them find good matches for their client base of music users. Sync agents work with record labels, music publishers and independent music creators across a range of genres. It is advisable for music creators to pitch their music to sync agents along with a brief outline of how their music can aid visuals. This can help the sync agent to realise the potential in a song and where it could be placed. Sync agents can vary in scale and size from boutique genre-specific companies with a small and manageable catalogue to high-level heavyweight libraries that supply to motion picture production companies in Hollywood. While some sync agents like to work with an artist's wider body of work, most prefer to work with independent music creators on a song-by-song basis by offering a single song deal to exploit a recording. There are a range of sync agents that operate with creators on a global basis, and many can be easily found through internet search engines or on music industry listings pages.

Broker Agencies

A growing range of music sync companies aim to connect music creators with opportunities for their music by collecting and receiving leads from music users (eg, ad agencies, music supervisors) and making them accessible to independent music creators on a subscription basis. Companies such as Music Gateway, Music X-Ray and Taxi Music have established themselves in this sector and have proved to be valuable in connecting many music creators and rights holders with music sync professionals. These companies can play a crucial role for many music users, as they tend to filter out unsuitable pitches on their behalf. There is a growing trend for many brokers to implement their own diagnostics which determine the mood, theme and genre of a song; and to offer services such as a review function to determine the potential of a song pitch, together with the additional option of pitching songs to multiple music users once more data on a specific song has been established. This can be useful to some music creators, as it results in objective feedback on suitability and refinement on placement and potential users.

These types of agencies usually require a subscription to their service and sometimes a split on licensing fees. In many ways, for music creators, this option is comparable to working with a music publisher or sync agent; but you are paying them – which is not necessarily a bad thing, as you have flexibility in your rights as opposed to being restricted to one company's pathway.

Music Publishers

There are a range of avenues that a music publisher can exploit, including TV companies that create programmes for both cable and network channels, film production companies, ad agencies, videogame companies, corporate campaigns and much more. Either a music publisher will be licensed by a rights holder (songwriter) to exploit their music for sync opportunities or a songwriter will have assigned copyright control to the music publisher. In both cases, the music publisher will look to exploit songs and instrumentals for commercial purposes in a way that ensures both they and the creator benefit. The music publisher will also look at how best to administrate and collect on backend royalties from the use of songs in media projects.

Traditionally, music publishers would not have expected to see any of the upfront licence money for the use of a recording; but in recent years, many independent music publishers have begun taking a commission on the licensing of a master recording if they find the placement, rather than a sync agent. This is especially true for music creators who are not signed to a record label. This is something that can and should be negotiated in the agreement between a songwriter and a music publisher. Fundamentally, the music publisher will seek a partial split of the copyright of the song and a split of any fees that are attached to the use of the song rather than the use of the recording.

Music Supervisors

Undeniably the Holy Grail of the sync business, music supervisors are responsible for selecting and sourcing songs for TV and film. They are at the top of the chain of gatekeepers and are highly influential in their positions. Music supervision is an artform – and an admirable one at that. Consider the tension and grit that Amelia Hartley's supervision skills added to the hit TV series *Peaky Blinders*; the dramatic, regal curation that won Alexandra Patsavas her Emmy nomination for outstanding music supervision on the hit series *Bridgerton*; and Nora Felder's sublime choice of Kate Bush's 'Running Up That Hill' on Season 4 of *Stranger Things*.

The discipline of knowing which songs to choose and where to use them is defined by finesse and sublime vision. Music supervisors can break an act and change the course of their career forever. They are therefore considered to be the hardest people to elicit responses from, due to the sheer number of people vying for their attention. Their duties include not only sourcing music but also creating the path for usage, which includes obtaining clearance on recording rights with record companies and negotiating rates of pay for songwriters, composers and music publishers, while remaining within the project's budget. To locate and identify suitable songs, music supervisors often use filtered searches – which is why a music creator's metadata is so important.

Advertising Agencies, Digital Agencies and Branding Agencies

Often referred to as 'creative agencies', these companies design and execute marketing plans for businesses. Promotion and marketing techniques can take a range of dynamic forms in the modern era, but the basic principles relate to building awareness of a business and its products or services. One of the most effective ways to achieve this is through music, which makes these companies key gatekeepers when it comes to opportunities for music creators. A plethora of businesses across a range of sectors could be used as examples of successful brand and band alignment, but let's focus on alcohol products and the role that music plays in their PR and marketing.

Example 1: Jägermeister

Up until the 1970s, Jägermeister was a traditional German *digestif* consumed largely by pensioners to aid digestion. However, American businessman Sydney Frank acquired the import rights in 1973 and by the 1980s, it had become a mainstream hit with shot-drinking college students in the USA due to its popularity among heavy metal bands. Jägermeister became a key sponsor of numerous rock and metal festival stages and tours, in addition to endorsing key bands of that era, such as Motley Crue, Metallica, Slayer and HIM. Fast-forward to the 2020s and Jägermeister, with its striking orange branding, has become a mainstay of rock and metal culture all around the world. This a perfect example of what music can do for a brand.

Example 2: Bacardi

Back in 2009, alcohol brand Bacardi sought to raise brand awareness among a younger audience by licensing the song 'Daylight' by New York-based duo Matt and Kim for its TV ad campaign. The upbeat feel of the song aided the ad's visual. By associating its product with an uber-cool indie duo, Bacardi came to be viewed in a new light. Bacardi was also seen to be breaking an act to a wider audience, which is also excellent brand PR.

Let's explore this from the perspective of the act, Matt and Kim. The duo had previously had a sync placement for their song 'Yea Yeah', which was used by Virgin Mobile for a Canadian marketing campaign in 2007. While this did not bring mainstream global awareness to the song, the duo began to see the ripple effect of having their music licensed in synchronisation with an ad. The duo were working hard to gain a following and had created an impressive live show that they wanted to share on a wider scale. The impact of the Bacardi campaign changed their careers. A 30-second clip of their song in the ad, which was screened in numerous countries, resulted in a huge amount of exposure. Matt and Kim were able to scale up their touring plans to a global level, reach new audiences and gain further placements for 'Daylight' in the videogames NBA Live 10 and The Simms 3: World Adventures.

Film Directors

Film directors play a key role in the use of songs for movies. It can sometimes be the case that a film director hires a music supervision team to find and clear songs for many parts of a film project. However, it is often the director who personally chooses the key songs for a movie theme and soundtrack. Wes Anderson is known to film some scenes with specific songs in mind. Cameron Crowe curated a very important scene of the movie Almost Famous by having many of the casted actors collectively sing the song 'Tiny Dancer' to enhance the emotion that was needed for the scene. Quentin Tarantino is renowned for his great ear for music in much of his work; and songs are a central part of many projects for Martin Scorsese too.

Micro Licensing

A growing area of music sync is micro licensing – loosely defined as a sub-sector of the music sync market which licenses music to independent web-based projects. This is particularly useful for independent film makers, YouTubers, personal projects and small businesses that need music for their visuals. The cost for a micro licence is much lower than what a TV production company, a videogames creator or a music supervisor would be expected to pay because the use of the music is limited to a smaller audience. While micro licensing does not pay rights holders as much as mainstream sync use, it does allow for many music creators to have their music used on a non-exclusive basis in exchange for micro licensing fees. When combined with audio detection applications such as Shazam, which can help music consumers instantly stream a song they have discovered, this creates new paths for independent music creators to have their songs discovered.

Micro licensing is still a relatively new phenomenon and it may take several years for it develop, particularly when it comes to the collection of payments for rights holders. However, in 2022, YouTube incorporated micro licensing into its YouTube Studio, which allows uploaders to use a range of music provided by record labels and music distribution companies. Many emerging music libraries accept submissions specifically for micro licensing use, so this could be a good option for music creators to explore when trying to establish new income streams. Music creators should also ensure that they choose the right digital distributor when releasing music: many distributors are now providing micro licensing access to numerous digital partners, which is why so many distributors now build in social media content IDs and delivery to social media and multimedia platforms as additional options. In essence, the gatekeepers for the use of music in the micro licensing sector are the public.

Interview: Bryan Hinkley, Owner, Gratitude Sound, USA

Gratitude Sound's diverse team of established artists have provided premium music to advertising agencies and production companies since 2014. Their attention to detail and client satisfaction have earned Gratitude Sound a reputation as one of Boston's premier music companies. Services include composition and production, music supervision, sound design, a music library and a record label.

You have done a great job of expanding your services at Gratitude Sound over the years. You're active in music supervision, sync, creative services and music publishing; and you now have a label too. What changes have you seen in the sync sector since you first started a decade ago?

When I started the business in 2014, we focused on creating original and bespoke music compositions, and I quickly identified that there was also a need for existing tracks. Usually, these were requested when there was no time, direction or budget for original compositions. Over the past ten years, the most dramatic change has been the volume of media that is being produced. More agencies and brands have established in-house production departments that allow them to provide less expensive content for social media. It's no longer a side hustle. Therefore, the amount of music that is needed has increased; and along with that, a variety of new music libraries and subscription services that provide affordable music have emerged. While these new libraries come with some challenges, the music they offer has come a long way from the 'stock' music of the past. The tools that are required to create quality-sounding music have become more widely available and affordable, and there's a flood of new music being created every day. Because of the overwhelming amount of music available, the ability to communicate and decipher a brief with creatives has become more important than ever.

What has being a provider of music to ad agencies taught you about the discipline of music supervision?

Because there's a subjective element to music, on occasion, brands will need some guidance in making a decision about the subtleties of the musical direction. Finding ways to utilise music beyond a simple background track is more important. Often, brands are interested in aligning with an upcoming artist in order to associate themselves with their credibility and momentum. Other times, they want a recognisable song to lend a feeling of trust and familiarity. They usually have a direction in mind and I try not to overstep my role; but I do have opinions about what's effective and why. When asked, I'm happy to give my input. I've learned that a lot of time and effort are put into campaigns that may never be aired. There are often multiple changes in direction after work has been created.

I've learned to be patient and believe that the end result will be the end result and it's not something that I can control. I do my part and do my best to make other people's jobs easier. Keeping a steady demeanour and a positive attitude is crucial.

You have been enhancing your artist roster and their catalogues. Is there an added value of pitching an artist's work for projects rather than just songs?

It typically depends on what the client wants. If they want a 'real artist', there's an added value to that. They are looking to find someone who has an existing following and can become a brand ambassador for them – someone who will play a role in establishing their brand identity. The real challenge is: if it gets to the revision phase, can that artist put down their attachment to a track and make changes according to the request? That's easier said than done. In licensing, an artist's music is something that could be defined in different ways, but I think of it as 'music created for the love of music', versus music that's made to be licensed. The added value of an artist's song is an authenticity and a truth that cut through where catalogue can be somehow lacking in soul. That's not to say it doesn't jam! I love some of the tracks in our catalogue. I don't mean to sound too 'New Age', but when music comes from an ethereal inspiration rather than merely the desire to be appreciated, there's a difference. There is something different about a track that was toiled over with love and care. I believe that's something that adds value when a song is attached to a brand. There's a time and a place for everything, but the magic of true inspiration is hard to replicate.

On a creative level in the studio, is the goal always to work towards creating product that aids a visual?

Most of our artists' music is produced outside our studio. We use our space primarily for custom work or passion projects. I often have people ask me what styles of music they should write and how to make music that's more sync-able. My feeling is if you want to make sync-able music, it needs to be simple and consistent. Lyrically, it must be abstract and applicable to multiple scenarios. It should also sound complete without any lyrics. My advice is: if you want to make good music, make music that you love. If you want to make pre-existing music for ads, it will need to be somewhat generic sounding. Because of the transient nature of advertising, each project tends to be unique. While there are some brief guidelines provided (eg, upbeat, cinematic tense), it's challenging to anticipate what will be needed.

What changes do you foresee ahead of you in your sector of work?

Since we started, a divide has emerged between the jobs that require a music company and those that need some music to go in the background. For the latter, more and more solutions are being provided and I don't see that trend reversing any time soon. So we are focusing on providing a service that will add value to a project through understanding and creative direction. Our experience and relationships are at the root of the value we provide. We are not trying to grow into the biggest music house around or to have more clients than we can handle. Although an aspect of that sounds appealing, we thrive in the work we do because of people and relationships. Once we've developed a working relationship, the work becomes easier and better. There's a trust involved that underpins the whole project; but with the massive catalogues, I don't think a personal approach can exist. There's a ton of work to be done and constant opportunities for new media and different ways to incorporate music into the fold effectively. I've come to realise that we can't do everything for everybody, so let's enjoy what we do and be the best at it.

Contractual Considerations

Figure 31.2 Types of Sync Licensing Contracts

Contracts can differ quite considerably in terms of what the offer is to music creators. This will also depend on who you are dealing with: it could be a sync agent, a broker service, a music publisher or perhaps even a music supervisor, a film director or an advertising agency.

Many sync agents will look to secure 50% of the upfront fee that the music user is paying, with the other 50% going to the rights holder or independent music creator. Some sync agents will not ask for any of the music publishing share of the backend royalties that are generated once a TV show airs, while others will ask for a percentage split of the publishing rights for a set length of time. Some sync agents offer an exclusive agreement, while others offer a non-exclusive agreement which allows the music creator to enter into similar agreements with other sync agents on a non-exclusive basis. Some sync agents will look to 'retitle' a song's recording. This is a term more commonly heard in the USA whereby a sync agent gives a song's recording an alternative title to differentiate between its work and the work of another sync agent working the same song. This means that a music creator could have one song with multiple titles being pitched by multiple sync agents. It could be argued that this practice is becoming dated and tired, especially in the age of algorithmic detection of a recording's unique sonic identity. Before long, widespread advanced software technologies will start to erode this type of practice, so it is not advisable for creators to consider this as a sustainable option. But it is nonetheless something which still exists, so be cautiously aware of this when entering into a non-exclusive agreement with a sync agent.

A music publisher's primary interest lies in exploiting and collecting on a song's use, while a record company's interest lies in the use of the recording. Both generate fees and royalties. The percentage split on sync placements with either a music publisher or a record company will be outlined in the contractual agreement that it enters into with a music creator.

Broker agencies are usually very transparent about what their offer is to music creators. It is always a good idea to read their website before you pitch to them so that you know what kind of deal you could be entering into if you avail of their services. There is a subscription fee involved with broker services and sometimes even a percentage split on a master sync licence fee, although this will generally be a smaller percentage than what a sync agent would expect. Generally speaking, a broker service would not expect to see any backend royalties as they are remunerated through the subscription fee and any percentage split of the master sync fee.

Knowing What to Quote

Knowing what to quote can be a challenge. Many creators will have poured their heart and soul into creating something special and meaningful, which then becomes useful to others. It is difficult to suddenly expect to put a price on that. However, this is a business and it needs to be done.

You will have to quote on sync fees only if you are working directly with a music supervisor, a director, a TV production company or an advertising agency. If you are going through a music publisher, a sync agent or a broker service, the negotiations will take place without any need for your action or negotiation.

The best advice when negotiating is often to start by asking what the client's budget is. This takes the pressure off you and shifts it to the client. Also, there will be a budget – there always is. Song selection and clearance is often the last part of the completion process in TV and film, and there will almost certainly be a specific budget in mind. Budgets can vary dramatically, depending on whether the project is a small indie flick, a Hollywood blockbuster or something in between. It is unlikely that you will have any idea of what the budget looks like for the whole project and how much of that budget has already been spent. But if you start by quoting too low, your offer will be gratefully accepted. Even trying to gauge a ballpark figure can be difficult if you have no idea of the intended usage of the song and its prevalence in the project. Therefore, asking about the budget is key to starting the negotiations and agreeing on a fee.

There is also another consideration: what are you quoting on? It is likely that this will be an upfront fee which covers the master recording use, rather than the use of the song. Perhaps there is a separate fee for the use of the song, but perhaps not. Many music supervisors know that songwriters and music publishers will collect their royalty collections through their PROs and therefore the budget covers only the use of the recording. It is important to be clear about this because it is difficult to know what to quote if you don't know what you're quoting on. There may be additional factors which contribute towards the fee. For instance, full songs with vocals often command higher fees than instrumental versions of the same songs. Perhaps the song is central to a story's essence or is crucial to a specific scene or character. When dealing directly with the source, understanding how the song will be used can be helpful in determining its value to the user.

Blanket Licensing

This relates to a licence which is acquired by a company or entity that pays a blanket fee to cover the use of a wide selection of music in TV and radio broadcasting or live performance. It could relate to an orchestra that performs well-known songs; or to a radio station or TV production company that would otherwise need multiple permissions from controlling copyright holders. A blanket licence is a simple way for a company or entity that uses a lot of music to obtain permission to use a wide array of songs.

The company or entity pays a fee to the relevant PRO, which then distributes the payment (in the form of itemised royalties) to the copyright holders of the songs that are used. It is the PRO that issues the licence on behalf of the copyright holders.

This can be a rather tricky subject to unpack, as there are so many variables to it that can vary dramatically, especially from country to country; so let's look at how this works in the UK.

Blanket Licensing Case Study: The UK

It could be argued that blanket licence agreements are best suited to the use of production music (sometimes referred to as 'library music') in the UK.

This is music specifically composed for sync use. If a song is released commercially (ie, in the public domain and available to consumers), a music user will need to check whether the song is registered with PRS for Music and Phonographic Performance Limited (PPL). In the UK, PRS collects and distributes money on behalf of songwriters, composers and music publishers; while PPL collects and distributes on behalf of performers and record companies. Music users can search the databases of both organisations to find out whether a song is covered under a blanket licence. If the song in question is not found, many music users will look for other options, which will include other songs that are covered under a blanket agreement and registered with PRS and PPL. This can be a lengthy process for many music users and a rather time-consuming one at that – especially when the use of a specific song is crucial to a project they are working on.

PRS for Music has deals in place with many major broadcasters and a smaller blanket contract is also available for independent production companies. The fees for blanket licences between broadcasters and PRS for Music are not usually disclosed; although PRS for Music provides transparency to copyright holders regarding the rates that are payable to them through downloadable PDFs which are published on its website. The documents list low and high peak times, the TV and radio programmes that operate under blanket licensing, and what copyright holders can expect to receive per minute of usage on their shows. However, there are still discrepancies. Rates differ between broadcasters. For example, music users working with Channel 4 will be expected to pay a fee for each track used; whereas the BBC pays a larger lump sum to the collection societies each year rather than an individual fee per song. If a music user is looking to license music for a TV show that is broadcast in the UK on the BBC, the blanket licence route is a good option. However, difficulties may arise if that programme is to be licensed outside of the UK, as the blanket licence may not extend into other territories and additional rights will need to be cleared.

In summary, blanket licensing in the UK is a little simpler because there is only one PRO (PRS for Music) which controls blanket licences. The position is similar in Canada, where blanket licences are controlled exclusively by SECAN. In the USA, by contrast, blanket licensing is more complex and thus less common, as there are a range of PROs and an even wider range of broadcasters.

32
Artist Merchandise

In a world where music has largely shifted to the digital domain, experiences and merchandise are tangible products that music fans still can't resist. Creating, selling and distributing merchandise signify a professional intention that extends beyond the music itself; but it is tough for many artists to understand when the right time to start selling merchandise is and how to go about it.

The difficulty for some artists lies in knowing which physical items they could sell outside of the standard tote bags, t-shirts, and hoodies; while other recording artists have just as strong a vision for their merchandise line as they do for the music itself. Some recording artists don't start creating and selling merchandise until they have the support of a booking agent behind them to generate the kinds of audiences that will enable them to start shifting product. Then there are others who start early on in their careers with self-crafted novelty items.

As in many other areas of the music industry, specialism and partnerships are key. Working in partnership with the right company can be crucial in understanding an act's potential in the merchandising marketplace. Many companies now have their own e-commerce capabilities that can be built into an artist's website, streaming and social platforms. Some even provide artists with the tools they need to run things for themselves. One thing is for certain: merchandising an artist's brand is key to marketing and financial self-sustainability.

Interview: Tersha Willis, Co-founder, terrible*

How would you describe your client base?

We work with a variety of artists at different stages of their careers, from those who are starting out to those who have been making music for decades with a huge back catalogue. We don't have any specific genres we work with; rather,

DOI: 10.4324/9781003452119-37

we work on projects that we like, love or believe in, and with teams who we know to be excellent at what they do.

What changes have you noticed in recent years regarding the kinds of merchandise you make?

The black t-shirt is still the most popular merchandise item the world over, but we believe that this is mostly because artists make this item the most. In recent years, we have seen a lot more knitted socks, scarves and art prints. Demand for unique items has grown massively with artists and fans alike – everything from plushie toys to custom-scented candles, bobble-head figurines, Barbie dolls, bespoke clothing ranges, footwear like sliders, sticker sets, colouring books, bespoke bags and accessories is on offer, and often these products sell out far quicker than t-shirts.

Making products that are meaningful to both the artist and their fans means looking beyond traditional soft merch items and dreaming a little bigger. Everything is possible with enough time and budget.

When is a good time for artists to start their merchandise line?

Unsurprisingly, there is a magic moment for artists to start making and selling merchandise – usually somewhere between releasing singles and EPs and being able to sell 200 tickets to a show. It's usually best to start selling merchandise at shows ahead of selling online, mostly because the margins are far slimmer selling online due to the many additional costs involved.

Selling merchandise at shows is a lot more compelling because the energy is high and live music creates a whole range of emotions that we want to hold onto, and merchandise is often the only way that we can capture the emotion of the live music experience.

Do you work in partnership with artists on their vision for their merch?

Absolutely – the best merchandise is created in collaboration with artists. Some artists have a specific vision of what they want and we have to work hard to make it a reality. Others need to go on a journey with it: touching and seeing new products; experimenting with techniques and different variations of artworks and colours; seeing other things we have made; or letting us suggest what would work really well with the themes they have given us. We have design and production teams who work closely with artists throughout.

Artists rightly see merchandise in the same way as they see their album artwork and put as much, if not more work and time into creating products for their fans.

The best-selling products are always those which the artist loves the most themselves. Generally, we would always advise artists to make something they love, and most of our work in this process involves getting that done on time and on budget.

What role does merchandise play in how artists are perceived by their audience?

Merchandise is often one of the first financial investments that fans make in an artist, outside of buying a ticket to a show.

Once a fan makes that investment, the relationship between fan and artist becomes more serious. Because of the nature of this exchange, making this relationship last means making something with care and ensuring that it offers value for money.

How an artist makes a product – whether it's sustainable, high quality, thoughtful and relevant – plays a role in what fans think of the artist and how much more they engage with them. It is very much like any brand/consumer relationship, where loyalty is earned through what the product is and what it represents.

Tersha's insights are invaluable for artists who are looking to start or expand their merch range. In terms of when is the best time to do so, Tersha's suggestion of 'somewhere between releasing singles and EPs and being able to sell 200 tickets to a show' is particularly helpful. This is aligned with the views of many others when asked this same question. Also, in an age when technology is enhancing creativity, Tersha's insights on the evolution of merchandisable products should be very useful to many music creators. So many acts today are creating products that capture experience, novelty, loyalty and the uniqueness of a specific artist.

33
Funding Opportunities

Creators often reach a point in their career when funding is required to take the next step. A key factor here lies in knowing what that next step looks like and how you would spend the money if you had it. If you can answer those questions, looking into funding grants may be a good option for you.

All around the world, there are funding bodies that award grants to those seeking to be enterprising and bold with their creative decisions.

- **Case Study 1 – PRS Foundation:** As one of the UK's leading charitable funders of new music and talent development, the PRS Foundation plays a crucial role in helping creative music talent to emerge. PRS for Music is the performing rights organisation for the UK market and it helps to fund the PRS Foundation. The foundation is primarily funded by the interest earned on royalties that are awaiting distribution from PRS for Music to its members. Since the PRS Foundation was created in 2000, it has awarded over £40 million to almost 9,000 new music projects. Many of the music creators who have received funding have gone on to become hugely successful names in UK music. Creators such as Sam Fender, AJ Tracey, Imogen Heap, Little Simz, IDLES and Glass Animals were all awarded grants to help kickstart their careers in their early days. The foundation supports individual talent from all backgrounds and genres, together with pioneering organisations, live music venues, festivals, promoters and talent development organisations.
- **Case Study 2 – Music Moves Europe:** The European Commission is the European Union's independent executive arm, which implements the decisions of the European Parliament and the Council of the European Union. It also funds the Music Moves Europe initiative, which aims to promote creativity and diversity among the 27 EU member states, especially in the wake of the Covid-19 pandemic.

DOI: 10.4324/9781003452119-38

- **Case Study 3 – NZ On Air:** With the aim of boosting homegrown public media in New Zealand, NZ On Air funds a wide range of creative projects, including the creation of original music. Its objective is to reflect and celebrate the range of diversity and culture in New Zealand society. Funding can be applied for to create original music, with funding rounds running multiple times per year.

All funders have their own requirements, which can vary considerably, but the concept tends to be the same: enabling the next generation of music creators to flourish and find their path. There are funders ready to fund music projects in all corners of the world, so be sure to do your research on the most suitable options for your geographical location.

It is important that music creators have a good understanding of how they would spend the money if they received a funding grant, because the way to obtain a grant is to explain exactly how the money would be used. Funding bodies like to see a full breakdown of how the funds would be used and what the projected outcome would be. A project needs a purpose. For instance, when the PRS Foundation awarded a funding grant to Sam Fender, it was to aid the recording of two singles, a video and a small UK tour. This is a project which would have needed serious planning in terms of logistics, timescales, personnel and costings. It was a project with a purpose: a promotional campaign that blended recorded music and live events. Once a project has been planned out and the costs have been factored in, this adds scale, realism and the ability to measure the outcome against the purpose, which helps funders to decide on the suitability of the application.

All of the abovementioned case studies state that the costs of the creator must also be factored into the funding application. This helps music creators to understand the value of their own time, which is an important part of the learning path. The EU guidelines specify a minimum fee of €70 per day for the creator; other funders tend not to state a fixed fee but do fund day fees which are much higher.

The prospect of obtaining a grant might feel unrealistic or unachievable for some creators, but it is entirely possible, provided that there is a purpose and there will be some benefit – even if that is merely the artistic development of the creator.

34
A Guide to Building a Portfolio Career: Understanding the Gig Economy

By *Meldra Guza, BA(hons), PGCert, MBA, CMgr, FCMI, FHEA*

Meldra Guza is a Latvian-born, UK-based music industry professional who has embraced the discipline and flexibility of a portfolio career. Meldra is the director of UK-based production company The SongLab Ltd. She is also a published songwriter, a senior lecturer at multiple universities, a performing musician, a voice talent and a music business consultant. Meldra was a teen star in her native Latvia, where she toured and released music as an artist in her own right. She has also been a session guitarist for various acts including Sir Rod Stewart, CeeLo Green and Dappy. Having spent two years as a songwriter for TV projects in the USA, Meldra also voiced a wide range of singing toys for Fisher-Price/Mattel. As her career has continued to evolve according to how she shapes it, Meldra chose to focus on the importance of music creators embracing a portfolio career in her MBA thesis.

What is a Portfolio Career?

A portfolio career encompasses multiple part-time jobs, roles, projects and activities, rather than a single job.

Music creators have a great deal of opportunities within their reach. Their fusion of skill, knowledge and usefulness presents a plethora of working options. It could be suggested that music creators are their own brokers in creating new working opportunities. However, creators might experience significant pressure to make informed decisions in a variety of specialisms that may not necessarily fall under their area of expertise.

This chapter looks at ways to manage various areas of skills development in order to develop and maintain music industry connections and opportunities. These skills include creative expertise, music industry know-how and business

DOI: 10.4324/9781003452119-39

and administrative skills that are transferable to any industry. The importance of interpersonal or 'soft skill' development is also explored in the context of how a creator builds and sustains a portfolio career.

Embracing a Portfolio Career

A portfolio career is a choice, lifestyle and strategy that music creators can develop to create a unique combination of revenue streams while continuing to explore their creativity. A portfolio career allows creators to work on multiple projects, utilising various skills while remaining in charge of their time and commitments. It can also be a strategic decision to work on better-paid projects using expert skills while also taking on other projects that require a more speculative approach. For example, a songwriter might choose to run their own business creating signature wedding songs and charging a significant fee per song, while also working speculatively (without receiving immediate payment) in collaborative environments to build their catalogue and pitch for sync licensing or artist cut opportunities. This could also apply to a touring session musician who balances life on the road with following their passion for electronic dance music production. creating instrumental tracks on the tour bus, in hotels and during any available free time. Or it might apply to a bass player in a metal band who started out as a classically trained pianist and has since added the creation of orchestrated arrangements for film and TV through the use of sample library technology and MIDI to their portfolio career.

The same professional might have one or two different day jobs, run their own business or be self-employed, while also finding time to commit to projects that will build and expand their future income streams by becoming rights holders.

The essence of a portfolio career is for creators to define themselves and capitalise on their strengths while continuing to develop and evolve their practice.

Self-management and Responsibility

Balancing different projects requires specific skills (more about that later in this chapter), including time management, attention to detail and determination. If creators can work towards self-imposed deadlines, overcome procrastination and be strategic about the projects they take on, a portfolio career can work exceptionally well in today's gig economy.

What is the 'Gig Economy'?

The 'gig economy' is an ecosystem in which work is often available on a free-lance or outsourced basis. Creators with high-level expertise in their field can pitch for opportunities, apply for specific grants, work in partnership with other creators and organisations, and adapt to the changing landscape.

The gig economy environment allows creators to take on work based on their availability, suitability and skill level. Fees should be agreed in writing between the creator and the client. This could also extend to an online plat-form or app. A non-music-related example of the modern gig economy is the concept of working for an app-based food delivery service or taxi service – or perhaps even both at the same time. It is important to note that in this con-text, the party that hires the professional is the client, and not the employer, if the professional is self-employed or working for their own company.

Creating, producing, recording and performing music have always been critical elements of the entertainment industry. With the development of technology and the fast pace of modern life, the 'gig economy' is a term now widely used to describe taking on additional work which is often discovered or facilitated through app-based technology and often completed remotely.

Analogue versus Digital

Modern music professionals have plenty of opportunities to generate work for themselves in a face-to-face environment. Whether through performance, ar-tistic expression, live workshops, community-focused creative work, recording or teaching, there is scope for them to collaborate and innovate. Funding is also available for the exploration of these themes.

Today more than ever before, creators can also generate a significant portion of their revenue from remote work that they complete in their own time. The power of the online environment and some dedicated high-level platforms al-lows people to network, collaborate and hire professionals from all around the world for projects that bring together the best teams to fulfil the vision of the client. This is especially true in the context of recorded music and the abun-dance of working opportunities for those who can self-record.

How Do Creators Set Up Remote Work Opportunities?

Typically, creators can focus on a particular set of skills that may be useful to others. These could range from instrument expertise to vocal technique, recording ability, compositional approach and production style, which together represent some critical sonic values. Once a specific niche has been identified, it can be easier to make oneself visible online.

It is crucial for those who are not producers to learn how to record their instruments (including their voice) and to appreciate the technical specifications that a client might require when delivering files back to them. While not all creators need be expert engineers and producers, when taking on remote work that requires recording skills, it is of paramount importance to deliver the stems/tracks/files precisely as required. This extends to the flexibility to make fundamental edits and changes to a project once completed.

Taking Time to Understand Each Other

It is fun to work on a new project and add a personal touch, and a creator's own improvised artistic interpretation can often yield satisfying results for the client. However, a considerable amount of remote work requires creators to follow a brief and fulfil instructions as per the initial agreement. It is easy to lose track of time and objectivity in seeking to achieve the set goal. While a slightly different idea might sound impressive, creators should be mindful of not imprinting their own preferences when working on a specific brief, unless they truly match the client's requirements.

Working for the Music

A portfolio career can allow creators to actively pursue their artistic aspirations while also taking on other projects. As more creators manage their own careers, there is also perhaps greater pressure to separate their artistic integrity and aims from their personal views. Creators must be able to separate their attitudes, emotional attachment and immersion when working on their own individual projects from their approach to specific external briefs over which they have no creative control. An artist might be working towards releasing their debut chill house single while doing session musician work playing banjo for a major artist. Both pursuits are important. With their artist's hat on, a creator can take their time and be picky and perhaps even indecisive at times; but when playing the role of session musician, they must make assertive decisions as part of the team they have joined and work in the team's best interests. When booked for a session, a music professional is there to do a specific job, not to get involved in matters that they were not hired for. Wanting to look useful and resourceful can sometimes be an unwelcome move that could bring a working relationship to a premature end.

Identifying Your Niche

Transitioning into a music professional can be difficult. Perhaps a good way to start is to pick one specific skill that the creator excels at and then think of the multiple ways in which that skill can be useful to others. For example, a vocalist can perform with their artist's repertoire; but they can also sing in a function or cover band or take on specific session musician positions, such as touring backing vocalist. TV and promotional work, or singing on a cruise ship, are other routes that may be desirable for that same professional. The same vocalist could also work as a demo vocalist for a variety of producers (face to face or remotely); and could use their voice to create sample packs and topline songwriting work in genres they excel in but don't regard as their preference. Finally, that same vocalist could also take on some private students, mentor other vocalists and work with educational organisations. As the vocalist's career progresses, they can become more selective about which routes offer the greatest creative fulfilment and focus on those which they enjoy the most.

The same approach can be applied when considering any other skill that a creator might have.

Additional Skills

A portfolio career can bring a lot of excitement and joy; but it also requires careful time management in order to earn enough money, have sufficient rest and – most importantly – leave enough space in the schedule to avail of unexpected opportunities. Gaps in the schedule can also be strategically planned to allow creators to spend some time reflecting and deciding on what to do next. Creators should also be mindful of how they respond to the professional world around them, and this extends to how they interact with other people. It is crucial for creators to build an amicable, productive and sustainable network of professional relationships.

Some people secure more work than others because they have mastered the balance of utilising four different skill sets to a point where interaction with them is always seamless and productive. The simplest way to describe this is that they are easy to work with:

- They excel in their area of specialism.
- They have a solid understanding of the music business.
- They also have a reliable set of general business skills: they understand how the music fits with product development, can generate invoices and are organised in basic bookkeeping.

- Most importantly, they are highly self-aware, respect other people's time and maintain their good reputation.

A creator's unique combination of skills and knowledge sets them apart from others. Although many creators can apply themselves to various projects, professionals become a 'go-to' person for a specific type of work. A creator can have versatile income streams through carefully nurtured professional relationships.

While not every creator will find the time to become an expert in the finer details of the music industry, a solid understanding of the music industry will make it much easier to navigate a portfolio career. For example, a good grasp of contractual language and expectations will prepare the creator to utilise a lawyer's advice more productively. Going into a meeting with an understanding of what a contract says enables a creator to figure out what they will gain from the agreement. Furthermore, appreciating the intricate professional networks of the music industry ensures that creators can remain mindful of the variety of roles within the music industry.

An understanding of expectations and the appropriate music industry vocabulary equips a creator with the confidence to contribute to conversations and negotiations. Alongside prior success and expert skills, an informed understanding of the industry and the ability to use the right language allow creators to progress throughout their careers.

Do it Yourself or Outsource?

There is so much that creators can do themselves. However, they may also wish to consider outsourcing some of the jobs they need to complete. Knowing what needs doing and the value of specialist expertise can enable creators to make informed decisions and use their financial resources wisely. Responsibilities that could be outsourced could include such things as digital marketing, product design, branding and accounting. Key professionals could be hired to undertake these tasks; or creators could extend their knowledge base by embracing these skills themselves. There are also artificial intelligence tools that exist to make one's life more manageable.

It is arguable that outsourcing important tasks to suitably qualified professionals can make a real difference – and for some tasks is perhaps even essential. For example, at some stage in a creator's career, they may wish to work with an accountant, as although this is an additional expense, a great accountant will be aware of legal changes and will be able to save money and support good practice in running the creator's career from a financial point of view.

Interpersonal and Soft Skills

Reputation and recommendations play vital roles in fast-tracking careers. Somebody can recommend a creator for an opportunity, but the creator must then deliver quality results to build their reputation. Furthermore, the person recommending them is putting their own reputation on the line when making such a recommendation.

Soft and interpersonal skills include time management, communication skills, proactivity, practical leadership skills, emotional intelligence and the ability to reflect on one's performance in order to improve. For instance, becoming more productive as a producer will involve the utilisation of time management techniques to create and finish tracks on time, while avoiding procrastination and developing approaches to overcome professional challenges. Other examples of soft skills development include having the confidence to talk about money and being able to turn down projects and explain why in a useful and constructive manner.

The Positives and Negatives of a Portfolio Career

Running a portfolio career requires the creator to be assertive and mindful of their longer-term goals while thoughtfully balancing their day-to-day work. There are numerous positives of a portfolio career, including the ability to:

- control one's own time;
- select projects that appeal;
- develop a reputation as a 'go-to' person for a particular type of work;
- oversee the pricing structure for one's services;
- make time to explore creative expression; and
- work towards long-term career milestones.

However, there may be challenges to overcome and it is good to be aware of these in advance and plan accordingly, so that you can be flexible in how you deal with them. Examples of potential challenges in a portfolio career include the following:

- A creator who worries about not having enough work may take on too much and not have enough rest.
- A creator may suffer a financial hit if they can longer take on or complete work due to unforeseen circumstances.
- As with careers in many sectors, creators must spend some time building their reputation, which requires an unpaid speculative time investment.
- A creator must be aware and stay on top of financial management.

- At times, a creator might have to pitch for opportunities in their own time (highly likely unpaid), with the risk that the time investment might not have a direct or immediate effect.
- A creator will ultimately need to say no to projects if they no longer feel connected to them, need to improve their work-life balance or focus on the development of a different area of expertise.

Suggestions for Getting Started

- Follow the money: Do some research on where investments are being made in the music industry and on what is happening in different territories of the world, and try to make some predictions of how these trends might move.
- Music funding and grants: Each country has its own policy on finance for arts and often a variety of organisations are looking to develop exciting initiatives to give voice to music creators. This can be approached in two ways. First, the creator can build their own projects and apply for funding for them. Second, the creator can investigate organisations that have recently received funding and look for ways to work with them to deliver their projects – for example, utilising their skills to develop and deliver songwriting or production workshops, or up-skilling up-and-coming music makers.
- Remain vigilant to updates on innovation and regeneration that are supported by wider policy and available to participate in cultural projects – for example, initiatives that support live music, heritage-based projects, multi-genre explorative projects or educational projects.
- Many creators struggle to decide on pricing, but this can be approached in the same way as any other competitor research. Creators can investigate what other similar creators offer and what their price point is. It is not recommended to purposely undercut others, as this ultimately reduces the value of the sector. It does, however, allow creators to become informed of their market value.
- Perhaps do not offer discounts on first encounters. Do not presume that more business will arise from the opportunity. Charge the appropriate fee. Consider offering a discount once the client has exhibited a certain degree of loyalty and delivered a specific volume of working opportunities. It is important to set a precedent for how much your work is worth.
- Do not worry about your fees being higher than what you would expect to earn per hour. Remember, your price reflects years of skills development and often admin time which you cannot charge for separately. Your fee includes all your communications with clients; however, your time still has value and this must be reflected in some form in your offer.

- Remain mindful of the need to save money for your tax bills and of your other responsibilities, including having the appropriate insurance cover for the work that you are carrying out.
- Sometimes it can all feel a bit daunting when starting out – particularly if you feel surrounded by people who all appear to be more confident, louder or more experienced than you – so focus on you. There is a good reason why you are part of the team or have been invited to bring something new to the project. That has been gained on merit; so, even if you don't feel like it, you do belong.
- We do not always have to share all of ourselves in a professional environment. It can be exhausting and make you feel more vulnerable. Just as artists build alter-egos, a creator might consider building their best representative who can face the world. This requires a creator to find and give themselves time to rest, relax, heal, rejuvenate and regain their strength.
- Finally, there is no single correct approach to work. You need to figure out what works for you. Many resources are available that support personal and professional growth, self-management, professional happiness and ways to increase productivity. It is worth exploring those options and trying out various work approaches until you find the combination of methods that works for you. This could be as simple as figuring out what time of the day or night is most productive for you, or whether you can be productive throughout the whole day. It may be that you need a reward system to keep motivated, however small the reward might be.

Scenarios of Portfolio Career Professionals

Scenario 1

A creator starts out as a highly experienced live musician who then establishes a home-based project studio set-up to new build income streams without the need for continual travel. They still go on tours and dep for other musicians (to 'dep' is to 'deputise' – that is, to take over someone else's gig if that person cannot make it). The creator also teaches privately from their home studio and creates content for YouTube.

Scenario 2

A student is focused on their songwriting career, but they quickly develop high-quality production skills and work with as many of their peers as possible to gain experience recording different voices and instruments. By the time they graduate, they have developed a reputation as a nice person to work with who has their finger on the pulse regarding sonic values and techniques. They can also play a few instruments and can often take on function and cover gigs, as well as dipping their toes in session gigs. As a recent graduate, they take on every opportunity to build their reputation; and within a few months, they have developed favourable income streams. Working with so many people has allowed them to develop skills to get the best out of performers, so they can now expand their practice by engaging in community music work and supporting others in unlocking their creativity.

Scenario 3

A music professional composes production music two days a week, teaches one day a week and runs an evening music workshop two days a week. They also have a weekly residency as a DJ and collaborate with topline songwriters to continue to build their brand by releasing new music on a variety of dance labels.

35
Reaching Out to Music Industry Professionals

The thought of communicating with music industry personnel can be terrifying. Many creators struggle to understand who to reach out to, and what to say and how to say it when they do. Like many aspects of life, the prospect is often far scarier than the process. If you have a firm understanding of the purpose of the communication, it becomes easier to know what to say, who to say it to and how to say it.

Speaking Different Languages

It is important to be able to change the terminology and tone that we use when dealing with different people. This is something that comes naturally to many people, but others perhaps need to become more mindful of it. It is not innate to everyone: some people have a gift in how they interact with others. In fact, those who don't change how they speak to others may be highly valued for this. How we speak to our next-door neighbour might differ from how we speak to an old friend we rarely see. How we speak to a toddler might differ from how we speak to an elderly person.

Similarly, in the music industry, how a music creator speaks to a recording engineer will differ from how they speak to a promoter. How they speak to a music publisher will differ from how they speak to a fan. This is not just because they are talking about different topics; it's because there is a distinct change in terminology and tonality.

The questions that a music creator must ask themselves are the following:

- Who am I going to try and connect with?
- How?
- Why?
- What do I say?

DOI: 10.4324/9781003452119-40

The first question is researched based. The second question dictates the mode of communication. The third question relates to the benefit for the recipient. The fourth question relates to how you sell the intended message.

The Codes and Modes of Communication

It is important to respect the mode of communication that is used. In an era when it is so easy to send a private message on social media or reply inside a thread, it is sometimes important to resist this temptation in favour of a more professional approach. Email is the business world's professional mode of communication because it is formal, legally binding and the preferred communication mode of many professionals. While social media communication is more acceptable to some than others, there is often a pattern of lighting the sparks of communication on social media and then moving to email once the conversation becomes more formal – although this can vary depending on age and generation. Phone calls are rapidly falling out of fashion; as is the concept of voicemail, which has been rather rapidly replaced by app-based or direct message mobile voice notes.

Many businesses have strategies on movement and redirection for communication, and it might be important for you as a creator to think about your own. For instance, it might be okay for fans to communicate with you through your private email in the early days of your career; but as your popularity grows, it will become impossible to reply to everyone and those fans from the early days may accuse you of having changed. It's a tough balance to strike, for sure. There are many examples of how people seek to redirect communication and engagement elsewhere. Many artists have an email address in their Instagram bio for business enquiries and a link to their music underneath; these are two simple examples of ways to funnel communication and engagement.

It is always important for creators to investigate submission policy guidelines when submitting songs to music professionals, as there is often a specific way in which people wish to receive songs. This could be through a 'songs@' or 'submissions@' email address, a specified link to upload files or perhaps even an external web-based company that administrates submissions, such as LabelRadar or SubmitHub. A submission policy is almost always stated on a company or individual's website.

Beware of Premature Introductions

Web-based platforms offer instant pathways to communicate with others, but it is important to beware of the risk of premature introductions. It is easy to spot people online that we want to connect with, but when that connection is made is just as important as how it's made. Perhaps there is a specific music publisher or artist manager that a creator would like to connect with, but they should wait until their pitch is ready and their new music is available before making contact. We are now in an age when we often meet people only to discover that we are already connected online. There's nothing morally wrong about that at all, but it can be awkward for a creator if an in-person introduction is made with someone they have already private messaged and got blanked by. Patience is key – it's part of your strategy.

The Email Pitch to a Record Company

There is no right or wrong way to send an email, in the same way as there is no right or wrong way to write a song. But there are more effective ways to yield the desired result and this often comes down to thoughtfulness.

Scenario

A rock band want to pitch themselves to record companies. They were formed 18 months ago and have played several shows at a local level, and they have started to release some singles. The singer is good at writing press releases, which has gained them some decent press pieces without spending any money. They have started pitching their music to sync agents to try to gain placements in TV and film. They have new music recorded that is unreleased. They want to use their growing reputation and momentum to entice a label to invest in their work.

Considerations: What type of record deal are they looking for? Do they want a record company to advance them the money to record an album? Why? There's arguably not enough traction to dive into this step yet. Perhaps they would be better off working towards two or three EPs that each have their own single releases. Each EP can have its own release campaign and different promotion and marketing approaches can be tested out and compared to see what is most effective. This expands the band's discography and feeds the nature of algorithmic streaming growth. It also means they pull back on the big debut album marketing punt until they have a better understanding of who their market is and what their fans want.

Another consideration to bear in mind is this: the band have new music that is recorded and unreleased. They could seek a licensing deal with a record company rather than a traditional record contract. The band own their own master rights, so they are free to share these with a record company in exchange for the label's input into the promotion and marketing of the record; as opposed to a record company having to fund a recording project. This changes the pitch, as the band's offer is clear.

Email Pitch Style 1

Hi,

Check out my band's demo pls.
LINK

Artist Name

Email Pitch Style 2

Dear ___,

I have recently looked into the work you did with [name of act] when researching record companies. Congratulations on all that is being achieved and good luck moving forward.

The reason for my email is because I am looking to secure a record contract for my band. We are an indie rock band in the same style as Blossoms, The Night Cafe and Sundara Karma. We have so far partnered with various promoters and radio stations on a local and regional level, and have achieved some good press features in recent months which neatly reflect our PR aims while we carry out a continuous waterfall approach to our multi-single release campaign. We are ready for growth and are looking at potential partners that we feel we could work with in a mutual beneficial fashion as we seek to build our reputation and visibility on a national scale before we start to work more of the continental territories. We have started to engage with sync agents as we plan to gain exposure for our catalogue through TV and film projects while we enhance our listener base with the digital service providers. We are in interested in licensing our newly recorded but unreleased music to a record company and believe this partnership would be a good fit. We currently own all our own masters. Please find a link to our music and electronic press kit. ___

We look forward to hearing from you. Good luck with all your projects and keep up the great work! Thanks for your time.

Warm wishes,
Name of the band member
BAND NAME
LINKS

Email Pitch Style 2 speaks the language of the record company and is much harder for the record company to ignore. There is a professional intention in the email, accompanied by a sense of knowledge about the music industry. The label can see that there is no need to teach this band how the music industry works: they already possess a basic understanding, as is evident from the wording they use in their email. The offer is clear: the band are looking to license their music to the record company. It is also clear that the band have a solid understanding of their place in the market because they've name-checked other bands that are similar in style. Truthfully, they are very early on in their career and have barely got going, but the language they are using shows professionalism. Wording such as 'we seek to build our reputation and visibility on a national scale before we start to work more of the continental territories' is very important. It softly says, 'We are going to make this happen with or without your involvement,' but in a completely unthreatening manner. They're confident, not brash. They're polite. What is also interesting about the email is that it invites the record company to start potential negotiations on a deal between them. In addition, at no point do the band plead with the recipient to listen to their music. They don't ask for help, which is crucial in how they are perceived.

By contrast, Email Pitch Style 1 is lazy and unhelpful. It achieves very little and can be easily ignored. It's the same band, the same music and the same people, but a completely different outcome – and that's all down to how they communicate.

The Email Pitch to a Music Publisher

The language that is used when pitching to a record company will be specific to a record company. It will talk about master rights of recordings and who the artist is. When pitching to a music publisher, the language needs to switch to the subject of songwriting copyrights and the style of the songwriter.

Scenario

A songwriter wishes to write songs for artists. They secretly harbour the hope of having an artist career themselves one day but wish to break into the music industry by writing songs for other acts. The songwriter is also a producer and collaborates with other writers, producers and artists. They wish to partner with a music publisher to enhance their network and opportunities for collaboration. The songwriter predominantly writes R&B and pop, and can sing. They have a showreel of songs on their SoundCloud account. Most of the songs feature the songwriter on vocals, except for two which are performed by local artists they have collaborated with.

The songwriter wishes to use the showreel to exhibit their skills to the music publisher.

Considerations: The songwriter has a lot to offer. They can write, sing, produce and play. This is someone who plays multiple roles in the creation of songs and therefore might be suitable for various collaborations.

> *Email Pitch Style 1*
>
> Hi,
>
> I'm a songwriter and I need help in getting my music out there. I desperately want to write for other artists, and I think I can! Here's my Sound-Cloud: LINK
>
> Best,
> NAME OF THE WRITER
>
> *Email Pitch Style 2*
>
> Dear ___,
>
> I am a UK-based songwriter who specialises in R&B and pop. I'm a topliner and vocalist, and I also produce to a professional standard. I am looking to pitch songs of commercial value to several different territories. I also have a selection of instrumentals that I would be interested in pitching for sync opportunities. All my catalogue has clearance and I have split sheets with all collaborators.
>
> Here is a LINK to three songs which are labelled with metadata that links to tempo, mood, genre and examples of artists that the songs could fit to. Below is a link to a wider showreel of my work. I am interested in finding a suitable publisher to assign my copyrights to or a publisher that I can work with on single song agreements.
>
> Best wishes,
> NAME OF THE WRITER
> LINK TO FURTHER SHOWREEL

Email Pitch Style 1 could yield results – it's not impossible, but it's less likely. As in the previous example, Email Pitch Style 2 reflects a professional intention with a mutually beneficial outcome for both parties.

The offer from the songwriter could be made clearer if they expanded on market and territory-specific knowledge linked to the music publisher's activity. For example, if they had said to the publisher that they are witnessing growth in R&B in Africa and Asia and would like to write for those markets, and that their research has shown that the publisher has connections and a track record in those territories, the chances of an immediate conversation between the parties would increase. Music publishers like it when songwriters are specific about what they can offer in terms of specialism. This give the publisher a better understanding of how they could collaborate. The songwriter mentions single song agreements – this is a great way for songwriters and publishers to test the waters with each other, one song at a time. The writer also has a secret interest in being an artist. Perhaps the publisher can sense this either from the showreel or from talking to the writer. This creates opportunities. If the singer is a strong vocalist, they could do features on dance label releases and write and sing their own lyrics to tracks created by DJs and labels that engage with the publisher. This could become a route to market that the writer had not previously thought about and which therefore was not included in the selling pitch.

The Email Pitch to a Sync Agent

Once again, the language shifts in a different direction when pitching to a different type of potential partner. This time, the email pitch is to a sync agent. The language to focus on concerns the master rights and the suitability of the music to aid visual media such as TV, film, games, ads and corporate music.

Scenario

A US-based production duo that predominantly create hip hop music wish to explore other business options for their music. They create tracks together and they work fast, with a high output of two new tracks per week. They lease and license their tracks online to potential users but wish to build more awareness of their work. Their aim is to work with artists directly but they are struggling to make this happen. They have switched their attention to the sync market as a way to expand their income streams, their portfolio of clients and their reputation. They have researched some sync agents that could potentially be a good fit for their work and, reading the submissions guidelines on a sync agent's website, they have found the correct email address to submit to. In addition, they have read on the sync agent's website that the sync agent takes 50% of any licensing fees gained as a result of any placements. The sync agent does not ask for any backend royalties on publishing. This means that the royalties that the creators gain from any placement need not be split with the sync agent. The sync agent only takes its cut from the fees that come in for the use of the recording. The sync agent therefore needs to know the status of the master rights and is less interested in the publishing side of the pitch. The duo are acutely aware that this type of arrangement could benefit their plans because they own the master rights, plus any placements that they gain from the sync agent will generate royalties. This will give them leverage in talks with music publishers further down the line, as their catalogue is active and earning.

Considerations: The duo are in a strong position here. They have the contractual freedom to trade freely in this manner. There are two things that could strengthen their pitch. The first is their ability to demonstrate an understanding of the moods that their music represents and thus the types of visuals that their catalogue could aid. This allows the sync agent to immediately understand the contexts to which their work may be aligned. Second, the duo must be aware that if they are using any uncleared samples, this could be damaging for their pitch. If the duo are using samples that are royalty free, there is no issue. However, if the duo have sampled copyrighted material, they are at risk of infringing a third party's rights. If the sync agent knows this, it will be less interested in the pitch. The sync agent doesn't need the hassle of sample clearance duties or the risk of letting down one of its media clients. If the duo were to sign with the sync agent, there would almost certainly be a disclaimer in the contract regarding the admission of any uncleared samples.

An additional consideration for the duo is whether the sync agent signs music non-exclusively or only on an exclusive basis.

Email Pitch Style 1

Hey,

We are a hip-hop duo looking to get into sync. Check out our beats. We have a Drake style, Kendrick style, etc: LINK

NAME OF THE DUO

LINK

Email Pitch Style 2

Dear __,

We are a two-person electronic production team from ___, USA. We have a range of hip hop music which we are looking to license into film and TV opportunities. We have visited your website and gained a good understanding of what you do, and we believe we could be a good fit to your existing roster and add value to the catalogue you represent to your client base.

We own our masters, so clearance is nice and easy. We have a tempo range of 90–140bpm and predominantly support the following moods: chill, energetic, party, dark and dangerous. Please find this LINK where you can hear the tracks that we currently have available. We are continually adding to our catalogue of available music with tracks that are consistent with this style.

Is this something you would be in the market for?

Best wishes,

DUO NAME
LINK

Email Pitch Style 1 sounds very much like the duo are trying to find a home for their unwanted beats. They are using language that would be more appropriate for platforms such as YouTube and Beatstars rather than a sync agent. This pitch style says very little and yet so much. They admit that they have no experience in the sync market – and therefore perhaps don't understand how the business works – when they say they are 'looking to get into sync'. Email Pitch Style 2, by contrast, achieves a great deal. Even if the duo have no experience in the sync field, it doesn't matter because they are using the right language. At one point, they refer to tracks that are 'currently available'. This is professional language: it not only makes the offer clearer, but also implies that the duo have a catalogue that is active and popular. The email concludes with a question that creates a call to action and yet remains professional: 'Is this something you'd be in the market for?' It might sound simple and obvious, but using the word 'this' in this context is interesting. They don't say 'our music' or 'our art'; they say 'this' – which makes it sound more like a business prospect that is only temporarily available.

Lazy Language and Generational Gaps

The use of the recipient's name at the start of the email is interesting in the above email examples. Informalities such as 'hi' without using a name can often annoy people from a certain generation. It also could be seen as a lazy copy-and-paste technique. Using the recipient's name takes no extra time but adds a human touch. It's human nature for people to use each other's names and it's not overly familiar to use someone's name if you don't know them. Text talk and abbreviated language might be the norm on social media; but in a formal email with a professional, it is important to try to formalise one's approach. In time, perhaps this will evolve to the point where text-style chat becomes commonplace in emails as younger generations wash through and older generations retire; but for now, there are a great deal of people in the music industry who remember life long before mobile technology and social media, and these people are often irritated by informality and lazy language.

Considerations for Artists Pitching to Record Companies

Record companies will ask many questions about a potential recording artist before they consider working with them and artists should do the same.

Here are ten key points that an artist should research about a label:

- the size of its roster;
- who it distributes through;
- its genre specialism;
- the number of people who work there and the roles they play;
- its reach potential;
- its approach to marketing and promotion;
- its partnerships with tastemakers;
- its reputation;
- its approach to artist development; and
- its ability to demonstrate survival through evolution.

If the goal is to secure investment from a record company, you have no choice other than to show that a market exists for what you do and where your place is in that market. This is often best achieved through the less glamorous tasks.

It is so important to build organic growth. This demonstrates to a record company that you are willing to work hard and are on a profitable path. It is all too easy to often *feel* like you are doing the right things as opposed to *actually* doing the right things.

Scenario 1

band play a gig. The atmosphere is electric and typifies what their career path is all about: being in the moment. The band have the following options straight after the gig:

- Chill out backstage and do nothing.
- Go and stand by their merchandise stand for the 'hot 15 minutes' immediately following their performance.
- Walk around the venue talking to their fans and collecting their email addresses.

What's the best option? Certainly not doing nothing. That's perhaps the desirable option, but this is a business. The correct option is surely a combination of the second and third options above. The band members should split up and share these duties between them. Once the work is over, they can relax. This is a professional mindset which is more investable.

Scenario 2

A band are playing a gig tonight. They arrive early for the soundcheck. They are worried that not many people will turn up, as they are in a town where they are less well known. They have a couple of hours before they need to be back at the venue after the soundcheck. The band have four options:

- Sit backstage and worry that nobody will turn up. Maybe have some food too.
- Post on social media that they are playing tonight.
- Pick up their flyers and walk around the town handing them out to people.
- Pick up their flyers and walk around the town searching for people who look like they would enjoy the show by discreetly examining their clothes, age and appearance. The band know who their market is and who to approach. They don't just give out flyers – they talk to people and invite them to the gig.

It is the last option above which makes a true impact. Those people in the street may one day reminisce about how they first met the band when they were handed a flyer before going to see them at their first gig. The band have put their egos aside and done what is best for the band. They are not scared of rejection in the street; they are fearless and confident. The band that chooses this option are investable.

Scenario 3

A house DJ has been perfecting her craft for some time now and her debut single is ready for release. She has two options:

- She ramps up momentum on social media for her release. Her friends and family all get behind the release and share like crazy on release day. Her streams spike to over 2,000 on the first two days of the song being released. She has family in Australia and France who all stream the song.
- She doesn't push her release to her friends and family. Instead, she spends three hours a day for four straight weeks researching key tastemakers to

pitch her release to. She knows her sub-genre of future house very well and has gained support from some key record companies which are playlisting her track on their Spotify and Apple playlists. She has also secured the support of a valued YouTuber who she connected with through SubmitHub. The YouTuber was granted a premiere to the track the day before the official release and it gained 215,000 streams overnight before it was released to the public. The song subsequently gains support from DJs.

It's the same song, but the strategies yield completely different results because the creator adopts a professional mindset in the second option. In the first option, her friends and family play the song because they love her, not her music. The peak in her streams falls as quickly as it rises and provides confusing and useless data to the digital services providers because the people who streamed the track are not generally listening to other tracks of this style. It will take the creator much longer to establish a foothold on a platform like Spotify as a result, because the platform won't know who to introduce her music to. The second option fast-tracks her success and she can then use her data as leverage to gain record company interest for her future releases.

36
Songwriters Pitching Songs to Recording Artists

A songwriter does not need to be an artist. There are many songwriters who create songs for commercial opportunities and recording artists. There are also recording artists who write songs for other artists. Many songwriters create songs that could work in different genres with a variety of artists. Songs can often be arranged and recorded with a set of production values that determines the style after the song has been composed. The line between where songwriting and music production sit in this context can be blurry.

There is a tendency for many creators to compose some songs that naturally seem to follow a different direction from others. Therefore, songwriters often have partial songs or song ideas that can fleshed out further down the line. Many writers have an informal category inside their catalogue that 'sits on the shelf' until the right project comes up. It could be that those songs have potential commercial appeal but don't fit the style of the projects that the writer is working on at that specific point in time. Then there is more purpose-led songwriting, where a writer composes a song for a specific project; this could be for or even with a recording artist. When it comes to writing songs for recording artists, it is important to consider who needs songs. Ed Sheeran and U2 don't need songs, so there is little point in writing for them. They're both acts that write their own songs. They collaborate with others, but they don't look for outside songs as such. However, there are many artists who do need songs. Record companies and artist management companies often seek songs for their acts, and this is where partnerships between songwriters and music publishers are important.

Suitability

Suitability is key to being a commercial songwriter. It is important for a songwriter to understand what kind of writer they are, as there are several different roles that can be played. There are writers who excel at writing lyrics, writers

DOI: 10.4324/9781003452119-41

who excel at creating melodies but are less strong with lyrics; writers who relish the role of intermediary between the artist and the producer; writers who work best on their own; and writers who work best in a collaborative setting. Some writers work well as an initial song starter that begins a session with a concept and a title; while others work more reactively, responding to suggested ideas with improvements. A writer should understand what role they play best – even if they are capable of playing all of these roles. Many of the best writers can adapt their role to suit who they are working with and the best interests of the song.

Another key consideration in terms of suitability is genre strength. The late British-Canadian songwriting great Ralph Murphy had hits spanning five decades across a wide range of genres. He once said: 'A great song is a great song. It's just a question of switching the vocabulary to fit the genre.' When a song is stripped to its bare bones before production begins, it's easy to see what Ralph meant; but in the modern era, technology and music production very often sit at the heart of song creation, which can sometimes dictate the genre earlier on in the compositional process. This is where genre specialism becomes relevant to modern songwriters. Let's assume that a songwriter that has a natural sway towards R&B: is it the ballad side of R&B or the dance side of R&B? Is it the contemporary side of R&B or is it really neo soul that the writer sits most comfortably in? Again, the lines between music production and songwriting can be blurry, but these are all worthy questions for any creator to consciously consider. A songwriter's creative cognition links to being comfortable with familiarity; but expansion of the mind is always possible through exposure to new styles and approaches.

Research

The word 'research' tends to be associated with academia, but it needn't always be. Research is something that we all do in different ways. Commercial songwriters tend to thrive when they understand what makes people tick, but that doesn't always come naturally. It often takes effort – in the form of research – to understand the latest trends in song structure, melodic construction and rhyming schemes; and that's just the musical side. The business of songwriting also requires research. Let's imagine that a songwriter has just finished collaborating on a song with an artist. A few weeks go by and the artist and their manager say that they've had a change in direction and the song no longer fits; but the songwriter has been reading up and listening to what works well in the Chinese market and is aware that the song is a natural fit for that market. It's examples like this that make songwriters so useful to music publishers. The song gets pitched and cut with a Chinese artist and label; and the writer and the original artist get the kudos and the royalties, while their stock in the music industry rises. The original artist's PR is happy because they have a new PR angle to run with too. And all this because the writer did their research and spotted an opportunity for what was otherwise a rejected song.

If writers are willing to put the graft into research, the rewards will follow. A big part of the research for writers lies in understanding who to pitch to. Working with music publishers who supply songs to labels and licensors is often key, so searching for the right publishers that work in the writer's specialist markets and genres is a crucial part of the job. There is a big, wide world out there and there are opportunities for songs every single day.

Interview: Ricky Hanley, Songwriter, Producer and Vocal Arranger, Hanley Music

Ricky Hanley is a multi-platinum-selling songwriter who composes songs for a wide range of recording artists in various territories around the world. Ricky has enjoyed huge success in Asia writing for a range of artists in both the Japanese and South Korean markets, including Arashi, Shinee, E-Girls, TVXQ, EXO and Generations from Exile Tribe. Ricky is also a renowned vocal arranger and works behind the scenes on primetime TV shows, as well as for a range of household-name recording artists.

You play several roles in the music industry, but let's zone in on your role as a songwriter for other artists. How did that start for you?

As a session singer, I had a regular session at a studio in Chelmsford and one of the producers there was asked to write for a band. He asked me to help, so we tried and it went very well. The band's management asked us to write for a 16-year-old girl from Newcastle that they were looking after. We agreed and wrote several songs for her. That girl was Cheryl Cole and as interest was building in her, we started getting offers from publishing companies. We eventually chose Global and Ashley Tabor.

How important is the role of music publishers and sub-publishers in your success?

Huge! I signed first to Global and Miller Williams, who ran the company, would bring so many opportunities to us. Also, I simply wouldn't have had the success I've had in Asia without my sub-publisher, Soundgraphics.

You have found a great deal of success by composing songs for artists and labels in Japan. You write the songs in English, but they are then usually translated into Japanese. How does translation affect the creative process and what considerations do you make for this when composing?

Very little, I would say. With the ballads, I am conscious that the Japanese like very emotional toplines; but I rarely think about the lyrics translation when writing.

Do you think it is more effective to have a niche as a songwriter or is it better to take a multi-genre approach?

Many A&Rs like to pigeonhole writers and will make up their minds as to where you fit as a writer. It's something that I've always had a problem with, but that's just how it is. It is important to do what you do best, though.

Have you any advice for emerging songwriters who are looking to create and pitch songs for artists and labels?

Know your marketplace; remember it's about the song more than the production; and of course, stay positive. It's a tough business.

Pitching

The preferred method of communication for music publishers is email and a writer's email to a publisher need not be long. The email should focus on who the writer is, what the song is, and who and where it could fit; and should then let the publisher decide whether they can see potential in working together on it. There is little need to send a bio or photos – it's not the same thing as an artist pitching themselves to a label. The publisher's interest is in the song and the writer, and not so much in their backstory or future plans. A songwriter can do single song assignments with a range of different music publishers, which can widen their network and their knowledge base. With this kind of approach, songwriters tend to start receiving lead sheets from music publishers offering details on labels and artists that need songs. These take the form of briefs which give detail on the requirements for the songs that are in demand. The brief guides the writer on what to create for both current and future projects, and gives them insight into the projected landscape of the music industry in the months ahead.

Pitching one song at a time is preferred by many publishers, although this does vary and each will have its own preferences when it comes to submissions. Some prefer MP3s attached to an email while others prefer links that don't clog up their inboxes. It's healthy for writers to think like publishers do, so they should consider sending as much information as possible regarding the suitability of the song. This usually includes the genre, the intended artist or project and a comprehensive but simple breakdown of the copyright details in the body of the email – for example:

- the song title;
- the writers' names and percentage splits of the song; and
- the names of the publishers of the co-writers (if relevant).

Some publishers prefer to receive the above details in the title of the MP3 file name, as that saves them the hassle of doing this task themselves before submitting a batch of songs to a record company. This approach allows information to be quickly retrieved on the alignment of a song title with writer splits, rather than sending an additional Excel document.

Who Else Can Songs be Pitched to?

A variety of subscription-based platforms enable songwriters to pitch songs for the consideration of various projects, including artists and labels that need songs. US-based Taxi Music and Music Xray are among the platforms that match songwriters with song opportunities. *SongLink International* (www. songlink.com) is a longstanding UK-based publication which has served songwriters and music publishers since the 1990s, providing a monthly tip sheet listing the artists and labels that are looking for songs each month. What makes this publication particularly useful to songwriters is that it is not a broker service. The publication provides the contact details of the artists and labels that are seeking songs, allowing writers to pitch directly to the artist or label. This gives songwriters who are looking to extend their network the opportunity to build their connections themselves through their own communications, rather than getting clogged up inside a filtered submission system.

Interview: David Stark, Editor/Publisher, SongLink International, UK

You play a vital role in linking those who create and pitch songs with those who need them. What was it that made you want to set up SongLink International?

In the late 1980s, there was a three-page photocopied tip sheet called *Songplugger* which I subscribed to. As an occasional songwriter myself, I was also extremely interested in the song pitching, production and recording side of the industry. I knew the publisher – an American guy living in London – and he eventually asked me if I wanted to take it over when he decided to return to the USA. Around the same time, I was offered a good job by *Billboard* magazine to move to their Amsterdam office (aka *Music & Media*) and run their new European music industry directory, *Eurofile*, which I did for nearly three years. On my return to the UK in 1991, I ended up working for a company called the Music Industry Research Organisation (MIRO), which by coincidence had bought *Songplugger* during the interim period. I then developed it into a popular monthly magazine for music publishers and songwriters, including the all-important song pitching leads for many name artists back in those days. MIRO sadly went out of business in July 1993, at which point I decided to go independent, changed the name to *SongLink International* and published my first issue in September 1993, to a great response from the industry.

SongLink International facilitates a greater sense of autonomy within the music industry because it allows people to connect directly rather than going through a filtered system. Is this one of the values you wanted to create with the service?

Yes indeed – the model was always based on getting information about which artists are looking for songs from their A&R person, manager or producer, and then publishing their direct contacts for subscribers to pitch their songs to. Before MP3s and web links became industry standard, this meant sending cassette tapes and CDs by post. This has always worked very well in most cases; but in recent years, I have started to filter a small percentage of the leads – especially those from major artists or labels that don't want to be bombarded by emails from songwriters or publishers.

You have seen many independent songwriters find success with their songs through your service. This must give you a great sense of satisfaction. Are you aware of many of the success stories that your platform has created?

Yes, I am – in fact, there is a page on the *SongLink* website titled 'Success Stories' (http://songlink.com/songlink-international-success-stories.html) which does exactly that, including testimonials from *SongLink* subscribers as well as many artists, labels and producers who have found songs through the service.

What changes have you witnessed in the song pitching business since SongLink International started?

As mentioned, the biggest change for subscribers pitching their songs was the submission method from CDs to MP3s; while the emergence of platforms such as Soundcloud, among others, has also changed how songs are pitched. The other big change is that many major artists and labels now use their preferred writers and producers for their projects. This has made it quite hard for new or unsigned songwriters to break into this segment of the industry, unless they have some track record as a writer/producer or even as an artist themselves. Because of this, *SongLink* has to some extent become more focused on indie artists and labels – of which, luckily, there are still many around the globe which are happy to receive good songs and quality demos from unsigned writers or independent publishers. I also publish *Cuesheet* (www.Cuesheet.net), a separate tip sheet covering film, TV, commercials and other multimedia projects requiring songs or music.

What advice would you give to emerging songwriters and music publishers who are looking to find suitable homes for their catalogue?

It's all about doing your research, which *SongLink* can obviously help with. We make all our leads as informative as possible, with plenty of information about each artist, their style of music plus comparisons to other artists, complete with reference tracks or videos. If you have specific artists in mind to target your songs to, that's fine, as long as you know the correct contact person; but pitching blindly to A&R or artist managers these days is almost impossible – unless you get lucky, of course, which can still happen. Collaboration and co-writing are also very much the name of the game, so be prepared to network like mad: go to as many industry events as you can and make yourself known in a positive way without putting people off. There are good opportunities in this ever-changing business, but in most cases you have to make them yourself. And always remember: it's a business, so you need to be aware of publishing contracts, percentage splits, sync and broadcast rights, and all the other elements which make up today's often highly complicated business.

Networks

Building a network doesn't need to take a long time if your efforts are well thought out. As in any other area of the music industry, songwriters need their own network of managers, labels, publishers and artists. This is a people-based business, after all. It's not just emerging songwriters who need to be at events, networking opportunities and expos – even songwriters who are signed to major publishing companies are continually seeking out new projects. Relying on leads and briefs can only get a writer so far. Attending songwriting camps is a great way for writers to extend their networks and their opportunities. These camps take place regularly all around the world, so it is a good idea for songwriters to research those that are relevant to their geographical location and, where possible, travel to other countries to work with writers from other cultures.

The Mysteries of Ghostwriting

The term 'ghostwriter' is used quite liberally, yet it remains rather ambiguous, as it has different definitions depending upon who in the music industry you are speaking to.

The term originally referred to the role played by someone who creates literacy works on behalf of an intended third party. That third party could perhaps be a public figure who subsequently gains the assumed credit for the work. This could take the form of journalism, political speeches or a variety of other forms of text creation.

In the music industry, the term 'ghostwriter' is used by some to describe songwriters who create songs for other artists even though their names are still mentioned in the credits of the song. It could easily be argued that this is not ghostwriting at all; it is merely songwriting. The term 'ghostwriter' is more accurately used to refer to a creator who is paid for their work but is not included in the listed credits. Traditionally, there have been songs that have been bought out in part or in whole by third parties; but this has started to fall out of fashion in favour of listed credits as it negates the need for a 'buy-out', which reduces the risk factor for the third party.

In the modern era, the term 'ghostwriter' is more often used to refer to music producers who create tracks on behalf of well-known producers. This is more typical in electronic genres such as house and hip hop. Ghost producers are contracted more due to the time it takes a well-known producer to create work of the desired standard, rather than because the well-known producer is not sufficiently talented, as some might believe. This is especially true if a producer or DJ is on a big tour with lots of travel and less spare time, with the added pressure to continually deliver new releases within that schedule.

There are also cases of ghostwriters or ghost producers being contracted to contribute to music library projects, sample packs, sample libraries and/or software plugins. Projects of this nature perhaps blur the lines a little further, as in some instances creators are paid a one-off fee for their work while in others they may receive royalties from the sale of licences. A listed credit (or lack thereof) will no doubt be part of the deal, and this may dictate whether a work becomes a quiet piece of a creator's portfolio or a marketing tool to help aid other areas of their work. In many cases, the term 'ghost' is often used, which can be confusing to creators; so it is always worth trying to understand whether a project involves 'ghost creation' in the original sense of the term.

Summary

Being a songwriter is a very popular career route. It can be developed alongside other creative pursuits, such as being an artist, a producer, a DJ, a band member or a music teacher. It is essential to be serious, multifaceted and non-judgmental about the projects you write for. Songwriters can add immense value both to each other and to the music industry. It is a blend of both creativity and music business acumen that defines a songwriter's path.

37
The Expected Standards of Song Presentation

There are various expectations of music creators in the modern era, not least in relation to song presentation. Many music creators feel that it is perhaps unfair to expect them to deliver high-quality recordings of their music. However, with so many affordable portable recording solutions available today, coupled with the wealth of free educational content on YouTube, there is no excuse for failing to do so. Regardless of your perspective on this subject, the undeniable truth is that high-quality song presentation is expected today. This does not mean that all music creators must be experts on music production; it just means that they need to be a little more informed.

Chapters 28, 29 and 30 of this book explored what is possible for music creators when they have the ability to record themselves. There have never been so many opportunities available to those who have developed these skills. In today's gig economy, musicians are turning professional more quickly than ever before, and a key factor in this is a creator's ability to create content in a self-sustainable fashion.

Demo Recordings

At a time when so many of us are in a rush and there is a sense of urgency in creating a final product, there is often a tendency to overlook the importance of a demo before a recording takes place. Digital audio workstation (DAW) recording processes can take a demo to a finished master within the same project. However, this does not mean that a demo is a pointless exercise. Many demos capture a sense of excitement and magic. Some get released and become hit records. Demos form part of the pre-production process – a point which can be improved on. This could be as simple as a band recording in their rehearsal space with their phone. Demos give an informed perspective. Demos demonstrate progression; and in some cases, they can be useful tools to pitch to specific professionals.

DOI: 10.4324/9781003452119-42

Pitching to Record Companies

Before pitching to a record company, it is healthy to ask what the intention is. If the goal is to showcase the capacity to be a great recording artist and there is unreleased material that represents the songs and the artist, then pitching a high-quality demo would be relevant. However, if an artist is looking to pitch product to license to a record label for release, the product must be finished in order for the label to consider it. In this case, the label is considering not only the suitability of the artist but also the capability of the product.

Pitching to Music Publishers

Again, the purpose of the pitch is hugely relevant here. There is little point in sending songs off without intention and purpose in the hope that someone will email back with great news and a contract. There needs to be a reason as to why a song is being pitched to the person you're pitching to. For instance, if a songwriter wants to show a music publisher that they can write great songs but they lack good collaborators to produce them, then perhaps the music publisher would gladly receive a Soundcloud link to some demos showcasing skills that can be developed in a collaborative setting. However, if the songwriter is pitching a song that they would like to get cut with an artist on a label, it needs to be the final polished end product. There are two primary reasons for this. First, the pitch needs to demonstrate why the song is a good fit for the intended artist, which requires the song to be produced in a way that sounds relevant, interesting and professional. Second, if the label likes the song, it may wish to buy the production, which means that this needs to be finished before the song is pitched.

Pitching to Artist Managers

This perhaps is more dependent on the preferences of the manager and the musical genre that the creator is working in. For instance, in the case of a pop act that has lots of interesting hooks and song ideas that could be embellished further with the aid of a producer, a short exhibition of their work could be appreciated by a manager. On the other hand, many artist managers want to see that an artist has already established themselves to a certain extent, and this means having released product to share that exhibits their style. Bands that have a solid understanding of their genre and audience will do far better by pitching finished and released music to managers.

Pitching to Songwriter and Producer Managers

If a songwriter, a songwriting producer or a producer who specialises in production and arrangement is pitching to a potential manager, they should ensure that a portfolio of their work is available online for the manager to access. The expectation here will usually be a track record of success, together with perhaps an idea of what their next career steps might look like and where the manager can fit into the plan. The creator will also be expected to specialise in a genre.

Pitching to Sync Agents

A sync agent will always expect to see the finished product. It is unlikely that a sync agent would show interest in a song and ask for the arrangement or production to be reworked. Their decision on whether to collaborate will be based on the potential not only of the song but also of the recording. A sync agent is generally looking for finished product that they can pitch into licensable opportunities.

Pitching to Producers

If an artist is keen to work with a producer, it is pointless to pitch a final product. However, the artist could pitch a self-produced project showcasing ideas and arrangements which could be re-recorded and/or further embellished by the producer. Some producers would prefer to receive a roughly recorded acoustic demo as a starting point for a recording project. It's always worth remembering that a producer will ask similar questions to a manager, an A&R or a PR. 'What is your genre?' and 'What style are you wanting to achieve?' will inevitably come up, so artists should dig deep into some self-discovery before seeking to work with a producer. There's nothing wrong with a producer offering a vision to the artist – especially if it's informed by industry practice rather than just opinion. However, if a producer misinterprets the artist's style, the artist will then be stuck with the wrong vision. Often artists don't know what they want for their sound until they've explored all the options. Some artists don't know what they want unless they try things out and can then eliminate certain options from their artistic self-enquiry. This can get expensive, though.

Pitching to DJs

If an artist or writer is looking to pitch their song to a DJ producer who will put a track together around a vocal, there is very little point in pitching an entire production. A piano and vocal or guitar and vocal will please most DJs – or perhaps even just an acapella labelled with the tempo and the key of the song. This gives DJ producers all they need to build their work around it.

Outsourcing

Putting together an entire arrangement relies on having the right parts in the arrangement. This may involve outsourcing an aspect of the arrangement to a specific musician, who can add immense value to how the song is presented. There are plenty of reliable web-based platforms such as www.soundbetter.com and www.airgigs.com where some excellent self-recording musicians can be hired to play on your song. For example, a creator may wish to have a real trombone player re-record the exact part that they have arranged in MIDI. The goal here is to have a real instrument player replicate a part that has already been created. Alternatively, a creator may wish to hire a guitarist to record some parts but not quite know what parts are required. This is where sending references tracks of existing songs can be useful to a session musician: there is less room here for interpretation and the creator still plays an important role in the stylistic output.

Loops, Samples and Plugins

The music creation software marketplace is evolving at a rapid pace, with some truly pioneering steps being taken every year. A seemingly endless array of sample libraries, software instruments, effects plugins and synthesis and re-cording outboard emulations are now available and in constant demand. As the market grows, competition follows, which tends to make price points even more appealing to creators. Sample packs give music creators instant access to the building blocks of a specific genre or style, which they can then utilise in their own creative works. Outstanding-sounding software synths are also read-ily available, and a combination of these tools can unlock potential in creators and inspire many to achieve more with their music. It is entirely possible today for a drummer to record their drum parts and then replace all of the drum hits quite quickly with the sound of a completely different drumkit. Processes like this can increase the sonic potential of self-made records, which can then com-pete in this fiercely competitive marketplace.

Mixing

Many music creators are becoming more comfortable with the processes of re-cording and arranging their music projects. However, the process of mixing a song is perhaps a step beyond their comfort zone or skill set. This is where out-sourcing the mixing process to a professional mix engineer can be useful. This can make a big difference to the overall quality of a recording and subsequently its chances of success.

Mastering

Audio mastering is the final step in the production process for a song before it is released. It involves a signal chain process that includes compression, limit-ing, equalisation, saturation, stereo imaging and volume and loudness control. This is a crucial step for a song to sound as professional as possible. Loudness control is especially relevant for streaming. If a song is too loud, the streaming platforms will turn it down when they optimise the song file for their platform. Most streaming platforms have different thresholds for loudness and there is no standardised set level that they all adhere to. Therefore, mastering a song's loudness is a crucial step when releasing music on digital service platforms. Mastering is achieved by many professional mastering engineers using software, while others still use hardware to achieve the desired result. Mastering soft-ware suites tend to be more expensive than the average instrument and effect plugins, but mastering engineers can be hired for reasonable rates through var-ious online platforms.

Stem Flexibility and Delivery

It is a good idea to be organised with the stem files of a recording project and have each track on a balanced setting and exported without any mix bus pro-cessing. This allows tracks to be revisited without the need for the original DAW recording project. This is also useful when edits are needed for sync pro-jects, alternative mixes for promo material and potential remixes. When work-ing with a producer, it is good practice to have them export all the stem files from the completed recording project and store them safely somewhere (along with a backup). This means you won't need to keep going back and forth to the producer as and when edits, revisions or remixes may be required. Having stems readily available for songwriting producers is important because it makes for a speedy delivery to a record company if you sell the production rights after gaining a cut with an artist.

38
Production Music and Media Composers

What is Production Music?

Often referred to as 'stock music', 'library music' or simply 'royalty-free music', 'production music' is instrumental music that is composed and produced primarily for use in a variety of media projects such as films, TV, podcasts, corporate presentations, ads and more. Production music is a desirable choice for music users that need to license music to aid a visual project but lack the budget and time to commission custom-made music. It is not just the composition but the recording of that composition that is covered under a licensing agreement. Often production music is either composed or compiled in a thematic form – perhaps in the form of an album or a collective body of work that falls within a specific mood or style. Production music is typically quite versatile in its structure, giving music users the flexibility to use it in several ways when trying to add emotion to a visual.

Who Uses Production Music?

Production music is used every day across a wide variety of media, including TV and film. The customers in this context are the media professionals who wish to use the music to aid a visual source. Production music can be a great option for many music users because it is readily available, the rights are pre-cleared and it is often covered under a blanket licence with a performing rights organisation (PRO). It's also generally more cost effective when compared to using commercial music (ie, music that is commercially released in the public domain). Earlier in this book, we looked at this in the context of PRS for Music and the BBC in the UK.

Unlike commercial music that is used for sync, production music does not require the permission of the rights holders; instead, it is licensed quickly and easily.

DOI: 10.4324/9781003452119-43

Production music tends to cover a diverse range of styles and moods, and often has quite descriptive titles, enabling users to identify the option that is best suited to their needs. Production libraries typically have a range of metadata on each piece of music and filters to facilitate searchability. These include factors such as tempo range, instrumentation, mood and theme. Trends in production music are noticeable in the same way as they are in commercial music. However, music from all genres and time periods is needed to cater to this varied range of media needs.

Rights and Usage

Rights and usage typically vary depending on the agreement, which means that a music user may be limited in terms of how they can use a specific piece of music. This could relate to geographical location, the length of the music used and the types of platforms on which it is used.

How Are Creators Paid?

There are generally two ways in which creators are paid for their work, although this can differ from country to country depending on how licensing is set up with broadcast partners:

- Licence fees: Upfront fees paid by a media company that cover the usage of the recording.
- Performance royalties: Royalties that relate to the composition being played in public which are collected and distributed by the PRO that the composer is a member of.

There are some key factors to bear in mind, however. In the USA, it is often the case that a library pays a one-off fee to a composer. This then allows the music library to take 100% of the licence fees that it receives from that point onwards. There is a sense of risk for both parties with this approach. By contrast, in the UK, upfront licence fees for the use of a recording are typically split between the composer and the music library.

Licence fees can vary significantly, from small fees for temporary internet usage and scale to considerably higher numbers for use on major networks.

Performance royalties are effectively paid by the broadcast partners, which have annual contractual agreements in place with the PROs. Although the media companies do not have to pay the costs of performance royalties, they still have an obligation to declare what music they have used; this information is then submitted to the relevant PROs so that accurate royalties can be distributed to the creators and the library that the creator is published with. For clarification, performance royalties here are split between the creator and the music library that they are contracted with for their musical works. The music library is a music publisher. The royalty rate split between the music library and the creator will be dictated by the contractual agreement between them but is typically a 50:50 split. If there is more than one composer and there is a 50:50 split agreement between the creators and the library, the library will collect 50% and the remaining 50% will be split between the creators according to whatever split they have between them (which will almost certainly have been declared in advance when the contract was issued to the creators by the music library).

Much like licence fees, royalty rates for usage can vary. Royalty rates are largely dictated by the number of viewers or listeners to a particular TV broadcast for which the music is used. Many PROs publish lists for various network and broadcast partners for both radio and TV for peak and non-peak times, so it is possible for music creators to try to guesstimate how much they might earn. The difficulty for creators (and libraries) that wish to estimate their royalties in advance is that they are often unaware of how and when their music will be used until it is actually used. Royalty statements are received by creators and libraries on a biannual or quarterly basis, depending on the PRO's protocol. It is at this point, when usage becomes clearer, that royalties are calculated and distributed to the rights holders.

Modern Advancements

One recent advancement in production music is in the addition of more flexible options for music users. A good example of this is UK-based interactive library Flexitracks, which is represented by Universal Production Music. Flexitracks offers music that can be flexed into various forms, as the tracks are split into groups of chords, drums, bass and melodies. This effectively allows users to remix production music on the fly inside of their own digital audio workstation (DAW) or video software, with a highly customisable approach. This can save time for music users, as they don't need to communicate back and forth with music libraries or composers on their requests for edits – instead, this is something that they can do themselves without breaking any terms or conditions.

Interview: Dr Paul Rogers, Media Composer/Producer, UK

Dr Paul Rogers is a UK-based media composer and producer who works with Flexitracks.

Do you compose solely to brief or does your creativity spark in ways that make you create ideas which you then document and return to when the right projects come up?

I create continuously. There is never a day that whizzes past when I don't have melodies, rhythms and harmonies emerging in my thoughts. Each time I pick up an instrument, rather than playing songs I've already learned, I just allow my mind and fingers to invent new ideas and wander over the instrument in a playful, explorative manner. This means I have an ever-flowing catalogue of ideas and music snippets (I try to make a rough recording of these ideas whenever possible, just on a phone or similar) which I can return to if I am working to a brief and I need some starting points. However, sometimes working with a brief can promote new and interesting ideas which I wouldn't normally think of, due to the stimulus aiding new ways of thinking. It's a misconception that working to a brief is limiting – in my experience, a brief can spark some beautifully creative lines of enquiry which push you beyond your normal ways of working.

Are there compositional methods that you use when it comes to how music theory supports specific moods and emotions?

There are tried-and-tested harmonic, melodic, rhythmic and textural elements which it is possible to turn to in order to create a desired mood, feeling or emotion. The obvious examples are descending melodies evoking melancholia; minor third intervals evoking sadness; and fast tempo and syncopated rhythms stimulating a feeling for dancing. There are countless more examples and many of these form part of the embodied knowledge that I draw on when writing. Waveforms, frequency bands and sound design also greatly interest me when seeking to evoke emotion. Even inaudible frequencies (eg, very low musical notes which can't be heard) can create sensation and emotions. I am always looking to use these methods – sometimes tacitly, sometimes overtly; but I also like to experiment to discover accidental combinations of textures and musical components which can often surprise you with how they make you feel.

Has your music ever been licensed to a project that has surprised you, in terms of how your music has aided a visual that you had not considered?

Often! I remember one theatre soundtrack where, for one section, they accidentally used a piece I'd composed for a different section, but the symbiotic and serendipitous coupling of the sound and visual was profoundly better and more appropriate than any of us had expected. Working with production music for TV is also eye-opening in this regard. For much of this type of work, I have no idea which of my tracks have been used on which TV shows until the royalty statements come in. I've found pieces I had composed and would have expected to be used for a gritty US historical drama being used on a UK daytime panel show. The combination of sound and visual is extremely complex and the reading or understanding of each can be drastically altered by the other.

What success or knowledge did you need to exhibit to gain the attention of Flexitracks before you were signed?

Production skills, first and foremost – the ability to record, mix and master your own material is essential; or the ability to work closely and successfully with a producer who can help facilitate the complete production, from writing to finished product. They knew I had production skills; but alongside this, I happened to have a focused aesthetic area of specialism, which they were also looking for. There are arguments for being widely adaptable in writing for media; but there are also arguments for focusing on what your passions and interests are and becoming the best you can be in your own niche area. It's the latter which has worked for me – most of my media work has resulted from being asked to deliver something which is relatively unique to me.

What advice would you give to any emerging media composers?

Keep making as much music as you possibly can: be prolific, be consistent. The more you make, the better you will get – I'm still learning new production and composition skills daily. Create high-quality private playlists of your new material, with consistent themes, so that you have suitable portfolio material ready to send links to anyone who needs to hear it. Listen, listen and listen some more!

What Kinds of Creators Tend to be Successful Media Composers?

Media composers for production music encompass a wide range of creators from various backgrounds – from instrument specialists to solo piano composers to rock guitarists to multi-genre producers and more.

Many media composers tend to work on their own and while this is not a hallmark of a production music specialist, it is interesting to understand why. As Dr Paul Rogers observes in his interview, the ability to record and produce music is a prerequisite; although he also notes that the ability to collaborate towards an end product is also an option. The latter relies on a solid under-standing between the co-creators of the ultimate goal, so that the aims of the project don't get confused with those of other music-related projects.

Example 1: The Musician Who Also Plays in a Band

Many bands have some very creative instrumentalists who are not considered songwriters in their bands because they don't write lyrics or vocal melodies. However, they can thrive as media composers, as their flair for both harmonic and melodic construction can be valuable without any requirement for lyr-ics. Add to this their understanding of music theory and recording technology and you have a skill set that makes for a successful production music creator. This describes many creative musicians who play crucial roles in bands when it comes to arrangements and musical compositional elements that lie outside the realm of traditional songwriting in the world of commercial music. Many creators fit this description and may not perhaps have considered how useful they could be to a brand-new client base in the media world.

Example 2: The Shy Pianist

There is a consistently high need for solo piano music of various moods. Let's imagine a piano player who doesn't wish to sing or take centre stage. Perhaps they are capable of composing and recording emotional pieces of music that could help to sell or aid key scenes in a TV programme. If this musician were to learn how to record their music using DAW software and study sound de-sign, understand the emotion of what they have created and then pitch it to music libraries, they could carve out their own career route from an otherwise insular path.

Example 3: The Sound Designer and the Instrumental Specialist

Collaboration is a key aspect of the music industry on a multitude of levels. What can work particularly well is when two creatives symbiotically comple-ment each other's skill set. Let's imagine a sound designer who can take a re-corded performance and turn it into a masterpiece through their distinctive approach to synthesis, sampling, mixing and creative productive techniques. Let's now pair them with a performing instrument specialist – for example, someone who can play a zhongruan, a sitar or a kora. Together they could make music that is unique to them. While in the world of commercial music, it can be challenging to create and take to market an area of specialism, in the world of production music it's a different story altogether. Imagine a TV series that explores India's influence on the Western world: the audience could be connected to this narrative through a rich sonic soundscape featuring a sitar, sounding simultaneously both authentic and modern. Niche areas of composition and recording can find a home in this context that increases the stock of the composers. The sound designer goes on to record a host of instrumental specialists, each of whose instrument is rooted in a particular culture. In due course, they become a go-to person for a series of documentaries, before going on to record and license a wide array of sample sounds for film, together with a partnership with a major software company that creates sampled instrument libraries.

Example 4: The Songwriter Who Can't Write Lyrics

Maybe there are some songs that are not supposed to have words. However, a songwriter might think they should. Imagine a songwriter who is determined to create commercial songs, but the lyrics just won't come to them.

If the songwriter steps back and starts to think about the assets and skill set that they do possess, rather than those they don't, they might just see that they have been a media composer in waiting all along. Perhaps by looking beyond the need for lyrics, they can see that their melodies sit best as instrumental pieces that can touch an audience. In time, the composer taps into what stimulates their creative thinking and what moods are naturally created by their style of composition: dark, still, complex and ambient. They go on to become a hugely successful media composer and producer who specialises in dark ambient music.

39
The Importance of Metadata

In the context of music, metadata is the crucial information that assists the audio content of a song, EP or album release. Think of it as a translator that helps the music to speak.

A metadata template is available to download in the assets and resources that accompany this book. This can be accessed at www.jonnyamos.com/music-industry-resources/.

The purpose of metadata is to allow music releases to be categorised and filtered in music libraries, streaming platforms and a range of other digital-based platforms. Metadata enables accurate identification and searchability. It also facilitates smoother royalty collection for rights holders. The use of metadata helps consumers and users to find music and allows for a cleaner revenue flow to rights holders.

The Key Components of Metadata

- Name of the release product;
- Type of release (single, EP, album);
- Name of the primary artist/s;
- Name of the featured artist;
- Release date and year;
- Primary genre;
- Secondary genres;
- Artwork cover;
- Track listing;
- Duration of the tracks;
- Names of the songwriters/composers and their Interested Party Information (IPI) numbers;
- Names of the producer/s
- Name of the recording engineer;

DOI: 10.4324/9781003452119-44

- Name of the mix engineer;
- Name of the mastering engineer;
- Names of any other parties involved with the recording or production processes;
- Names of the music publishers;
- Name of the copyright holders;
- Name of the licensor of the recordings;
- Name of the record company;
- Name of the distributor;
- International Standard Recording Code;
- Universal Product Code;
- Release version and remaster details (if relevant);
- Geographical region of the recording artist;
- Language;
- Lyrics;
- Whether the lyrics are explicit;
- Mood;
- Tempo;
- Keywords;
- Lyrical theme;

Metadata in Context

Different templates for metadata are used by different companies and these might vary in context. For example, music libraries that license music for media might want to know more about the characteristics of a song. They might ask for additional details on aspects such as:

- whether there are male or female vocals;
- a list of instruments used in the song;
- an enhanced description of the song story or message;
- a longer list of mood descriptors;
- the specific tempo of the song; and
- a classification of the tempo (eg, down-tempo, mid-tempo, up-tempo).

A music publisher might ask for further details on the song copyright. This could include:

- where the song was composed;
- where the song was recorded;
- when the song was composed;

- additional contributors to programming or instrumentation;
- the full names of the additional composers and their IPI numbers;
- the full names of the music publishers of the other composers and their IPI numbers;
- the names of any sub-publishers which are contractually linked to the composer's music publisher;
- the names of the collection societies of the composers;
- the role that each composer played in the collaboration;
- a detailed breakdown of percentage splits between songwriters;
- performance share and mechanical share of rights between songwriters and music publishers;
- any territorial exclusions for exploitation and collection; and
- the International Works Standard Code.

It is worth noting some of the key differences in the expectations of metadata. Record labels and distributors focus on recordings and product releases, whereas music libraries focus on the key filters that music licensors use when trying to filter through song options for media and sync opportunities. By comparison, a music publisher's interests more closely relate to the accuracy of the copyright information in respect to the composition.

Metadata helps music to become more discoverable and is also a prerequisite for digital download and streaming platforms, as it enables them to organise their catalogues and curate playlists with greater speed and accuracy. If incorrect metadata is submitted, songs may fail to realise their full discovery potential. Many digital platforms also use their own form of enhanced audio analysis to extract key features and characteristics of a song which further inform the platform of enhanced metadata that they can link to a song's identity. This is particularly useful for platforms in curating playlists and creating customised recommendations for listeners.

Part 6

The Future of the Business

40
The Global Marketplace

Ongoing technological advancements can make the world feel smaller. They can also enhance a music creator's understanding of their place in the international music market.

According to the International Federation of the Phonographic Industry's (IFPI) *Global Music Report 2023*,[1] industry revenue growth is up by 9% worldwide. In past years, it has often been the more dominant music markets that have boosted global figures; but as we move further into the 2020s, we are seeing growth across all major areas of the planet.

The Top Ten Music Markets in the World

- USA
- Japan
- UK
- Germany
- China
- France
- South Korea
- Canada
- Brazil
- Australia

Revenues from streaming, performance rights, synchronisation and even physical sales continue to increase; while digital downloads are experiencing

1 All statements in this book attributable to the IFPI represent the author's interpretation of data, research, opinions or viewpoints published as part of the IFPI's *Global Music Report 2023* and have not been reviewed by the IFPI. Each IFPI publication speaks as of its original publication date and not as of the date of this book.

DOI: 10.4324/9781003452119-46

an ongoing decline. Sub-Saharan Africa, North Africa, the Middle East and South America are the areas of greatest growth, while Asia is still performing strongly. Although North America and Europe are still seeing growth, they are perhaps starting to show signs of saturation which may lead to a plateau as we move into the latter part of the decade.

International Markets Expand as Homegrown Talent Develops

One of the most interesting developments is the explosion of interest in local cultures. As the presence of K-pop in the Western world has been normalised, we may now start to see other distinct musical cultures from Asia and Africa becoming more popular in Western society. Warner Music's Nicholas Cheung, the regional director of hip hop and R&B for Asia, observes that hip hop is influencing a new generation of music creators who are adding their own cultural elements and understanding to the genre:

> There's this local superstar based in Cambodia. He comes from a refugee family that had to go through some difficult things. He mixed a lot of the traditional elements with new hip hop elements and he raps about what he's been through. It's still hip hop but it's something different and not a replication of what's in the West.

This is one example of how Western influences can impact on other cultures. As consumption increases, so too does participation and stars begin to emerge from burgeoning new scenes. In the USA, hip hop has existed since the 1970s. It is an autobiographical genre through which storytellers from various cities share the struggles of their communities. In the UK, grime emerged from the garage movement of the early 21st century; and in the 2010s, we witnessed the birth of drill music – another rap-based form of musical articulation that has become popular in Western societies. These genres have been experienced by many music listeners in the Western world, but perhaps less so – or not at all – in other continents. Hip hop is brand new to some listeners, who have their own struggles and their own stories to tell.

Adam Granite – the chief executive officer (CEO) of Universal Music Group for Africa, the Middle East and Asia – believes this trend is still in its infancy: 'We are still at the beginning stages of development of this ecosystem on a global basis. There are literally billions of consumers we expect to enter in the coming years.' Granite also acknowledges that while these trends are exciting, the technologies and cultures must be available to make the market both fair and accurate in terms of royalty collection and copy-right. 'It has been decades of work as an industry to get to this stage and it continues every day,' he adds.

Calvin Wong, CEO for Southeast Asia at UMG, is committed to the growth of domestic talent: 'We can't just tempt artists with the promise of an international career – we must first stay focused on their domestic success, and then from there we can think about the impact on the global market.' It is also encouraging to see that CEOs such as Wong are mindful of the generation gaps between music executives, with their habitual tendencies, and the next generation of emerging music professionals needed to push evolving markets forward:

> We spend a lot of time and effort adding new, talented local executives to our teams. This is crucial as we are seeing a generational change in terms of artists and we must relate to this next generation. The way to do it is to find and develop brilliant young executives in every country.

When local talent and scenes are thriving and there are mechanisms in place to monetise and develop them, markets beyond the domestic become ripe for the evolution of new musical flavours. This is also perhaps due to the interest in global culture that younger generations are developing through social media channels. A good example of this is the emergence of the amapiano genre over the past two years, as managing director of Warner Music Africa Temi Adeniji observes:

> It reminds me of where afrobeats was maybe five years ago. It's interesting as it's not melody based. It's very much vibes and rhythm, and there are no real hooks that people can sing along to. We're seeing crossover hits in mar-kets such as Nigeria with artists incorporating a lot of amapiano elements into the scenes in other countries. It's going to be interesting to watch the trajectory over the next few years.

Adeniji is right: amapiano is a burgeoning genre that is now reaching huge audiences. As it gains in popularity in different markets, arguments as to its precise African origins have begun. This is a hallmark of a popular style, similar to the debate on where house music originated.

As outlined in Chapter 19, Emily Jackson of Horus Music in the UK predicts that these growing non-traditional territories will become increasingly promi-nent on the global music scene:

> I expect to see more territory-specific growth in the industry. This includes Africa, South America and even France and Spain. As dominant markets

such as the UK and the USA become saturated, it only makes sense that big players . . . move to where there is more room to grow and make money. This could provide opportunities for certain types of music – for example, the growth of amapiano or Latin music styles and other regional genres. This is an opportunity both in terms of the creation of music and from a marketing perspective, with growth mirrored in the number of playlists focusing on these genres.

It could be argued that focusing on which genres will trend has its limitations. Trends come and go: that is – and has always been – the reality. Eventually, they become dated, then retro, then rebooted. Perhaps the key focus for music creators lies in understanding not just *what* the trends are, but rather the *how* and the *where*. If a creator is making a style of music that is inspired by a different musical culture or country, it is important that this is noted in the metadata of the track, as it could help the song to find its audience – especially in today's rapidly expanding global marketplace.

Interview: Rudolfs Budze, A&R, Universal Music Group, Latvia

Rudolfs Budze has been a professional DJ for 22 years, playing numerous clubs and festivals across Latvia, Lithuania, Estonia, Poland, the USA, Malta and the Netherlands. He is also a founding member of award-winning act Bandmaster. In the 2010s, Rudolfs began working as a studio producer in his native Latvia, collaborating with a range of artists, while also serving as a talent judge on national television show *Supernova*, which selects Latvia's Eurovision entry each year. He was also the head of Latvian Public Radio until 2019. Around this time, Universal Music Group began to expand its operations into the Baltic region and Rudolfs became an A&R consultant for Latvia.

It is great to see the emergence of a major label presence in the Baltic region. How has the process been since establishing Universal Music in Latvia?

We started small, but luckily quite successfully. We signed a very young artist, Patrisha, and released her first single when she was only 17. Her first two singles were big hits and they now have 4 million views combined on YouTube, which is really an achievement for a small market like Latvia. After that, I went on to sign Singapūras Satīns, who are a local rap supergroup. We signed them right after their biggest independent hit and at the time they had already released two albums. Two further albums later, I can say that they have been our biggest success story so far, with fantastic results in the local market, both in digital and radio coverage. Overall, at this point we have eight signed artists for the Latvian office and it's balanced quite well: we have four pop acts – Patrisha, Aminata, Dons and Grēta (the X *Factor Latvia* winner); and four hip hop acts – Singapūras Satīns, rolands če, Prusax and BANDA BANDA. The digital market is still developing in Latvia, so radio plays a big role in our mainstream presence. This is especially true for our pop artists.

Since we launched, we have been lucky to have won the radio hit of the year with Dons at the Latvian music awards; and also best hip hop album (rolands če), best debut (Patrisha) and people's choice award (Grēta).

What has been the impact on artist development since the introduction of Universal Music into Latvia?

It is too early to measure. We have two developing artists and they get pretty decent radio airplay, but they have some work to do to establish their names in our industry. Other artists on the roster were already strong, with established domestic careers. Collaboration and cooperation with us will be key in taking their careers to the next level.

Scouting and developing talent are difficult; but then come the challenges of launching and marketing an artist's product while also building their PR. What have you learned about the domestic market through the process so far?

Our domestic market (when it comes to recorded music) can be split in two categories: radio and streaming (physical is very small). And they differ quite significantly. Radio tends to accept only very 'safe' music and hip hop is still not that well received by the radio stations, although it is growing on Spotify. Also, our artists (especially pop artists) must be very careful with their public messages. We've had a couple of PR crisis moments. Some of our artists have not been very careful with their statements about polarising topics, such as war and vaccination. They have lost sympathy from radio stations and got dropped from rotation, and they stopped getting invited to do promo interviews. We have since tried hard to make efforts to rebuild their image.

What is your approach to building repertoire for an artist? Do your artists have a vision for their sonic identity or is this something you co-create with them?

It varies, case by case. I would say that rap artists have a much stronger vision for their repertoire. Rappers have a strong identity and image. With pop acts, especially the younger ones, it takes time to develop them into artists. A lot of people on this planet can be good singers, but not a lot can become true artists. Since we are a major label, we must also be aware of the demands of the market.

You have been proactive in securing branding partnerships for your artists.
What considerations do you have regarding how to build synergy between a
brand partner and a recording artist on the label?

Brand deals are a good way to make some money in our market and they also
help in building the artist's brand. We've had some major campaigns such as
rolands če with mobile network Bite, Aminata with mineral water Mangaļi
and Singapūras Satīns with KFC. In all cases, the partnerships made sense.
Hip hop mostly appeals to younger audiences and with rolands če we did a
'back to school' campaign for the mobile network provider before the start of
the school year. It felt organic and rolands' face was on every street corner in
Latvia's major cities – which of course helped his artist brand and PR. Aminata
is into a healthy lifestyle – doesn't drink alcohol, loves sports – so cooperation
with a mineral water brand also made sense. The Singapūras Satīns/KFC deal
was also from the same book: kids love KFC and they love Singapūras Satīns.
In all cases it must make sense. It can't feel fake, because then it doesn't work
for all parties.

Sample-Driven Electronic Music Genres

Electronic genres have long been at the forefront of youth culture, due in part to
the desire of creators and labels to find innovative approaches to sound design
and sonic textures, and in part to the role that the use of samples plays. Today,
world music loops – and in particular, vocals and culturally specific instruments –
are gaining prominence in this regard. In a world where anyone with a laptop
can download a sample of the beautiful texture of a Mongolian throat singer
singing a vowel, a loop of the unique Japanese shamisen instrument or perhaps
an Arabic percussion kit, it becomes much easier for electronic musicians to
incorporate the sounds of cultures outside of their own compared to a guitarist
in a rock band. Diversity in styles and genres and growth in key markets can
only facilitate this further. Ahmed Nureni, general manager of Warner Music
for the Middle East, says:

> The diversity of musical genres is growing rapidly and each region in the
> Middle East and North Africa has its own creative musical soul. Our local
> team are closely engaging with these newly rising genres with a focus on
> discovering and helping the artists within them to build their careers locally
> and across the region. Artists from our region are hugely creative and we
> know that we can help them enjoy massive hits by forging collaborations
> with other performers, producers and songwriters.

This is paving the way towards a more evolved global music market in which lesser-known genres and styles can thrive. If we consider the trajectories of afrobeats and amapiano, we could yet see a fusion of new and exciting Arabic styles that the Western world has never heard before – especially when partnered with Western electronic styles. This decade feels like a golden age of hybrid genres, with style-bending ideas and new fusion genres emerging. This could ultimately result in a higher level of cross-cultural creativity, rather than being merely a passing fashion.

41
Artificial Intelligence in Creativity and Analytics

Artificial intelligence (AI) is not the future. It is the present. It is already here and it is changing many aspects of the music industry in a way that is difficult to fully calculate and consider. AI is a subject that has moved to the top of the mainstream agenda – not only in music, but in society at large. As the decade unfolds, we will no doubt see significant changes resulting from the use of AI.

The Role of AI in Creativity

It could be argued that AI has been prevalent in the context of music technology for many decades now. The concept of Musical Instrument Digital Interface (MIDI) messaging, which allows different musical components and devices to respond and interact with one another, has existed since the early 1980s. Tools that offer randomisation, generative composition and probability have been used in various electronic genres for quite some time now. However, in recent years, we have seen the belief that AI can improve compositional approaches take hold. Many developers have built tools for creators that can be used in different creative ways, which extends to the possibility of bypassing key areas of a creator's limitations, such as music theory and playing capabilities. Generative ideas allow music creators to artificially create sequences and arrangements using complex chord progressions, melodies, basslines and drum patterns without the pre-existing theoretical knowledge that was previously essential.

Composition and Arrangement AI Tools

Music creators now have a host of plugins that are available to them that can generate patterns for their song composition and arrangements. This is all achieved through research into genre-specific patterns and how they relate to mathematics. The results are turned into MIDI grooves, which can then be assigned to the software instruments of a creator's choice.

DOI: 10.4324/9781003452119-47

Genres and styles are studied for their typical patterns. These can range from chord progressions to melodic lines that are typical of specific genres. The results generate patterns that can be used as extracted MIDI data. Imagine analysing 1,000 hip hop songs for their chord progressions, drum placements and basslines. Patterns would emerge. Now try the same thing with 3,000 hip hop songs. The same patterns would emerge, while other patterns would also become apparent. These can then be grouped against specific time periods – for example, early 1990s gangster rap.

Using AI in this way gives creators several options. First, it frees up their budget because they don't have to pay specialist musicians for recordings. AI won't be offended if a creator rejects an idea, which also speeds up the process. Second, a creator's copyright ownership need not be split with other creators where AI replaces the role of a co-creator. Third, it allows creators to venture into new genres that they may not have previously felt comfortable to try. For instance, imagine creating deep house music for the first time. AI will suggest typical chord progressions in the genre, which can then be assigned to pad and piano sounds of choice. It will also generate options for typical basslines, melodies and grooves in that same style. It is then up to the creator to decide which to keep and which to blend with their own ideas.

Playability versus Suitability

It is easy for a music creator's judgement of a song to become compromised when they have been heavily involved in the creative process – perhaps especially if they have played an instrument or instruments in the arrangement. However, it is possible that AI may generate more suitable suggestions than a human when it comes to creating new parts for an arrangement. AI is not biased in the same way as a person. An individual's performance and idea generation are often conditioned by mood, sleep and personal taste. It could also be argued that a person's knowledge base further limits their options. This is not true in the case of AI. Just because a producer can play the piano doesn't mean to say they should. The suitability of choices is perhaps more important to a song's arrangement than who plays what or how an idea was created.

Extracting Artistic Tendencies and Replicating Artistic Traits

Let's now apply this same theory to music creators and how their data can be extracted. Most music creators use patterns in their compositional and arrangement style, even if they're not consciously aware of it. Running a pattern analysis on the use of chords, tempos, melodies and basslines will churn out results which could be called typical of that music creator. This process can be applied to many known artists and is already used by some software plugin developers. Today, any music creator can use AI to generate typical patterns in the style of an artist who inspires them. Perhaps over time, these grooves will be mass produced through intensive data pattern analysis and used for new AI-generated music projects. As this area develops, it could pave the way for music creators and labels to work in partnership with software developers to establish licence fees for the original artists. If, however, a mean average is analysed in patterns across multiple unnamed artists from different labels and styles, this becomes much harder to track and arguably sits outside the realm of traditional copyright values. The source material that is analysed to create AI products has its own IP; so too do the AI products that are created. In time, it may become more apparent that this is a very grey area that needs addressing. In Chapter 19 of this book, Emily Jackson of Horus Music raised some thought-provoking issues:

> AI could increase creativity and provide opportunities for artists to offer up their own work in order for AI tools to learn from it. However, this also poses lots of questions. Who owns a piece of work created by AI? Where does the owner of any work the AI learns from stand in terms of ownership or copyright, and how does licensing work in this scenario?

Perhaps the answers to these questions lie not so much in how data is extracted as in how it is recognised and licensed, with a fair price point and remuneration for the rights holders of the original IP.

Creativity versus Analysis

Creativity and analysis are both essential to the success of a creator, yet they are two different skills that engage different parts of the brain. Creativity taps more into the emotional right side of the brain; while analysis taps more into the logical left side. This is perhaps why some creators find it difficult to identify their best work: they are deeply immersed in the creative side and therefore lack the objectivity needed for analysis. Equally, it is perhaps the reason why some A&Rs are so good at picking suitable choices for singles from an album: it's not their own creative work, so there is less emotion involved in the decision.

Let's try reversing this process for a moment. Instead of creating something and then assessing whether it's worth keeping, let's flip it the other way around: first assess whether an idea is any good and then get creative with it. This process is applicable to many music creators and some are better at it than others. For instance, many electronic producers spend time listening to samples and deciding which ones to work with, and then get creative with them. Similarly, many songwriters and producers listen to song ideas from others and then respond to those ideas to improve what is being shared with them.

AI is perhaps not yet capable of offering feedback on whether an idea is good or not. It would be difficult to develop code that can handle such a wide array of subjective elements. However, what AI excels at is generating ideas for creators. This leaves the creators in a position where they can assess whether those ideas might be suitable for their project. This even extends to AI-generated lyrics. In the end, what defines the output is a series of decisions which are made by a human; but it doesn't always need to be a human that generated the suggestions which informed this process.

AI in Reactive Music Production Software

The 2010s saw the emergence of reactive music production software that can 'listen' to music and react by offering suitable settings on equalisation, compression, saturation and stereo imaging, among other elements encompassed in a digital audio workstation (DAW) project. In theory, this kind of software can bypass the need to fully understand the signal processes involved; although many music creators find that their learning is enhanced by absorbing what the AI does to the music, as it subsequently teaches them more about the process. This is perhaps comparable to having a teacher teach you how to mix. Reactive processing of this kind can be applied to individual tracks within a DAW project and even to a mix bus channel. AI of this kind also extends to audio mastering, which has the ability to render an entire mix and prepare it for distribution. While there are many mixing and mastering engineers who question the morality of this concept, it allows many music creators to create great-sounding results without the need to fully understand the skill set.

It could perhaps be said that AI is a time-saving, copyright-free assistant for music creators. As with many other subjects in the music industry, there appears to be a generational divide in opinion: many of the younger generation see AI as a natural part of their workflow that speeds up their productivity. On the other hand, there are growing issues around rights holders and likenesses which require further exploration. As always, there are two copyrights to consider in this context: the compositional rights owned by songwriters and music publishers, and the recording rights owned by the owners of sound recordings. The subject of compositional tendencies that are analysed in AI is an interesting issue, as it blurs the lines between what has been created and what could be created based on mathematical probabilities. Some developers and creators seemingly have no regard for those who own the underlying rights to their output. Then there are developers and creators who wish to take a more ethical route. There is also the perspective of the industry and its associated rights holders, who are looking for the best way to move forward that ensures parity and best practice for all. We're not there yet, that's for sure.

Ethically Sourced Data for AI Usage

We are now starting to see the introduction of ethically sourced, copyright-cleared datasets for AI music projects. USA-based tech company Global Copyright Exchange (GCX) is a pioneering organisation that caters to a diverse range of users, including AI developers that focus on generative music projects, media companies that want adaptive solutions, sonic branding agencies that enhance a company's message and more. The key is in the clearance and ethical sourcing of music.

Interview: Alex Bestall, Chief Executive Officer, GCX and Rightsify, USA

GCX and Rightsify provide a comprehensive and compliant dataset licensing framework to developers, music and entertainment companies and anyone else looking to train generative AI ethically. Rightsify's catalogue consists of more than 10 million recordings and compositions that are played in thousands of businesses every day and have been streamed billions of times globally.

What role can music play in helping businesses to help sell their products and services?

Music is a powerful tool in the business world – it enhances the customer experience, sets the mood and influences buying behaviour. Through the right selection and strategic use of music, businesses can reinforce their brand identity, improve customer retention and ultimately increase sales.

What should music creators consider when trying to get their music used by brands?

When considering their music for brand use, creators should ensure that it aligns with the brand's identity and the message they want to convey. It's important to maintain the integrity of their own artistic vision while being flexible enough to meet the needs of the brand. Also, creators should understand the rights related to their music and negotiate fair compensation.

What do you think the future looks like for performing rights organisations (PROs)?

The future of PROs is likely to be shaped by increased digitisation and globalisation. As music consumption continues to shift online, PROs will need to adapt their models for more efficient digital rights management, ensuring fair royalties for creators. In addition, with the explosion of AI-generated music, the role of PROs will likely continue to evolve.

How do you think the use of AI by businesses will impact music creators?

AI will profoundly impact music creators. AI has completely dismantled the barriers to entry for creating music. Now anyone can make music, regardless of knowledge or skill. This is both a challenge and an advantage for creators. The volume of music in the marketplace will inevitably increase, which makes marketing and creating connections with fans more important than ever. The licensing framework for AI is still in its early stages and creators should and will be paid for their music when it is used to train AI models and monetised commercially.

What factors do you consider when curating playlists for music users?

When curating playlists, we consider factors such as the intended audience, the mood or vibe of the setting, cultural and regional preferences, and the purpose of the playlist (eg, focus, relaxation, motivation). We also prioritise diversity in music styles and genres to cater to a broad spectrum of tastes. Lastly, we ensure that the selected tracks align with the image and values that the user wishes to project.

AI in A&R

As previously discussed, 'A&R' stands for 'artist and repertoire', but the role involves so much more than what is signified by these two words. It encompasses everything from artist development to the management of relationships, mediation between key partners, stylistic influence, management of expectations and talent scouting. It is this latter aspect in particular that has been dramatically improved through the use of AI.

A growing number of agencies can assist with talent scouting thanks to the smart use of AI. Each agency has its own set of proprietary and often patented methods of capturing data on emerging artists and trends on a global basis.

This type of machine-based learning enables record companies and artist managers to identify and track potential new artists. With such a huge number of musical releases on streaming platforms each week, these technologies analyse the songs and artists that are most likely to break and trend. This is based on a range of data that can be accessed through fee-based services, using filters relating to genre, geography, touring data and social media engagement, together with a cohesive understanding of the artist's market. Tools of this nature are invaluable for record companies which are keen to understand the dyamics of an artist's market and how best an audience can be developed.

While AI now plays a significant role in tracking emerging talent, it has not changed the other duties that are required of an A&R. In fact, it could be said that the core role of an A&R has barely changed. This sentiment is made clear in the International Federation of the Phonographic Industry's *Global Music Report 2023*, as Konrad von Löhneysen, managing director of Embassy of Music, explains:

> That side of what we do as an A&R department has never changed when we are discovering new artists. Right from the start we have to ask ourselves 'What do you hear in the music? What do you see in the artist? What is the special position this will have in the market and who is supposed to listen to it?'

UK-based recording artist Sam Ryder enjoyed a great deal of success on TikTok, which is what brought him to the attention of Parlophone Records, which he later signed with. Having gone into the 2020 Covid-19 lockdown with a sense of uncertainty, it was the social media platform that helped Ryder to find and connect with his audience before the record company came calling for his services. This is a reminder to music creators that they can build their audience with or without the support of major backing, provided that they have consistency, strategy and purpose. Just because major companies can track an artist's self-generated growth doesn't mean that the artist is always available or willing to sign to a label. Growth on social media and streaming gives an artist the leverage to gain their own sponsorships and build their own teams, and choose whether they wish to sign to a major label. It is interesting to note that Ryder left Parlophone in 2023 to rebuild his own team.

AI gives key industry partners a head start in tracking the talent that they may wish to invest in. Perhaps there is still a case for ignoring the capabilities of AI and going back to grassroots to find talent who have yet to build their audience. Or perhaps – much as with music creation – there is a balance between AI and human instinct.

42
Mental Health Awareness: A Creator's Understanding of Self-care

'Mental health' is a blanket term which covers the key elements of psychological, emotional and social wellbeing. It determines how an individual thinks, feels, responds, functions and behaves. Reported cases of mental health difficulties are on the rise in many parts of the world – as is awareness of mental health throughout society.

There is likewise a growing realisation of the importance of mental health in the music business and continual advancements are being made in this regard.

A music creator's career is rarely a regular nine-to-five pursuit. It can be an exhausting path of antisocial hours and unique circumstances that present a range of uncertainties. This can drain a creator of their energy and understanding as to where they fit in society – especially when compared to their friends and family. There are risks of burnout, isolation, malnourishment, disappointment and discontent on an adventure that can throw up many highs and lows.

Interview: Dr Adam Ficek, Clinical Psychotherapist, Counsellor and Musician, UK (UKCP/BACP, DPsych, MSc, MA, PG Cert, PG Clin Dip, PGCE)

Adam Ficek has been in the music industry for the best part of three decades, as both a performing artist and a DJ who has toured the world and found success with various Top Ten releases. In addition to his role as a creator, Adam is a highly respected clinical psychotherapist and consults for a wide range of music industry partners to benefit the wellbeing of music creators.

What mental health challenges do you see most frequently when working with music creators?

Mental health is a large and nuanced area. In the modern digital world of Tik Tok-esque pop psychology, it is important to remember the subjective

DOI: 10.4324/9781003452119-48

understanding of what mental health and mental distress mean to individuals. I think music creators are more prone to emotional overwhelm – whether this is nurture or nature remains to be seen. The existing research paints a mixed picture.

One issue which is more prominent in the modern music industry and for creators is the difficulty with social media. For most of the musicians I work with, social media can be a marketing blessing or personally toxic. The pressure to be on show and offer ourselves up for the consumption of others can lead to fragmentation if we struggle with a sense of self. In my own PhD research, I discovered how 'professional musicking' allowed people to feel both good and shameful about themselves. This rollercoaster of being self-influenced through the eyes of the other is the biggest struggle I see for musicians in the mental health environment. Working on a more solid sense of self is my one of my primary clinical objectives when working with this demographic; and it has also helped my own journey of mitigating the commercial demands of the occupational environment.

What can music creators do to ensure a greater sense of balance and mindfulness in their career?

Mindfulness is a big area and we know from the research that it works for some but not others. I think balance comes from self-knowledge and knowing our wounds. A greater sense of balance or resilience can be cultivated by regulating our emotions through reflective practice such as mindfulness, but also through self-exploration with a certified psychotherapist or counselling psychologist.

Knowing our own bumps and bruises and how we construct our worlds is vital when navigating a tricky environment such as the music industry.

What can creators do to help to balance their expectations in an industry that presents so many highs and lows?

One key component in navigating the volatility of the industry is knowing that success isn't necessarily about talent. Luck plays a huge part in many careers. This could be framed as meeting the right person at the right time, or even a wider cultural perspective of a particular genre being more commercially popular at a specific point in time. There is a need to be able to create and perform to the best of our abilities, and this does also feed into success; but we shouldn't forget the role that luck plays. We can, of course, influence our chances through networking and connecting also; but sometimes the stars just align or they don't. That's life!

How important is time management in the context of a music creator's wellbeing?

Time management is important in every aspect of life if we want to be professional and efficient. When it comes to wellbeing in general, having discipline is freedom. Within the domain of pop psychology, there is often the myth that creativity comes from a place of transcendence. I think this is true to a certain extent; but I also believe that we need to cultivate and optimise this 'muse' to give it the best chance of manifestation. I have personally found it valuable to carve out a specific piece of time on a regular basis. Whether ideas come to fruition is a different matter!

Are there any patterns in mental health that you have observed in particular age groups or types of creators?

From my experience as a musician and clinician, solo electronic or studio artists seem to struggle more, due to the occupational isolation that they encounter. Spending lots of time alone isn't particularly good for anyone, let alone a vulnerable creative. We need human contact in some form, depending on our individual needs and neurodiversity. This connection helps to regulate us emotionally and frame our connective creativity through other people.

I also believe that the young generation of creatives are potentially prone to struggle due to the toxic nature of social media use. As an older creative, I have more choice as to when to engage with social media. Today's youngsters are almost forced into this form of communication – which in part can be helpful but can also be synthetic and destructive. Social media can offer a semblance of connection, but it lacks the nuanced, holistic perspective of real interaction. On these platforms, we can be lured into projecting an idealised part of ourselves almost in competition with others. From my clinical work, this is the biggest stressor for young creatives.

Social Media: A Marketing Monster or a Toxic Tirade of Bragging Rights?

It is probably fair to say that social media is both of these – and much more. An undeniable truth for modern creators is that social media matters. This seems like a frighteningly obvious statement to make, but it is worth absorbing nonetheless. It could perhaps be suggested that avoiding social media outright – however noble or bold this may be – comes at the cost of a creator's visibility and accessibility. Much like many other subjects in this book, this can divide opinion between different generations. The younger generation have never known a world without social media; while the older generations have a basis for comparison – a 'before' and 'after', if you will. This perhaps creates a lack of empathy and understanding of the social media experiences of Generation Z – widely regarded as those born between the mid-1990s and the early 2010s. Gen Z are those who are most affected by the troubles associated with social media. So what has this got to do with music? Everything – because this is the next generation of music professionals Combine this with Dr Ficek's clinically informed observations of those who create regularly in isolation, and then add to this the rise of online gaming culture and the popularity of energy drinks, and we can start building inferences about patterns that exist in Generation X that no previous generation has had to contend with.

Being Accessible on Social Media

The power of social media is undeniable. It has changed the world because it has changed the way in which so many of us communicate with one another. Today, it is entirely possible to watch a TV show and then connect with the actor you've just watched. Being accessible has its advantages; but it also makes it harder to switch off. There is a constant anticipation that someone might get in touch who can change the perceived fortunes of a music creator. And with this comes the risk of being targeted by a range of service providers – many of which may not even be human, although they may appear to be. In an age when creators of music are easy prey for marketing firms, creators may presume that they have been approached rather than targeted. Being accessible to fans might seem like a key priority for music creators, especially those who rely on a direct-to-consumer strategy. However, being accessible at all times can perhaps create a sense of pressure that is unsustainable.

Being Discussed on Social Media

In Chapter 7, when discussing the importance of resilience, artist manager Denise Beighton from Upside UK stated:

> Every artist I've ever met will take the negative comments to heart. They can post a clip of music on a platform and if they have 99 great comments and one bad one, I can guarantee it's the negative comment they'll talk about and remember.

This is perhaps human nature; or maybe it is a particular trait of sensitivity or perfectionism possessed by some music creators. Denise continued: 'It's hard, but accept it: not everyone will like what you're doing.' This is an important message that is perhaps simple enough to understand in theory, but harder to incorporate in practice. In many ways, the media or the public offering negative comments about a creator is nothing new. However, in the age of social media, blogs and forums, this feedback not only is instantaneous but also encourages further debate in comments sections. Many platforms benefit from promoting conversational engagement between users. This generates higher levels of traffic and usage, which translates into increased advertising revenue. However, all of this can have a severely detrimental impact on an artist's wellbeing.

What is the Music Industry Doing to Offer Greater Wellbeing Support to Creators?

There is greater pressure on companies and organisations in the music industry to offer wellbeing support to creators. There is also a heightened understanding of the reasons why this is needed. This is perhaps because the younger generation of music professionals have a more progressive view of its importance. Many major record companies are now building teams of executives at a global level who can support an artistic vision while balancing the needs of the business against the difficulties that artists face in trying to prioritise both their productivity and their wellbeing. Record companies work directly with artists, of course, so it is notable that artist wellbeing is becoming more important to them. The first step for many companies in the music industry is perhaps to acknowledge the need; the second step is to act on it by developing protocols that can support artists in achieving their mutually aligned goals.

The International Federation of the Phonographic Industry's *Global Music Report 2023* reveals that Sony Music has launched an Artists Forward initiative. Senior vice president of artist initiatives and business administration Susan Moultrie explains:

> The goal with our wellness efforts is to ensure that our artists feel, as much as possible, that they're in a position to be at their very best as they proceed down their career path. As part of this, we provide access to counsellors around the world and they can have sessions with a licensed therapist, in person or virtual, depending in their need.

Confidentiality and stigma can be concerns for some artists, so it is interesting to note that Moultrie emphasises: 'The program is confidential – we don't get any details about the calls or the sessions.' This mirrors the standards of large companies operating in other sectors. This is an encouraging step taken by one of the world's leading music conglomerates and a sure-fire sign that times are changing.

Universal Music Group also offers support to artists and is cognisant of the issues raised by Dr Ficek earlier in the chapter, as executive vice president Selina Webb reports:

> Every artist that signs to one of our labels has the opportunity to check in with a counsellor. Maybe they want to talk about their relationship with social media; or they might need some additional support with the huge pressures which come with just being an artist – the volume of work, the intensity of the work and the scrutiny.

Key aspects of this work that cannot be professionally resourced in-house can be outsourced in the same way as, for example, distribution or marketing. Fabian Drebes, co-president of Warner Music for Central Europe, says:

> We can rely on our longstanding collaboration with the renowned mental and corporate health specialists at the Furstenberg Institute who have made coaching, counselling and support with a holistic approach available to our employees, and now also to our artists, with exceptional 24/7 access and services in 16 different languages.

It is not just the major record companies that are putting building blocks in place to support their staff and their creatives. Especially over the last two decades, contemporary music institutes have served as gateways into the music industry through partnerships and educational courses. Student wellbeing is at the top of their agenda in the 2020s, with professionals both on campus and in third-party clinical referral programmes providing support in a similar way to those at major label groups.

A Creator's Awareness of Self-care

To avail of these care packages, either intervention on the part of the company or the creator's foresight to seek help for themselves is required. Mindfulness – a meditative practice of self-awareness – is now practised by a growing number of music creators as a way to create a sense of balance. However, as Dr Ficek observes in his interview, while mindfulness may work for some, it may not for others. Perhaps it is too difficult to arrive at a uniform understanding of how to cope with the often-pressurised environments that characterise the creative industries. As a result, everyone should find their own ways to deal with their individual situations. Creators could perhaps begin by examining what exactly is happening to them when they are not functioning as they might wish to. By becoming more self-aware, they can equip themselves to spot the signs and pursue their own style of intervention that works for them.

43
Beyond the Horizon: Exploring the Future of the Music Business

What has happened in the past can help us to predict what might happen in the future. If we look at the developments and issues that characterise the music industry today, it paints a picture of change in the current landscape. The world around us is evolving at a quicker rate than it ever has before and the music business is no different. This chapter makes some predictions on the future of the industry in the decades to come.

The Boom in Artist Audiobooks

Over the past decade, Spotify acquired a wide range of tech companies with a strong focus on machine-based learning. These investments paved the way for Spotify to create the most advanced music recommendation system ever. Consequently, the conversion rate of users who have switched to the ad-free premium version of the platform has seen year-on-year growth for almost a decade. This is perhaps beginning to plateau in the UK and the USA, where the markets are reaching saturation point; but other international markets continue to grow (as outlined in Chapter 40). Since the start of the 2020s, Spotify has begun to acquire tech companies with a focus on the podcast and audiobook industry. Combined with the aims of many major record companies, this perhaps suggests that a new area of focus for recording artists may emerge, in the form of audiobooks. Life stories, creative memoirs, the truth behind the songs and the inside story of an artist's outlook and values – these are all narratives that forge a link between a new growth area in streaming and the current goals of artists and labels.

As Angela Lopes, senior vice president, strategy and development of Sony Music Group states in the International Federation of the Phonographic Industry's *Global Music Report 2023*:

> We're seeing generation Z want to embrace new way of engaging with artists. There continues to be a greater shift towards next generation

DOI: 10.4324/9781003452119-49

platforms, and we are seeing a rise in revenue streams from new categories. We think a lot about how to help artists enhance their direct to fan
relationships.

Audio products that are created by artists could enhance their relationships
with their fanbase in a new way. In an age when narrative can be created quite
comfortably through social media, and when deep fake technology is creating
a distorted sense of what is and is not real, authenticity is paramount. Artist
audiobooks help to tell a story and make an artist's account of the truth more
accessible than perhaps social media can. There is something deeply personal
about an audiobook, both in its connection with the listener and in its delivery
by the author. It is not a podcast series, which requires a weekly commitment.
It is a documentation of an era in the same way that a music product is. If it is
narrated by an artist with a flair for storytelling, it will surely be gladly received
by a fanbase who crave sincerity. Clips of stripped-back versions of songs coupled with stories, similar to those which used to be featured on TV programmes
in the past, could make for compelling enjoyment. Some music fans often state
that they miss the liner notes that used to accompany a physical music release.
Who played what instrument and where specific songs were recorded – these
are interesting nuggets of information which could help to enhance the consumer experience.

A clear strategic goal of recording artists and record companies alike is syn-
ergetic branding alignment and this also points towards its inclusion in the
audiobook format. As Bob Workman, senior vice president of international
brand partnerships at Warner Music and general manager of WMX UK,
observes:

> Our artists have a wide palette of interests, passions, and skill sets and that's
> where certainly within the field of brand partnerships, there's lots of oppor-
> tunity. We're often engaged in an area or activity that might not be funda-
> mentally about the music.

An effective way to establish branding alignment could take the form of spoken
brand endorsements in an artist's audiobook. We are already witnessing this in
the podcast market. The ability to pipe in artist-spoken ads mid-book could
potentially create a high-earning income stream for artists and labels alike.

The audiobook concept also allows artists to explore their views in greater
depth than is possible in their songs. Specific values that an artist holds and
shares can connect them with likeminded people in a way that can sometimes
be difficult to achieve through music alone. The artist audiobook model could
allow artists and fans to engage and share insights in a way that also benefits the
corporate interests of the major labels and streaming platforms.

What Else Can We Learn from This?

This points towards an additional inference: the basic framework of how music is consumed and delivered to new listeners might not be changing anytime soon, while Spotify focuses its efforts on new areas of dominance in the streaming world. This bodes well for artists and labels that seek to understand the algorithmic nature of the platform with a view to gaining enhanced visibility for their music content. This could mean that there will be no sudden changes to the fundamental flow of Spotify's algorithm – unlike social media platforms and search engines, which have exhibited more regular changes in recent years.

The Reconstruction of Values in an Artist-Centred Ecosystem

Artists have more career control today than they have ever had before. This applies to a multitude of aspects. Artists are now in a position where they can build their audience themselves if they know their market and have the right product. They can identify their market by experimenting with their sound, researching trends and building content. Artists can also create their own products at lower cost than ever before. Artists can connect with fans if they have the right know-how – and that know-how can be learned or hired. If artists are rights holders, they have leverage and they can keep their rights if they know how to handle them.

As new commercial opportunities drive new income streams, artists are becoming business-savvy content creators who share their lifestyles and interests as well as their music – the implicit subtext that underpins their story. Artists are changing how the game is played – and the labels know it.

In the 2020s, major labels are responding by revisiting the fundamentals of how they work with artists. They are working both for the artist and with the artist by paying close attention to the details that constitute marketable features.

In the past few years, labels have begun using artificial intelligence (AI) to scan the internet to search for trending artists. This makes perfect sense from the label's perspective, because an artist who has data has an established audience that product can be released to. This is a much less risky way of investing, from the label's perspective. However, many artists are starting to realise that they don't need to relinquish their rights to a major label if they have already built their audience themselves. This perhaps means that we will see an increase in A&R departments that blend online scouting protocols with a more grassroots approach to discovering talent.

Apart from this change in how talent is scouted, the way in which talent is developed is also changing. Artists now have more autonomy over their vision and typecasting is becoming less common. An artist's position in the marketplace is becoming more customised and less standardised. Gone are the music executives in their 60s trying to second-guess what might appeal to the younger generation – and frequently getting this wrong. Those people are increasingly being replaced by executives with a more informed approach to finding a balance between the organic artistic vision of the artist and the future of their audience engagement. There are now huge amounts of data that can be absorbed to make more educated predictions on change and suitability for Generation Z. Audiences are changing; artists are changing; but so too are labels.

Interview: Tilly Wellard, A&R, Creative Consultant and Co-founder, Bonded, UK

Tilly Wellard is a fine example of someone who represents the next generation of music industry executives. Tilly is an in-demand A&R and talent scout with an informed understanding of the landscape of the modern music industry, with a particular focus on how artists connect with their audiences.

In your role as an A&R, what have you learned that would be useful for emerging music creators to know?

Things take time. Even when you have a label and an experienced team, success doesn't happen overnight. A lot of emerging creators these days are working towards that one big moment on social media – for their latest TikTok to get 10,000 views in one day or for their latest release to go straight onto the A list of a big radio show. I've seen it happen, and it can help boost your profile, but it isn't going to sustain your career. The internet can create the illusion that artists' careers go from zero to 100 'overnight', when in reality there has most likely been a team working day and night for the last three years helping the artist to figure out their sound, their brand, their network and many other factors that play a role in building a solid foundation before essentially launching an artist. That's not to say artists are kept locked in a bunker honing their craft until they're ready to be a superstar; but I guess what I'm trying to say is to be patient and realistic when you are setting goals and releasing your art.

What changes in the landscape are you witnessing regarding how artists connect with their fanbases?

Active engagement is becoming more and more prominent. The internet is facilitating a lot of that: live Q&As, behind-the-scenes videos and the more recent trend of 'photo dumps'. Fans are always waiting for the next bit of content to be shared by their favourite artist. With that comes increased pressure for the artist – the pressure of trying to stay relevant, be constantly active on social media and live up to fan expectations – which I imagine can be pretty tough.

Fans are gaining a lot more power and influence. Their desire for that personal connection has always been there – they want authenticity and a relatable artist – but one major shift is the consumer's ability to detect when an artist is truly being themselves. There's no faking authenticity in today's landscape.

Are there any mistakes that any artists make when releasing music that you think could be avoided?

One thing I'd recommend is to have all your assets and links easily accessible before release. When promoting a release on social media, have the link for people to click almost immediately. When reaching out for press or distribution, have your electronic press kit, music and social links at the ready. Many sectors in the music industry have a lot of music sent to them and must be time efficient, so having things available all in one place can play a major role in the amount of attention your application is given.

Also, going back to what I said previously: things take time. I often see artists rush into an album cycle or an EP for their first release, but it's super-important to use the early stages of your career to test the waters, drop a few singles, see what works and what doesn't. You can always take down tracks later down the line once you've found your sound.

What advice would you give to emerging artists who are looking to build a team around them?

I truly believe it's all about the relationship when picking a team. Trust is super-important, so always ask yourself whether the team around you truly understand your vision. I always go by the saying: the artist doesn't work for the team and the team don't work for the artist – they work together.

What changes do you foresee in the future of the business?

One of the biggest changes I am noticing – especially with the rise of TikTok – concerns the ability to tell the difference between an artist with a hit and an artist who has longevity within their career; I think that may take a while to figure out. This has led to an increase in labels offering single deals rather than encouraging artists to sign multiple album deals. I can see that continuing in the future.

The Extension of Song Copyrights

Pop music as we know it emerged in the 1950s. Viewed from a broad perspective, that's not so long ago. The copyright of songs generally exists for a further 50–70 years (depending on the country) after the death of the composer. We will soon see the dawn of an era in which hugely popular songs fall into the public domain. This has already happened for various works of literature. Songs that are already in the public domain (and therefore copyright free) perhaps feel so traditional that many of us barely even consider the authorship. 'Happy Birthday', 'Rockin Robin' and '99 Bottles of Beer' are all examples of songs for which legal protection under the recognised copyright framework has lapsed. In the coming decades, this will happen to many songs that mean so much to so many, and one of two things may happen:

- Monster hit songs will become copyright free; or
- The legal protection of copyrights will be extended.

The second option above would certainly seem to benefit the long-term interests of rights holders. If we were to see a change in legal frameworks around the world, this would increase the value of song catalogues. If major music publishers – or indeed any entity that owns song catalogues – could lobby for new legislation, the subject of song catalogues could assume even greater importance than it has today.

What Might This Mean?

If song copyrights were extended, this could also result in the extension of sound recording copyrights. This would mean not only that rights holders held more value, but also perhaps that legacy artists might return to prominence in pop culture more frequently. In recent years, recordings featuring deceased artists such as Elvis Presley and Whitney Houston have become huge hits. An extension of sound recording copyrights would enable rights holders (more than likely record labels) to bring recordings to new generations who are less familiar with legacy artists.

Non-fungible Tokens

In 2021, non-fungible tokens (NFTs) were one of the hottest trending topics on social media. To some, this felt like a fad; to others, it was an exciting crypto-investment opportunity. As Emily Jackson from Horus Music stated in

Chapter 19: 'Blockchain and NFTs . . . seem to have fallen off the bandwagon; although, depending on who you ask, they may still be considered relevant.'

What Are They?

NFTs are digital assets that represent the authenticity of a unique item. In some cases, an NFT can be labelled as ownership of an item. It is a token of uniqueness with a unique identifier. An NFT can represent a collectable piece of visual art; a unique piece of clothing for an avatar in the metaverse; an image for a meme; a domain name; or even a unique code that gains a person access to an exclusive club or restaurant. They are non-fungible, which means that they are unique because they hold distinct and non-replicable attributes. If something can be replicated, it becomes fungible. If a person owns an NFT, it means that nobody else owns it. NFTs are particularly popular in gaming and the metaverse, where uniqueness of identity is key. These digital items are growing in popularity around the world.

Where Do They Fit in the Music Industry?

The key thing to think about here is whether an NFT holds rights or collectorship value. If something is a collector's item, it is the uniqueness and authenticity that sell. If it the sale of a right, it holds more value.

- Videos can be NFTs.
- Specific versions of songs can be NFTs.
- Artwork can be NFTs.
- Digital copies of handwritten lyrics can be NFTs.

Scenario 1: Collector Value

A band releases an album which can be streamed on all major platforms; but they also create a digital version of the album that holds a sense of uniqueness, such as a digital booklet with liner notes and lyrics, together with a download of the song files. This could be an NFT. A buyer is not buying the rights to the intellectual property (IP), but merely the rights to the uniqueness of the product. It is rather like buying a pair of rare Nike trainers: you own the shoes, but you don't own the rights to the brand or the model. The trainers are a collector's item. This is a limited run and each NFT has its own unique identifier, comparable perhaps to a visual artist's print run.

Scenario 2: Sale of Ownership

Let's now imagine that the same band release a music video and sell the ownership of that music video to a unique buyer. The buyer of that NFT owns the IP of the video. The buyer does not own the recording rights to the band or the recording rights to the song, but rather the ownership of the rights to that specific video. The buyer then exploits the video through their own means and collects the revenue from it. Let's imagine that the band sell the NFT for £50,000 and the buyer generates income of £200,000 over the next two years and still retains the rights to the video.

Unique Music Products

It is clear from the above scenarios how NFTs can be incorporated into the music industry. We are in the early stages of seeing how this area evolves. The idea of artists creating unique versions of songs that become NFTs is achievable, provided that it is the artist's vision which dictates the product outcome. If an artist compromises their integrity and surrenders their artistic values to create a unique version of a song that includes someone's name as a birthday gift, for instance, this becomes something more akin to a subscription-based platform where creators create bespoke material. There is a fine line here.

In a blog on this subject, MusicTomorrow.com stated:

> Right now, most buyers are crypto-savvy investors, and most NFT offerings can be described as simple digital collectibles. However, there's an undeniable potential for NFTs in music to become so, so much more. It's easy to imagine that as the market matures, more music first audiences will enter the space and if the NFT offers turn from digital memorabilia into real financial assets supported by music copyrights, we might be looking at a radically new way for artists to fund their careers and establish the value of their art.

It is difficult to argue with this assessment. The key factor, as always, is ownership.

The Evolution of Song Recordings

Songs come in all shapes and sizes. There are hit songs with short notes, long notes, short choruses, long choruses and no choruses at all. There are no rules, but there are patterns.

Trends

Song structure is something that tends to move in trends. In the early to mid-2020s, songs became shorter. We know why, so let's think more about how. In the Western world, intros have gone, outros have shortened and many bridge sections seem to have been cut in favour of a chorus breakdown. Intros, if they do exist, seem to have evolved into a snapshot micro version of the chorus and act almost like a trailer to keep the streamer streaming. But this will change again – it always does.

In recent years, we have seen other trends emerge through online communities. Songs that are sped up and songs that are pitched up and pitched down are examples of this.

One key thing to bear in mind here is that this is not happening to the song; it's happening to the *recording* of the song. There's a difference. The essence of the song remains. It's the way in which the recording is shaped and manipulated that evolves.

The Spirit of a Song

Songs are the lifeblood of the music industry. They serve a purpose to all of us. It is all too easy to associate our understanding of a song with a specific recording of that song. However, there can, of course, be multiple different recorded versions of a song – especially when interpreted by different artists. Many listeners can feel swayed by a certain artist's take on a song, which evokes certain emotions in them. However, a different take on that song – for example, a ballad that is sped up by a DJ and synchronised with a different track – can evoke different emotions. We recognise the familiarity, but we dance instead of cry. This reflects the flexible spirit of a great song, rather than a specific recording. It is not the spirit of the song which evolves, but rather how it is delivered to listeners.

Songs in Other Languages

Today, foreign-language films are excelling in English-speaking countries. On many of the major streaming services, films from overseas which are dubbed into English are enjoying great success; and increasingly, the same is true for songs. Quite simply, Generation Z consume content differently from any other previous generation. Songs in other languages are finding a place in the hearts and lives of many young listeners – perhaps due in part to a sense of global discovery as they connect with the world around them on their own terms through online communities.

The Proliferation of Microgenres

The artistic pursuit of uniqueness is gaining in intensity and genres are increasingly being bent out of shape in new and exciting ways. Today, some artists effortlessly shift between two or three primary genres with a sense of freedom and daring. When we mix red and blue, we get purple. We need the red and we need the blue; but people get bored. With purple, we get the best of both worlds because we get something new.

In addition, the underground emergence of new genres from around the world is on the rise. In years gone by, genres came in and out of trend. Today, we are increasingly witnessing fusion genres emerging. Add to this the element of artistic interpretation and the result is some surprising sounds that are often yet to be named and claimed. How someone from London interprets a North African percussion loop can create a musical part with a new context and meaning. How someone from Norway interprets a flamenco rhythm and changes its speed can create an innovative hybrid output. This is an era of acceleration for microgenres.

Non-traditional Growth in Sync Licensing

Traditional sync licensing for music mostly relates to TV, film and games. The overall sector is strong and has been for a long time. However, there is a growing need for non-traditional sync licensing, which sits largely in new media areas such as media campaigns, influencer music, the metaverse, YouTube and start-up film production companies and app designers. The need to adapt to new technologies presents both challenges and opportunities when it comes to licensing music. There is an opportunity for growth here in how digital distributors meet the growing demand from new types of music users.

Leveraging New Networks

TikTok in the 2020s is what MTV was in the 1980s. It is a star-making platform where the most committed and innovative can thrive. It perhaps even reflects the evolution of the music industry itself: the fundamental difference is an organic power shift that favours both creators and consumers. Many TikTok users are eager to discover new artists. This is a different culture from that of a playlist curator or a journalist writing a blog. There is a sense of silent or passive engagement on an audio streaming platform or a blog; but on social media, where visual content communicates quickly and effectively, there is a sense of ownership from fans and a sense of loyalty that grows.

We may start to see more breakout stars learn how to use this network to leverage greater opportunities for themselves. This is where innovative artist management is key, as the most profitable paths for artists may not lie with the traditional partners in the music industry. Instead, the optimal strategy may involve working directly with brands and sponsors and taking ownership of their own events and rights management. As artists learn more about how to build a strategy that favours their career, we could see a new era of organised, educated and driven music creators who build their own brands.

The Development of Live Streamed Events

As we progress through the 2020s, the cost-of-living crisis is cutting ever deeper. Ticket prices for live music events have continually increased over the past two decades and continue to rise in tandem with the soaring costs of touring. In 2022, just when live music was expected to rebound after the Covid-19 pandemic, many events suffered from a surprising drop in sales.

Today, artists are making more informed choices as to whether a tour is financially viable. Combine this with the development of immersive audio experiences and heightened concern for the environment, and it all points towards one trend: the growth of live streamed events.

There will be an overwhelming number of people who utterly despise the idea of the live music experience being replaced by an immersive one. However, those people need not be disappointed, because even if live streamed events grow, they can never truly replace the experience of a live music event. However, the two can coexist.

It is all too easy to think back to what live streaming looked like in Spring 2020 and how glitchy and unreliable the technology was. At times, it perhaps even felt charitable to persist with it. However, this kickstarted an entirely new way of building a live experience. Twitch and YouTube started to set the bar for audience-led experiences, but bigger things perhaps lie ahead. 'It feels like you're actually there'; 'It's actually better because you're always in the front row and you don't have to queue to get in and out' – these sentiments could well become commonplace in the near future as immersive audio, virtual reality and 4K resolution screens continue to evolve. Digital service providers (eg, Apple, Spotify, Amazon) are in a strong position to develop this model further; or maybe the giants of the live sector will start to acquire the tech start-ups that build this technology for the industry. We are already witnessing virtual meet-and-greets and virtual venues, so perhaps the live streaming of music events can further enhance the relationship between fans and artists. Technological developments already in test mode suggest not only an increase in live-streamed experiences, but also a decrease in audio latency, meaning that a live stream to the USA from Japan would be delayed by no more than two seconds at most. Perhaps as tours are planned out later in the decade, the logistics will cover not only the live events themselves, but also the live stream of the events in both audio and visual form. A live stream ticket might cost only a fraction of the in-person ticket for the event, which would not only allow access at a global level, but also draw in further income.

Today, environmental protection has become an urgent concern. Likewise, the drive for greater inclusivity is also near the top of the agenda for many people. Live-streamed events support both goals.

A related issue concerns the rights of the recordings and how these are governed, controlled and handled at an administrative level. If an experience becomes a digital document, it holds a value. The last thing the music industry needs is a return to piracy.

The Evolution of Audio Streaming Economics

In 2023, the Writers Guild of America went on strike from May to September over a dispute with the Alliance of Motion Picture and Television Producers. The strike caused a great deal of setbacks for a wide variety of media productions. In total, about 11,500 screenwriters were represented in the strike. The screenwriters may have set a precedent for the entertainment industry. One of the key things that the screenwriters were rallying against concerned the residuals from streamed media. They also wanted to ensure that AI would be used only for research and would not replace them in their roles.

Now let's imagine a boycott of that nature by rights holders in the music industry. It would involve far more than 11,500 people and the implications would be much deeper and wider. It is not beyond the realms of possibility to consider a creative or corporate strike against the major music streaming services, with rights holders lobbying for a larger share of revenue. The costs of such a campaign could perhaps end up being transferred to the consumer if the streaming platforms increased their subscription fees in response.

Combine this with the increase in content and the rising cost of living and we can almost certainly predict that the consumer costs of streaming music are set to rise. Let's stop and think about this for a moment and play devil's advocate. When you consider what music used to cost consumers and what it costs them today, it is clear that consumers are getting a pretty good deal. A monthly subscription to a premium music platform for a catalogue of music spanning multiple decades, cultures and genres costs less than a single CD album did in the 1990s. The tough financial times in the early 21st century were caused by piracy, which effectively ended so many physical sales of music. The streaming services rose from the ashes and partly saved recorded music. Maybe it's time to hike prices higher in favour of rights holders now that streaming has restored an understanding among the public that they need to pay for music they enjoy? That is a wider debate for another time, perhaps; but it seems likely that the price of audio streaming will ultimately increase as far as consumers are concerned.

44
Your Future

Hopefully, the chapters of this book have helped to add clarity and context to your ambitions. For the book to succeed in its aims, links must be drawn between the theory and the practice; and the reader must be able to build a picture of where they see themselves in the industry.

Some of the more traditional elements of the music business, especially those relating to intellectual property, can be difficult to fully absorb. These are the focus of Chapters 1–10: the bedrock of the business, from which everything follows. Becoming a recording artist is the ultimate shot at the title for some, but knowing how to navigate best practice can be difficult. That is addressed in Chapters 11–15. Creating music is one thing, but ensuring that music finds a place in people's lives is a key goal for many – this is discussed in Chapters 16–27. Perhaps the ultimate underlying goal of a music creator is the freedom to make a living from their passion, and Chapters 28–39 seek to support this. It is easy to become overly preoccupied by our immediate surroundings, but it's important to remember that there is a big, wide world out there – and there may be a place for your music further afield if you work hard enough to find it. That's why Chapter 40 exists. Artificial intelligence is dominating much of the mainstream agenda as we progress through the 2020s. However, we can start to see it as more of an opportunity than a threat if we learn more about its purpose, its place in society and its growing capabilities. Chapter 41 offers a contextual glimpse into this rapidly evolving subject. A career in the music business can sometimes be overwhelming, especially in the modern information age; Chapter 42 explores what you can do to safeguard your wellbeing. Chapter 43 considers what the future of the industry might have in store; while this chapter brings the book to a conclusion.

It is important to see that you have a sense of control in how you respond to all of this. It might perhaps sound like a cliché to say that you control your future; but the reality is that you do. The chapter of your life that you are in right now,

DOI: 10.4324/9781003452119-50

as you read this, may form part of your legacy; but perhaps it may not. Maybe you're still working out what your plan should look like. In any case, there is no need to rush – especially in an era when age is not as important as it once was. A music creator's career is very rarely defined by a single stage; instead, it is a collection of stages in which music means different things at different times. A creator's musical output is often dictated by the circumstances surrounding them at the time. It will evolve over time, and creators are not always the best judges of what defines their best work.

If your goals are clear to you, be aware that your ideals will change as you change.

If your goals are still unclear, be aware that you have several options – but the need to be assertive is not one of them.

Good Things Come to Those Who Wait

While again, this may sound like a cliché, it is nonetheless true. Nothing happens quickly – and even if it does, it's rarely sustainable.

English singer-songwriter David Gray released his fourth studio album, *White Ladder*, in 1999. It was self-financed and recorded in his flat. It initially enjoyed big success in Ireland, but made less of an impact elsewhere. However, after a re-release, the popularity of *White Ladder* gradually began to build, to the point where it eventually became one of the biggest-selling albums of the 2000s. This also brought David Grey's back catalogue to a much wider audience. While this change in fortune was doubtless due to Grey's talent, it was also due to graft, tenacity and perseverance. In some people's eyes, Farrokh Bulsara was born to be Freddie Mercury. However, this perhaps overlooks the courage and voyage of self-discovery that were needed for Freddie to become Freddie. Before Lizzo's brand of quirky, upbeat, fun music found its audience seemingly overnight, Melissa Viviane Jefferson had been grafting for years to prepare for this. The list could go on; but the point is that creators create in order to be who they want to be. Creators create music and creators create themselves. Many factors have transformed this industry in recent decades, but one thing has remained constant: hard work is everything. Once a goal becomes clearer, it provides direction, and it then becomes easier to find the motivation to see it through. The misconception perhaps lies in thinking that success depends exclusively on how good you are, when the reality suggests that it is more about how badly you want it. That said, some beautiful, fascinating and captivating things can happen when music creators least expect it – as is outlined in the following interview.

Interview: Kevin Charge, Songwriter-Producer, UK

Kevin Charge is a multi-platinum-selling music creator with decades of experience and a passion for an array of musical genres and eras. Kevin has travelled the world co-creating songs with a wide variety of international collaborators and exhibits an admirable work rate and attitude towards his work.

You had a great deal of experience in music creation for several decades, composing, performing and recording. Then suddenly – and seemingly out of nowhere – you found your niche in the J-pop market later on in your career and went on to achieve a total of 61 Number 1s (and counting!) across Japan and South Korea. What age were you when you had your first hit in Japan and how did this come about?

It's hard to believe now, but I was 52 years old when I got my first cut in Asia!

I had been a musician for many years, touring, doing studio sessions, gigging and basically learning my craft working for other people and doing their songs. However, I became disillusioned with the music industry in 2008 and so decided to give it up. After not touching my keyboard or entering my studio for eight months, a chance conversation with a music friend of mine resulted in him convincing me to go to his studio for a writing session, where I also ended up being the producer. That one session made me realise how much I missed music; and now I was doing my own material and production, it was like a breath of fresh air.

My friend was published by TG Publishing of Denmark, which ran a writing camp called DPop. He spoke to them about me and convinced them to let me come along to one of their songwriting camps.

TG Publishing and I hit it off straight away and soon after, I was signed to them. They were one of the first publishers to look at the Asian market and invited Soundgraphics head man Hide Nakamura over to Denmark to an Asian song camp. I was lucky enough to be invited to that camp and immediately struck up a great relationship with Hide and the Asian genres. Hide and I became very good friends, and he mentored me and helped me to understand the approaches required for the Japanese music market. This allowed me to truly understand what they required. The rest is history!

You have continually evolved and developed at a rapid pace and showcase a multi-genre approach across your catalogue. If we compare the hard-hitting electronic groove of 'Alligator' by K-pop stars Monsta X with Shinee's fresh and innocent track 'Your Number', we see a big variation in mood and style; and yet it still sounds and feels like you. What is your philosophy towards shifting between styles and emotions?

This is where my many years of playing with all types of bands and music styles have really helped, because over the years I have played every type of genre I can think of and I know and understand them all. I love Frank Sinatra and Tony Bennett as much as I do Justin Timberlake and Dua Lipa, and that means I never limit myself. I can party to a hi-energy track and cry to a beautiful ballad; and when I sit down to create a song, those emotions are with me. In my opinion, great music comes from within and if you feel it, that comes across in the music.

You have seen huge stadium audiences in Asia singing the songs you've co-created. How can you describe that feeling? Is it something you thought could happen earlier in your career?

Being a songwriter requires a high level of self-belief, so to some degree I have always felt that with the right break, I could be successful. However, never did I believe for one moment that it would come so late in my career.

It's hard to describe how it feels to be at a live concert with 55,000 people going crazy to your song. It's something that a songwriter-producer only ever dreams might happen, but when it does . . . Wow! It's a feeling like no other. It's basically a confirmation that all the years of hard work and determination to keep trying and trying were all worth it.

At that moment, I told myself that if this was it, I was proud to have achieved that at least once. Thankfully, that wasn't it – not because suddenly everything fell at my feet, but because from that point onwards, I worked harder than ever before to ensure I got more of it!

What kinds of professional relationships in the music business have played an important role in your success?

The most important people have been John and Lotte Aagaard of TG Publishing, for sure. They initially saw my potential and gave me a chance, and they introduced me to Asian music. They have been there with support and friendship from the beginning and I'm sure things would have been very different were it not for them.

Hide Nakamura from Soundgraphics has also been the most amazing mentor and friend, and I would not have had the success in Asia I have had were it not for his guidance and belief in my music.

I also have to mention all the amazing writers, topliners and musicians who have worked with me over the years. Most of what I do is down to collaboration with great people, and I have been extremely fortunate to have met and worked with some seriously talented artists and friends.

Do you have any advice for emerging creators who are looking to find their feet in the business?

The best advice that I can give anyone is to say that the dream is out there, but it won't come to you unless you work hard and never give up. When you have written one track, don't sit there waiting for it to become a hit; write another one, and another, and another. Every time you write another track, you'll get better and people will start noticing. When you approach a record company or a music publisher, you will have a body of work to show them, so that they can see that you're not messing around and are prepared to do what it takes.

Then they will start believing in you as much as you believe in yourself; and from there it grows and grows, until one day you are sitting in Tokyo Dome or Wembley Stadium listening to your song being played to 55,000 people and the dream becomes a reality.

It's rewarding to hear stories like Kevin's – and there are so many others just like him who find their path later down the line in their career. It's worth noting that while Kevin may have experienced a lucky intervention that was followed by an invitation, that only happened because he had already proven his worth. By the time he attended the songwriting camps, he was ready – and he delivered because all his previous hard work ensured that he was well prepared. So many music fans in Japan have had their lives touched by Kevin's creations – and yet he came so close to giving up his musical endeavours altogether just before his inspiring chart run started. Kevin was presented with a choice. He could have turned down the invitation to attend the song camp because he had become disillusioned with the industry. However, his journey up until that point had taught him more than a thing or two about tenacity. He still had hope – and it proved to be the decisive factor that enriched his existence and meant that his name and catalogue will now be forever etched into history.

May your future be your own. Never give up!

Conclusion

From a detailed study of complexities, simplicities begin to emerge. Patterns become noticeable and paths become clearer. If that hasn't happened yet, don't worry – it will.

Something I figured out many years ago was that if you leave a trail of professionalism behind you with every step, new paths will emerge in front of you. By this, I am referring to both kindness and professionalism. It takes effort. Remembering people's names takes effort. Being positive takes effort. Being negative takes no effort at all. In the introduction, I quoted Mark Twain, so I'll bookend by quoting him again here: 'Kindness is the language which the deaf can hear and the blind can see.' Twain was inspired by others, just as you are inspired by others who have come before you. It is up to you now to inspire others by doing what you were put here to do.

I remember the dark times of the early 2000s, when rampant piracy upended the industry as we knew it. Music industry executives looked puzzled by this shift in the landscape, as the younger generations were listening to more music than they had ever done before but were paying nothing for it. It was the beginning of the mainstream digital age and it changed everything. Before long, audio streaming had become the new way of consuming music. It didn't save the old recorded music industry; but it did kickstart a brand-new one that acknowledges intellectual property. From the ashes of the analogue era rose a plethora of new ways for people to communicate in a much more progressive and informed world; and meanwhile, social media emerged, as a result of which the music industry evolved even further.

'One who believes in themselves has no need to convince others' - Laozi

I have never been afraid or ashamed to have started something from nothing in music, and I never will. I think it's because I'm not scared of failing. I once co-founded a rock band with some friends. We went from playing to a handful of people to playing to sell-out crowds inside of less than 18 months.

We grafted hard and we were tough on each other in the most productive ways possible. We went from red carpets and global magazine features to a much more mundane existence in the working week as we tried to make ends meet. It was character building. If only we had known the business like I know it today. I've started numerous music companies and projects; some have worked and some haven't. I've created songs that I didn't think were very good but that found success and songs that I think are great but that have not yet found success. The world of copyrights is a fascinating one, as you never know what surprises will pop up. Although the days of earning 'forever money' from one song are perhaps behind us, it still only takes one song to change someone's life forever. I've seen that happen to so many and it's a beautiful thing to witness. Songs open doors in ways that hands can't.

Don't step quietly in this business; walk with passion and pride. We only get to do this life thing once, so go and do something amazing and leave a legacy behind you. Be happy and believe.

Glossary

A&R 'Artist and repertoire' – a department and/or person that works for a record company or music publisher to scout and develop creative talent.

Advance Money paid in advance to a music creator by either a record company or music publisher in accordance with what has been agreed in a contract. The payments can be spread over a term throughout the contract. Advances are usually non-refundable and are recoupable against future royalties.

Airgigs A web-based platform where music creators are hired on a freelance basis to record musical parts for other creators or creative projects.

Algorithm An often-patented process developed to perform complex tasks using a computer. In the context of this book, algorithms largely relate to data processing, optimisation and recommendation patterns in the context of audio streaming.

Assignment of rights The transfer of ownership or control of certain rights from a songwriter to a music publisher.

Audit An inspection or examination of accounts and data.

Beat leasing The concept of music producers creating instrumental tracks which singers and rappers can use in their own commercial releases. The 'leasing' of the beats refers to the contractual arrangement for the use of the track, alongside the terms of use and financial remuneration for the producer.

Blanket licence A broad licensing agreement between a performing rights organisation (PRO) and clients such as broadcasters and production companies. A blanket licence allows clients to access and use a wide catalogue of songs without the need to liaise directly with the rights holders. A PRO grants a licence for the use of rights holders' work.

Content IDs A rights management protocol which allows for the creation of a digital fingerprint of a recording or a music video's identity to be tracked on digital platforms.

Control Administrative and/or creative control of the ownership of musical compositions. Control can be held by a songwriter or by a music publisher if the rights have been transferred to it by the songwriter.

Copyright The legal protection granted to the creators of musical works (songs). The main aspects of a song's copyright relate to sole or shared ownership, exclusivity, licensing, royalties and the duration of legal protection. The word 'copyright' can also be used in the context of sound recordings, which are often referred to as 'master rights'.

Collection societies An organisation that represents songwriters, composers and music publisher members. Duties include royalty collection and distribution, usage tracking and licensing. Also known as a PRO.

Collection management organisation (CMO) An organisation that administrates copyrights on behalf of multiple rights holders. CMOs handle similar duties to a collection society or PRO, as well as additional duties such as synchronisation and mechanical rights.

Cue sheet A document that outlines the use of music in audiovisual productions such as ads, television and film.

Cut A term used to describe the process of a songwriter getting their song recorded by a recording artist.

Digital service provider Streaming platforms such as Spotify, Apple, Amazon, etc.

Digital time stamp A mechanical process which creates proof of song ownership in a digital and tangible form.

Download In the context of this book, songs that are downloaded for purchase by the public.

Exploitation The efforts of a rights holder such as a music publisher or a record company to gain exposure for a song or song recording in order for it to gain growth and visibility. One form of exploitation is the use of a song in a TV programme or ad.

Imprint label A small label set up by an existing label to create a separate brand.

Infringement The use of copyright without the permission of the rights holders.

Intellectual property A creation of the human mind that requires legal protection. This could be a song, a recording or a video copyright. It could also be a patented idea, a design or a trademark.

Inter-band agreement A written agreement between members of a musical group or band. The agreement can cover a variety of negotiable items, such as ownership of assets, member roles and duties, decision-making processes, financial liabilities, plans, rights of members, commitments and termination.

Interested Party Information (IPI) A code which is associated with songwriters, composers and music publishers. The IPI acts as a unique identifier of a person or a company and is issued by a PRO after they become a member.

International Standard Works Code (ISWC) A unique and universally accepted identifier code assigned to a musical work (song).

International Standard Recording Code (ISRC) A unique and universally accepted identifier code assigned to a sound recording. A recording can have multiple ISRCs for one ISWC (song).

Label services provider An organisation that partners with record companies and artists by offering a range of services, such as distribution, promotion, marketing, plugging, product development and/or strategy.

Master rights The rights that relate to the ownership of a sound recording.

Metadata Descriptive text that accompanies a song or recording. Metadata enables music to become identifiable, filtered and efficient.

Meta tagging The specific descriptive tags that represent and assist a song or recording. The term is often linked to a song's title and the names of recording artists, but it also encompasses other aspects that aid the full metadata of a music product.

Music licensing organisation An organisation that manages, licenses and administrates royalty collection for sound recording copyright (also known as master rights) holders and the rights of performers on sound recordings.

Music supervisor A person or company responsible for choosing and clearing the use of music and songs in conjunction with audiovisual productions such as TV and film. The role includes budgeting, collaboration, licensing and song selection.

Non-fungible tokens A unique digital asset that represents either the ownership or uniqueness of a specific product.

Performing rights organisation An organisation that represents songwriters, composers and music publisher members. The duties of PROs include royalty collection and distribution, usage tracking and licensing. They are also known as 'collection societies'.

Perpetuity A term largely associated with the music publishing sector and songwriters, which relates to a songwriter assigning control of a song to a music publisher for the entire life of the copyright.

Pitch In the context of this book, the submission of a song or recording for an opportunity.

Playlist A collection of songs on a compiled track list which is available for streaming. Playlists can be curated by humans or algorithms.

Points Percentage points on the copyright of a sound recording which can be given to a specific individual or entity such as a music producer.

Portfolio career A career that involves multiple part-time roles and jobs. This is especially common among music creators, who can pursue multiple pathways with their skill set (eg, performance, recording, composing and teaching).

Press release An announcement of news which is directed towards suitable media outlets, tastemakers and other interested parties. In the context of this book, a press release is most commonly linked to a new music release or a musical event.

Production music Music which is specifically created for use in audiovisual productions and signed by libraries and music publishers, which then look to exploit its potential with media companies. More commonly referred to in the USA as 'library music'.

Revisions Changes, amendments or edits to a work. The term as used in this book refers to the changes that music creators agree to undertake as part of their offer in recording projects. The term is also useful for music producers.

Sample packs A royalty-free collection of sounds, loops, stems or MIDI data inside a digital download pack. Sample packs are often specific to instruments, genres and moods. Sample packs are created by music creators and made available to other music creators.

Song split The division of credit and royalties where two or more music creators share ownership of a song copyright. Percentages are used to identify shared ownership.

Soundbetter A web-based platform which facilitates the hire of music creators on a freelance basis to record musical parts for other creators or creative projects.

Stems The individual recording files inside a music recording. Stems can be individual instruments (eg, bass, guitar, synth) or grouped instruments exported by classification (eg, vocals, effects, drums).

Sync A widely used abbreviation of the word 'synchronisation', which relates to how music is used to aid a variety of audiovisual sources in media.

Tastemaker An influential person who aids the discovery of new music, such as a playlist curator, a radio presenter, a blogger, a YouTuber or a journalist.

Topline Most commonly, the combination of lyrics and melody in a song.

Universal Product Code A unique barcode used to track a release of a recording in the marketplace.

Index